The Psychology of Sexual Diversity

The Psychology of Sexual Diversity

Edited by Kevin Howells

Basil Blackwell

First published 1984

Basil Blackwell Publisher Ltd
108 Cowley Road, Oxford OX4 1JF, UK

Basil Blackwell Inc.
432 Park Avenue South, Suite 1505,
New York, NY 10016, USA

British Library Cataloguing in Publication Data

The psychology of sexual diversity.
  1. Psychosexual disorders
  I. Howells, Kevin
  616.85'83   RC556
ISBN 0-631-13669-X

Library of Congress Cataloging in Publication Data

The psychology of sexual diversity.
  Includes index.
  1. Sexual deviation. 2. Psychosexual disorders.
  3. Sexual behavior in animals.   I. Howells, Kevin.
  [DNLM: 1. Paraphilias. 2. Sex Behavior. 3. Sex
  Behavior, Animal. 4. Sex Disorders. WM 611 P974]
  RC556.P745 1984   616.85'83   84-12474
ISBN 0-631-13669-X

Typeset by The Spartan Press Ltd, Lymington, Hants
Printed in Great Britain by Redwood Burn Ltd, Trowbridge, Wilts

Contents

Acknowledgements

Wladyslaw Sluckin provided support and encouragement in the preparation of this book. Rita Benford and Margaret Frape helped me with more jobs than I can even recall. Marguerite and Caitlin Howells were the tolerant recipients of disrupted evenings and weekends. I am indebted to them all.

Kevin Howells

Introduction

Editing a book provides a rare opportunity for academic self-indulgence. I have used this particular book to further my own education, in the hope that what will be useful to me will also be useful to others. The various authors' contributions fill four of the more obvious gaps in my own knowledge and resources.

The first gap has become obvious to me in teaching a course on human sexuality for medical students. Students following this course have often approached me to ask for more advanced reading than that provided by introductory textbooks on topics such as homosexuality, gender dysphoria, fetishism or general attitudes to sexual deviance. It has always been difficult to direct them to a text in which what is known about such variations is summarized in an accessible way. The present collection is intended to meet this need.

The second gap occurs in the course of clinical work with sexual deviants. It is my own experience that clinical psychologists, psychiatrists, social workers and others engaged in clinical work with deviant groups often focus on one particular class of deviant behaviour. Some work with clients whose homosexual behaviour has become a problem for them, some with sexual offenders, such as rapists, and others with the sexually dysfunctional. The separation of these diversities is unhelpful. There is much to be learned by extending our knowledge of sexual behaviour and its determinants through focusing on the theories and findings of those working with different, but often related, groups. In the long term, the processes underlying sexual development in general are likely to be revealed by this breaking down of boundaries.

Thirdly, humans are not the only animal species whose sexual behaviour shows marked variation. Polemical contributions in the field of sexual diversity often contain bold assertions that some particular sexual variation (for example, homosexuality) is rare, or alternatively pervasive, in the animal world, and such a fact may be used as evidence to support a particular theory about human sexual behaviour. The literature on sexual diversity in animals is often hard to find, and even harder to evaluate, for those whose main focus is human behaviour. I have attempted to include some discussion of sexual behaviour in animals in this book, for this reason.

Finally, psychologists, doctors and other scientists are often poor cultural and temporal relativists. Ideas about what sexuality is and what forms of it are 'normal' change considerably over time *within* cultures and show marked variation *between* cultures. Psychological and medical interventions with the sexually deviant are part of a general societal response, based on particular assumptions, beliefs and values which may not be fully recognized and acknowledged. I have attempted to introduce some sociological discussion of this sort into the volume.

Before outlining the contents of particular chapters, some comment must be made about the problems of terminology which exist in this area. In the past, the topics discussed in this book have often appeared in texts with titles including the terms 'sexual abnormality', 'sexual deviation', 'sexual deviance' or even 'sexual perversion'. The vocabulary used to define an area of study is of considerable importance. Words such as sexual 'abnormality' and 'perversion', in particular, do more than *describe* behaviour, they suggest ways in which the behaviour is to be viewed, studied and responded to. Petras (1978) suggests that such terms 'detail a plan of action towards the phenomena, others, and more importantly, ourselves'. Many of these descriptions are pejorative and have implications of pathology and of the need for medical intervention.

Most of the sexual behaviours discussed in the chapters could be categorized as instances of 'sexual deviance'. They are deviant in the sense that they are 'unapproved' (Petras) by many in society and violate what appear to be accepted rules as to how sexuality is to be expressed. They are not deviant in any absolute sense in that a plurality of rules and values may exist within a society, and systems of rules may vary across societies and subcultures, and also change over time. Whereas, for example, masturbation may have been considered 'deviant' in the nineteenth century, it is far less likely to be viewed in the same way today. Many of the sexual behaviours described in the book may change, or have already changed, their status in a similar way. For these reasons I have used the term 'sexual diversity', which is free of many of the connotations of the alternative terms.

Homosexuality has been the form of diversity most studied by psychologists, doctors and social scientists. What is known about the homosexual preference, from empirical work, is reviewed by Philip Feldman in chapter 1. Feldman draws attention to the definitional problems that exist and the heterogeneity of homosexual groups. The primary/secondary distinction he proposes appears to be an important first step in establishing meaningful typologies which can be related to aetiological theories.

The literature relating to homosexual behaviour in animal species has rarely been critically reviewed and evaluated. Patrick Tyler does this, and explores the usefulness of the comparative approach, in chapter 2. His analysis reveals how incomplete the evidence is on a number of important issues. Tyler's review also indicates a marked variability in the prevalence of homosexuality among species, an observation which precludes broad generalizations about homosexual behaviour in animals.

Harry Brierley's contribution (chapter 3) focuses on diversity in the area of gender identity and gender-role behaviour. Understanding deviance in this field requires comprehension of the important conceptual distinctions between such terms as sex, gender and gender role. Brierley maps the differences between these concepts and goes on to propose a model of how gender identity, gender role and sex-object choice are integrated within a general homeostatically balanced psychological system. How cross-dressing, fetishism, asexual transvestism and transsexuality can be assimilated into such a model is discussed.

Fetishism, in a broader sense, is also the focus of chapter 4 by Chris Gosselin and Glenn Wilson. These authors review published work in this area and report work of their own with particular deviant groups before attempting to describe some of the factors which may have aetiological significance for this particular form of sexual expression.

Most of the patterns of sexual behaviour discussed in the book are consensual. Sexual behaviour can also be coerced, as when force is used to produce sexual compliance. The present author reviews work relating to coercive sex (mainly rape) in chapter 5. Three specific areas of controversy are isolated and the available literature in each of these areas is assessed. The complex nature of the aetiology of coercive sexual behaviour is revealed by this review – a theme which recurs throughout the book.

Sexual inadequacy is not typically considered in writings on sexual deviance. It shares with the other diversities, however, the attribute of being 'unapproved' and rule-violating, though in this particular case these attributes are internally generated. It is the dysfunctional person him/herself who dislikes his/her own behaviour and who believes that it violates the rule that one must be sexually competent. Derek Jehu's analysis (chapter 6) describes the major features of inadequacy, the major historical and contemporaneous causes of the behaviour and some of the components of treatment.

Human sexual dysfunction has rarely been related to work with animal species, even though corresponding behaviours seem to exist. Jehu discusses comparative issues in chapter 7, with particular reference to primates, and brings some novel perspectives to the study of human inadequacy.

What we know about the human sexual diversities is usually based on observations, assessments and measurements of both 'normal' and 'deviant' behaviours in a number of contexts. The information and theories derived from such observations have little validity unless the methods of study themselves are reliable and valid. Richard Laws (chapter 8) critically evaluates the major methodologies used in research into sexual diversity. Laws' review indicates, once again, the patchy nature of our knowledge, but also gives directions for providing more precise and valid answers to the questions that are being and will be asked.

Finally, Ken Plummer (chapter 9) brings a sociologist's perspective to the themes that run throughout the book. Plummer's analysis highlights the discontinuities between animal and human sexual behaviour and reveals the assumptions underlying much work in the field. Plummer's chapter brings to the volume a consideration of social reactions to, and social constructions of, sexual diversity.

REFERENCES

Petras, J. W. (1978) *The Social Meaning of Human Sexuality*, 2nd edn, Boston: Allyn & Bacon.

1
The Homosexual Preference

Philip Feldman

INTRODUCTION

It is notoriously difficult to secure reliable, generalizable information on heterosexual behaviour. The problems are even greater concerning the homosexual preference. Earlier research used samples of homosexuals in prisons or hospitals – and then compared them with heterosexuals drawn from the population at large. More recent studies have had access to homosexuals leading normal lives, often in gay communities. This is clearly much more satisfactory, but many homosexuals who are still in the process of 'coming out' will be missing from such samples. We do not know if their absence affects the findings of such research studies.

A further problem has been raised by Suppe (1981). He has pointed out that 'until recently the vast majority of studies of homosexuality were conducted by heterosexual researchers . . . who have been acculturated into the values and behaviours of the dominant heterosexual culture. The homosexual male has also been reared in that culture and learns somewhat different ones during the lengthy process of coming out and acculturation into the male homosexual sub-culture' (Suppe 1981, p. 79). Suppe concludes that this acculturation requires 'significant promiscuous male homosexual experience' and that this is inevitably difficult 'unless one has a homosexual orientation'. In support of his basic assertion that heterosexuals are ill-equipped to research into homosexual behaviour Suppe cites Bell (1975): 'I am convinced that we have failed to tap important dimensions of the homosexual experience . . . more contact with our subject populations would probably have enhanced my own self-awareness of the diversity of homosexual experience; our studies would then have been at once more objective and comprehensive' (Bell 1975, pp. 426–7). Suppe discusses the problem and possible solutions at some length and suggests as a way out of the difficulty the 'combined collaborative input of professionally competent heterosexual and homosexual researchers' (Suppe 1981, p. 79). Each will compensate for the blind spots and biases of the other.

The establishment and continued vigorous existence of the *Journal of*

Homosexuality is part of the generally enhanced status and self-confidence of the homosexual community. The *Journal* is now in its seventh year and is an important focus for empirical research on all aspects of male and female homosexuality, covering a wide range of academic perspectives from biology to law.

It is clearly vital that descriptive and explanatory data are as unbiased as possible. A great deal of time and effort has been expended in developing theories to account for data which turn out to be the product of distorted sampling, inadequate research designs, faulty or biased research instruments or of researchers unacceptable to the homosexual community. The growing self-confidence of the homosexual community and the increased participation in research of researchers whose sexual preference is homosexual are both likely to improve the quality of research in this field. It is also becoming clear that the true focus for future research should be the nature and development of sexual preference *in general*, rather than any particular preference. The biological and social influences which produce the homosexual preference are likely to be the same as those which produce the heterosexual preference. However, the extensive research done to date has largely been conducted with the homosexual participants as the 'experimental' group and the heterosexual ones as the 'controls' and such studies inevitably figure very largely in this chapter.

Before going on to descriptive and explanatory studies of the homosexual preference the homosexual community requires a special consideration, as to the historically based legal, occupational and social disabilities suffered by that community.

THE SOCIAL CONTEXT

The church

The attitude of the Christian church to homosexual behaviour, adapted from Old Testament sex codes, has been strongly condemnatory. The ecclesiastical courts had the right to punish homosexual offences and did so, by torture and death, until the French Revolution of 1789, the effect of which was a limitation of the penal code to such acts as sex with children. Since then the control of sexual behaviour, both heterosexual and homosexual, has increasingly rested with the lay, rather than the ecclesiastical, courts and a more liberal approach has very gradually developed. That it has still some way to go is indicated below.

Medicine

In the eighteenth and nineteenth centuries doctors followed the church in trying to limit all forms of sexual conduct (Bullough 1974). The general view was that non-procreative sex (masturbation and any form of birth control) was not only wrong but also harmful, bringing on a range of ills from fits to fevers. Homosexual behaviour was also seen as non-procreative and hence as deviant. Moreover, until very recently homosexuality figured in the standard classification of psychiatric problems. It was only in 1974 that the American Psychiatric Association removed it from its *Diagnostic and Statistical Manual of Mental Disorders*. This is a good beginning, but the attitudes of doctors themselves, rather than one of their representative associations, may take much longer to change.

The law

The severe legal disabilities long suffered by male homosexuals have been much lightened recently. For example, in 1967 the United Kingdom Parliament passed the Sexual Offences (No. 2) Act which made sexual behaviour between consenting males in England and Wales (it was never illegal between females) no longer an offence provided it was conducted in private and both participants were over 21. The next target for British homosexuals and their sympathizers is a reduction of the age of consent to 16, the same as for heterosexuals. Public opinion is likely to move in this direction only very slowly. (In practice, there seem very few British prosecutions for homosexual behaviour when one partner is between 16 and 21, provided that the other is also at least 16.)

The same legalization of private acts between consenting male adults has occurred in the USA where developments have also taken place across a wide spectrum of other legal and civil rights. These are well illustrated by a special double issue of the *Journal of Homosexuality* (Fall–Winter 1979–80). An overview paper by Knutson (1980), a professor of law, illustrates some of the key legal decisions of recent years, particularly as they concern the right to employment in the public service, the right of a gay organization to official recognition (for example, in a university) and the rights to custody or visitation of gay parents. Over the last decade the response of the American judiciary to a surge of legislation which has challenged anti-homosexual laws and conventions has been somewhat mixed. According to Knutson the following conclusions are reasonable:

(a) the law and the legal process, which may either mandate discriminatory practices or permit a discrimination to occur without legal redress, seriously impinge upon the constitutional liberties of more than a million Americans; (b) the disarray in the decisional laws results principally from the differing perceptions and visceral reactions of individual judges with respect to the phenomena of homosexuality; (c) the refusal of the United States Supreme Court to provide guidance or leadership fosters and exacerbates the problem. (pp. 5–6)

Knutson isolates several key elements of such 'differing perceptions and visceral reactions' and illustrates them by reference to key cases in which they played a major part in decisions some of which have been unfavourable to the homosexual plaintiff.

1. The 'criminality' theory. Very roughly, this goes as follows: there are laws against sodomy; sodomy is *ipso facto* a criminal offence; therefore all homosexuals have criminal status; hence it is justified to withhold constitutional protections from them.

2. Homosexuality is self-evidently 'a crime against nature'. The circularity of this assertion is well illustrated by the response of the Supreme Court of Louisiana to claims of unconstitutional vagueness: 'these words [i.e. the crime against nature] have a well-defined, well-understood, and generally accepted meaning, i.e. any carnal copulation or sexual joining that is devious and abnormal because it does not conform to the order obtained by nature' (La. 1975, cited by Knutson 1980, p. 9).

Associated with the 'against nature' assertion is the equally 'self-evident' assertion of 'immorality', which appears for example in the statement of the United States Court of Claims: 'any schoolboy knows that a homosexual act is immoral, indecent, lewd and obscene' (Ct.Cl. 1969). Knutson illustrates the importance of the 'immorality' assertion by reference to the Gaylord case (Wash. 1977). The question was a simple one: whether a schoolteacher could lawfully be discharged solely because he was a 'known homosexual'. The Court posed the determinative issue as: 'was Gaylord guilty of immorality?' The Court recognized that 'in its abstract sense, the term is not and perhaps cannot be comprehensively defined.' Nevertheless, relying on the *New Catholic Encyclopaedia*, it found that since 'homosexuality is widely condemned as immoral and was so condemned as immoral during biblical times,' Gaylord's admission of being 'homosexual' constituted an admission of being 'immoral' and justified his dismissal (Knutson 1980, p. 9).

3. Dismissal from employment has also been justified by the social damage caused by homosexuals. This sort of justification was given in the judge's conclusion in the case of Drew *v.* Halaby (D.C. Cir. 1963). Dismissal was appropriate because 'to require employees to work with persons who have committed acts which are repugnant to the established and accepted standards of decency and morality can only have a disrupting effect upon the morals and efficiency of any organization' (Knutson 1980, p. 10).

4. The 'sickness theory'. As indicated earlier it was only in 1974 that the

American Psychiatric Association removed homosexuality from its list of mental disorders. The sickness assertion has been used to justify denial of security clearances to gay applicants (e.g. 9th Cir. 1973).

Despite the pervading nature of the perceptions and attitudes listed above it seems that much progress is being made and Knutson cites a number of landmark judgements. He concludes: 'it appears settled that the Federal Government in its role as employer cannot discriminate on the basis of sexual orientation' (Knutson 1980, p. 14). He cites legal precedent in California which indicate that laws enjoining equal employment opportunities apply to private as well as federal employers. He notes that the California Supreme Court is one whose opinions are highly regarded, often followed by other American courts. (However, discrimination remains strong in the armed forces. As the US Attorney-General argued in a recent case: 'tensions and hostilities would certainly exist between known homosexuals and the great majority of naval personnel who despise/detest homosexuality' (Ct.App. 1978).

So far as Britain is concerned, in July 1982 the senior policeman who served as the head of the Royal bodyguard resigned because his association with a 'homosexual prostitute' – as the person concerned was described in the British press – became public knowledge. There was no suggestion that he had performed his duties with less than complete devotion. Moreover, an attempt some years earlier by the partner concerned to threaten blackmail had failed when the policeman concerned told him to do what he wished with the information.

Social attitudes

Levitt and Klassen (1974) reported a section of a 1970 American survey on attitudes to homosexuality, carried out by the Institute for Sex Research, which involved a rigorously constructed national sample of 30,000 American adults. These results may be generalized to the whole American adult population. Homosexual behaviour was perceived as 'always wrong', even when the participants 'were in love', by 70 per cent of the sample and as 'almost always wrong' by another 8 per cent. (It can be assumed that the homosexual section of the sample can be numbered among the remaining 22 per cent.) Adultery was regarded almost as unfavourably, but adolescent heterosexual intercourse was considerably less disapproved of. Another question concerned in which of the professions homosexual men should be allowed to work. The results fell into three groups: a quarter supported homosexuals being judges, teachers and ministers of religion, and a third supported their being doctors and government officials; by contrast over three-quarters agreed that homosexuals should be allowed to be beauticians, artists and florists. Nearly half the sample 'strongly agreed' that it was dangerous to allow homosexuals to be teachers or youth leaders and that they are high security risks; over a third were equally firm that homosexuals seek out children for sexual purposes and a quarter that they seek to corrupt their co-workers. Other (and equally incorrect) stereotypes were even more strongly held. Nearly three-quarters strongly agreed that homosexuals act like the opposite sex and two-thirds that they have an unusually strong sex drive (a nice contradiction; other survey evidence indicates a popular belief that women have a weaker sex drive than men). While half or more were strongly opposed to homosexuals dancing together in public and to the existence of 'gay' bars, only a small minority favoured excluding them from church membership – this finding suggests that it is 'public display' which causes objections.

There has been no similar British large-scale survey. Hays (1978) looked at the views of a random sample of the population served by one Birmingham general practice. Their attitudes could be summarized as 'equal but separate': that is, homosexuals should be accorded most of the same rights as heterosexuals – although there was some doubt about their fitness to be employed as teachers – but social mixing between heterosexuals and homosexuals was undesirable; homosexuals should 'keep themselves to themselves'.

The homosexual community

Very broadly, homosexuals may be divided into those who lead overtly homosexual social lives and those who continue to keep their sexual preference secret, despite its greater acceptance in recent years by general society, and despite the greater confidence of the homosexual community. It is safe to say that homosexual persons, both men and women, are to be found in every occupation. The traditional stereotype of a special association between homosexual preference and certain occupations may be no more than a myth – due to the traditionally greater acceptance of homosexuals by some occupations (such as the arts) and the equally traditional lesser acceptance by others (such as the 'liberal' professions and the armed services).

By definition, persons whose sexual preference eventually emerges as homosexual are born into and are exposed to the social and sexual norms of heterosexual society. As they become aware of their homosexual preference (on average in their middle to late teens, but with a variation on either side) they may either conceal it or begin the long process of 'coming out'. According to Suppe (1981), for the male this

> usually results in being thrust into the available male homosexual sub-culture, completely ill-equipped and burdened with inappropriate values and instincts... one must learn to accept sex as primarily a recreational activity wherein going

home with a partner can be as casual and uncommitting as picking up a partner at the tennis court for a few sets. One has to learn to cruise . . . one must recognize that lover relationships are likely to survive only if they are sexually non-exclusive . . . the individual experiences an element of 'culture shock' followed by a need to acculturate to the new sub-culture . . . this is comparable . . . to a light-skinned black person, raised as white, who attempts to enter the black sub-culture as black. (Suppe 1981, p. 77)

Suppe refers to his extensive experience with 'newly out' gay college students. He considers that the reacculturation typically takes at least three years and may never be fully accomplished. According to Suppe the phrase 'coming out' has three major meanings. First, informing one's friends, family and employers of one's homosexuality and refusing any longer to 'pass' as heterosexual. Second, the process of reacculturation, and third, coming to accept that one is homosexual and that the well-known abusive terms refer to oneself.

The gay ghetto.   The development of the homosexual community in such North American cities as Los Angeles and San Francisco was documented by earlier writers such as Hooker (1967) and Achilles (1967). According to them the community lives in one specific area of the city and uses exclusively homosexual meeting places, particularly pubs and 'gay bars'. The latter were described as the key social centres both for sexual transactions and for more practical issues such as finding a job or a place to live. According to Gagnon and Simon (1967) the female homosexual community was less highly organized than the male and also placed less emphasis on transient sexual relationships.

A report by Levine (1979) concerns a careful study of a number of areas in major North American cities, popularly thought to be male 'gay ghettos'. Originally 'ghetto' was used to indicate the area of a European city assigned to medieval Jewry, who were banned from the remainder of the city. Twentieth-century sociologists use it to describe the more or less voluntary segregation of a cultural or ethnic group in a particular area. Applying current sociological criteria, an urban neighbourhood can be termed a gay ghetto if it contains gay institutions in numbers, a conspicuous and locally dominant gay subculture that is socially isolated from the larger community and a residential population that is substantially gay. Levine studied twenty-seven neighbourhoods in five major American cities and found three, one each in New York, Los Angeles and San Francisco, which met the key requirements for the appellation gay ghetto. There were also twelve which did so partially. He suggests that the transition to a gay ghetto is assisted by a modicum of tolerance which attracts gay men. The resulting concentration attracts other gays and a consequent heterosexual withdrawal. The process is the same as for the development of Jewish, Black or Italian neighbourhoods.

However, it should be pointed out that there is an important difference. Jews, Italians and other ethnic groups have distinctive histories, cultures, languages, religions, and so on. What are the distinctive features of the gay community other than their sexual preference and their consequent search for partners and the social display associated with this? It may be that when acceptance by the heterosexual majority has gone much further than at present, homosexual persons will 'reintegrate' into the various communities with which they have ties of non-sexual kinds – religious, cultural, ethnic, and so on.

DESCRIPTIVE STUDIES

Definition

It is difficult to arrive at an acceptable definition of many forms of human behaviour. Perhaps the least contentious definition of the homosexual preference is: sexual behaviour between members of the same sex, accompanied by sexual arousal, carried out recurrently and despite the opportunity of a heterosexual behaviour. (For a definition of the heterosexual preference amend appropriately – 'opposite' for 'same', 'homosexual' for 'heterosexual'. I exclude those who engage in homosexual activities only in prison or other settings which preclude access to heterosexual partners. The definition is clear-cut when we consider only those whose sexual activities and feelings are solely or almost solely homosexual or heterosexual, but what of the substantial number of persons who engage in sexual activities of both kinds? This brings us to the equally difficult topic of classification.

Classification

The simple division between 'homosexuals' and 'heterosexuals' is clearly unsatisfactory. The pioneering Kinsey studies (1948, 1953) used a 7-point scale, whereby o was exclusively heterosexual in behaviour and 6 exclusively homosexual, the points between indicating the differing proportions of homosexual and heterosexual outlets, out of total sexual activity. More recently, Bell and Weinberg (1978) suggested separate o–6 scales for both 'behaviour' and 'feelings' (the two are highly correlated but not completely so). The two scales are then summed so as to yield a 14–point scale.

Feldman and MacCulloch (1971) argued for a broad division between the primary and secondary homosexual preferences. The two groups are likely to shade into each other rather than being clear-cut, but for purposes of exposition it is convenient to retain the distinction. Primary homosexuals are those who have never experienced heterosexual arousal at any stage in their lives.

Heterosexual behaviour may have occurred occasionally but for social appearance only. Secondary homosexuals have experienced noticeable heterosexual arousal, together with some heterosexual activity. The secondary group varies within itself according to the relative proportions of homosexual and heterosexual activities: the more of the former the nearer the individual is to the '6' end of the Kinsey scale, the more of the latter the nearer to the 'o' end. Whereas most, but not all, of those occupying the o and 6 positions are likely to have done so throughout their lives, positions 1–5 are far from permanent, with much movement over time. The Kinsey data suggest polarization with increasing age, with progressively fewer persons occupying the mid-points. Finally, by definition, the Kinsey group o (and possibly some Kinsey 1s) may be described as *primary heterosexuals*.

Numbers

As yet there are no surveys concerning the sexual preferences of properly constructed samples of the general population. The Kinsey surveys of the 1940s had serious sampling errors although the quality of the interview construction and administration was very high. A rough analysis suggests that about 4 to 5 per cent of the white male sample in the Kinsey survey had been in the primary group from their earliest awareness of their homosexual preference to the time of the interview. Around 12 per cent had been in the secondary group for at least three years between the ages of 16 and 55. About 20 per cent of the remainder had more or less incidental homosexual experience. The homosexual proportions of the Kinsey female sample were markedly less – perhaps a half of the male in each case.

A much more recent report by Shively and DeCecco (1978) provides an interesting comparison. They surveyed the sexual preferences of just over 1000

Table 1   Behaviour and feelings in sexual preference

| | Behaviour | | | | Feelings | | | |
| | Females | | Males | | Females | | Males | |
	Number	%	Number	%	Number	%	Number	%
Homosexual	24	4.3	57	14.8	30	5.3	48	12.6
Bisexual	24	4.3	12	3.1	51	8.9	32	8.4
Heterosexual	515	91.4	316	82.1	495	85.8	300	79.0
Total *	563	100	385	100	576	100	380	100

* The totals in the 'feelings' columns are not exactly the same as those in the 'behaviour' columns; the authors provide no explanation.

of the nearly 22,000 students of San Francisco State University, but unfortunately give no details of the sampling method. They recorded data for both males and females on a Kinsey 0–6 basis, for both sexual behaviours and feelings and then combined the groups (0 + 1 = the heterosexual preference, 5 + 6 the homosexual). Their combined results for behaviours and feelings are shown in table 1 (somewhat reworked from the original data so as to include groups 2–4 ('bisexual') and to show behaviours and feelings in the same table.

The main conclusions which can be drawn from these results are:

1. Some of the results repeat those of the Kinsey findings of 30 years earlier. For example, the proportion of males who are homosexual is significantly higher than the proportion of females for both feelings and behaviour. (However, female sexual development may lag a little behind that of males so that a follow-up some years later might indicate more equal percentages of the two sexes as being more or less exclusively homosexual.)

2. There are several important differences from the Kinsey results.

   (a) Much smaller percentages of both sexes fall into the 'bisexual' groups.
   (b) In general about 80 per cent of the male sample and 85 per cent of the female sample are more or less exclusively heterosexual in both behaviour and feelings. This is about the same noted by Kinsey although the division between exclusive and bisexual is very different.
   (c) About 15 per cent of the males are more or less exclusively homosexual as against only 5 per cent who are bisexual. The proportions reported by Kinsey were the reverse of these.
   (d) About 4 per cent of the female group are exclusively homosexual in behaviour and the same proportion is bisexual. Again this is rather different from the Kinsey results though not so strikingly so as for the males.

Caution is needed in comparing these data with the Kinsey results. The Kinsey male survey covered the full range of age and education and the female one also covered the full age range (although two-thirds of them were college-educated). However, these results do suggest that while the *total* proportion of individuals who report the homosexual preference is unchanged, sexual choice is much more decisive and clear-cut than in earlier years with much less tendency to bisexuality – this is perhaps because of the more liberal climate for the homosexual preference, particularly in the Bay Area of California where the Shively and DeCecco survey was carried out. It should also be pointed out that not all of those labelled exclusively homosexual in the above survey fit the primary group of Feldman and MacCulloch. The Shively and DeCecco survey was concerned with *current* problems and feelings and not with life-long experiences.

DESCRIPTIONS

Introduction

This section reviews the evidence concerning descriptive differences on a variety of measures between persons of different sexual preference. Any differences which emerge might point to crucial explanatory variables. The main areas in which descriptive differences have been sought fall, as is usual in behavioural research, into two broad groups: biological and psychological.

Thus far the story is straightforward but at this point difficulties arise. The evidence concerning classification makes it clear that it is a gross oversimplification to regard groups of homosexuals as homogeneous, readily comparable with equally homogeneous groups of heterosexuals. Persons in general occupy different points on the spectrum from a life-long complete homosexual preference through the bisexual preference in different proportions to a life-long complete heterosexual preference. Some people occupy the same position on the spectrum throughout their lives. Others move about; perhaps as far as from one extreme to the other. At the very least we should employ research designs which involve three groups: group A, life-long homosexuals; group B, life-long heterosexuals; and a mixed group C – which has experienced both forms of arousal in varying proportions at different times. Even further subdivisions of the third group might be desirable. Such a design might indicate, for example, that group A differed from the other two (if at all) mainly on biological measures, while group B differed from group C (if at all) mainly on psychological measures. This kind of outcome is predicted by the Feldman–MacCulloch theory (1971) of primary *versus* secondary homosexuality, outlined at the end of this chapter.

Unfortunately the majority of the research at both the descriptive and explanatory levels has compared an undifferentiated group of homosexuals (groups A and C combined) with a group of presumed heterosexuals (group B). The detailed descriptions of certain of the studies reported provide clues as to differences within the homosexual groups employed and between such subgroups and the heterosexual comparison group. But the clues are thin and extrapolation to what might have resulted from a more satisfactory design is very uncertain.

Responses to heterosexual stimuli

The majority of homosexuals have had heterosexual advances made to them, as have almost all heterosexuals. A significant minority of homosexuals, possibly the primary group, have always taken strong evasive action (Kolaszynska-Carr 1970) and report unpleasant subjective reactions, particularly fear and anxiety. In addition, some female homosexuals report marked anger and disgust when they find themselves exposed to heterosexual advances. Both male and female homosexuals keep away from contexts in which sexual advances from a person of the opposite sex are likely, and they do so far more than heterosexuals (Ramsay and van Velzen 1968; Kolaszynska-Carr 1970). There is good evidence that male homosexuals get on better socially with women significantly older than themselves than do male heterosexuals, possibly because of the lower probability of a sexual approach or demand from the female concerned (Kolaszynska-Carr 1970). There is thus a clear picture of avoidance of heterosexual social stimuli by adult homosexuals of both sexes. There is good evidence that homosexuals show a decline in heterosexual arousal from adolescence to adulthood (Kinsey et al. 1948, 1953; Kolaszynska-Carr 1970). The primary–secondary theory asserts that the decline is confined to the secondary group; the primary group has never experienced any arousal.

Personality assessment

The theory that the homosexual preference is an indication of psychological disturbance goes back at least as far as Sigmund Freud, who related homosexuality specifically to paranoia. In a more general sense the view has been widely held that the homosexual preference indicated a neurosis, or a psychological instability of some kind. Indeed for many years the American Psychiatric Association included homosexuality in its list of psychological problems, along with various types of neurosis and psychosis. Of course, homosexuals may develop all kinds of psychological problems, as may heterosexuals, but is there any reason to consider the homosexual preference *in itself* as an indication of personality disturbance?

A number of studies have compared homosexuals and heterosexuals on self-report questionnaires of personality. The general finding is that when the homosexual group is in some special and restricted setting – a psychiatric hospital or a prison – and the heterosexual group is living in a normal setting, the scores obtained by the former do indicate greater psychological disturbance. This difference is almost certainly due to the variation in setting, rather than to differences in sexual preference. However, even when the comparison has been between groups both of which live in normal social contexts, the homosexual group tends to obtain scores indicating that they are more anxious than the comparable heterosexual group. There is increasing evidence that a major reason for this finding is the social rejection experienced by many homosexuals. One way to test this possibility is to ask samples of heterosexuals and homosexuals, both males and females, about their history of psychological problems. Kolaszynska-Carr (1970) asked members of these groups to attribute their psychological problems to a cause – sexual or non-sexual. Whereas there were no differences between the female groups, the male homosexuals were more likely than their heterosexual counterparts to have had a sexually connected psychological problem. When we remember that society is more hostile to male than to female homosexuality this result is entirely to be expected. Further evidence comes from studies of the relatively tolerant college environment. For example, Dean and Richardson (1964) found only a very small difference in psychological disturbance between student homosexuals and heterosexuals. It can be concluded that the presence or absence of a psychological problem is a most unsatisfactory method of distinguishing sexual preference. Providing that people are living in a social environment equally tolerant of both preferences, there is no reason to expect one group to be more disturbed than the other; the full range of psychological stability–instability will be found in both groups.

Physical measures

Body-build.   The conventional view of the male homosexual is that his build is rather 'feminine'; the opposite stereotype is held of the female homosexual. What is the evidence for these popular beliefs? Once again, it is essential to study people living normal lives in the community and desirable to divide the homosexual group according to whether they fall into the primary or secondary categories. A report by Evans (1972) approaches these requirements. He compared 44 non-patient male homosexuals and III heterosexual men for body-build, childhood behaviours and a variety of biochemical measures. Half the homosexual sample was described as having been exclusively homosexual throughout their lives (corresponding to the primary group). The remainder reported intermittent heterosexual activity (if we can assume that this has been accompanied by sexual arousal, they would correspond to the secondary group). Differences were indeed found for the body-build measures; the homosexual group, despite being slightly taller, were significantly lighter, less muscular, and were longer in proportion to their bulk (termed linearity). Their physique was less masculine on a combined measure developed and standardized by Tanner (1951). Moreover, the range of scores was much greater for the homosexuals than for the heterosexuals – exactly what would be expected of a group containing two relatively different sub groups – whereas some homosexuals had body-build scores as high (more 'masculine') as any of the heterosexuals, none of the latter had scores as low as some of the homosexuals. Evans also reported several interesting correlations between linearity and childhood behaviours (more effeminate in the high linearity subjects) which will be referred to later in this chapter.

Sex hormones. Early studies (Heller and Maddock 1947) failed to show differences in endocrine levels between homosexuals and heterosexuals. The methods were technically crude and, in addition, these studies all compared heterosexuals with undifferentiated groups of homosexuals. The issue was revived by a report by Margolese (1970) who carried out an analysis of serum androsterone and etiocholanolane in ten heterosexuals and ten homosexuals and found a clear separation in their values with no overlap, the levels of these hormones in the homosexuals being lower than in the heterosexuals. Evans (1972), testing the sample referred to in the previous section, and using refined methods of analysis, obtained significant differences in several biochemical indices between his groups. These included blood serum levels of testosterone and two of the products of androgen metabolism which are considered indicants of androgenic hormone levels, the values of all of which were lower in the homosexual group. Moreover, the range of scores was higher in the homosexual group, again suggesting, as did the body-build data, the very varied nature of the homosexual group.

Other studies have both used refined biochemical methods and attempted a rough division of their homosexual samples which approximates to the primary–secondary distinction. Kolodny et al. (1971 and 1972) studied 30 male homosexual students between the ages of 18 and 24, who were interviewed and assigned Kinsey ratings. The mean testosterone levels when compared to a comparison group of 50 heterosexual males matched for age were significantly below the control mean for homosexuals who were rated as Kinsey 5 and 6, but not for homosexuals with Kinsey ratings of 3 and 4. Unfortunately this report did not detail the extent to which the Kinsey 6s had been solely homosexual for the whole of their lives. Nevertheless, the findings, which replicate those obtained in a smaller study by Loraine et al. (1971) are of interest. Kolodny et al. point out that the depressed plasma testosterone levels of their Kinsey 5s and 6s could be the secondary result of a homosexual orientation (the relative absence of heterosexual activity might be the cause rather than the effect).

However, more recent studies of hormones in male homosexuals have failed to support these earlier findings. Examples of these negative results include reports by Pillard et al. (1974) and Doerr et al. (1973). Between 1972 and 1977 there were at least ten more studies in testosterone in male homosexuality, reviewed by Meyer-Bahlburg (1977). He states that most of the homosexuals who have been investigated had testosterone levels which were indistinguishable from those found in heterosexuals. There are however a small number of studies which show high or low testosterone levels and only two studies which examined the levels of unbound (active) serum testosterone.

It is known that testosterone levels fluctuate widely on both a daily and a weekly basis (Parks et al 1974), so that it is quite possible that any real hormonal differences between groups of homosexuals and heterosexuals may have been concealed by these fluctuations. Clearly, more sophisticated methods of sampling for hormone assay are needed and the failure to subdivide homosexuals into primary and secondaries may well be crucial to the exposure of serum hormone differences between homosexuals and heterosexuals (MacCulloch and Feldman 1977).

Meyer-Bahlburg (1977, p. 331) concludes that because of the inconsistency of the results on testosterone and the methodological shortcomings in many studies, it is 'premature to theorize on general mechanisms underlying endocrine deviations in adult homosexuals derived from individual studies. . . . The data available make it seem highly unlikely that deviations in testosterone levels and production in adulthood can be held responsible for the development of male homosexuality in general.'

The results of studies on gonadotrophin levels in male homosexuals also lack uniformity or any coherence, although Kolodny et al. (1972) and Doerr et al (1976) both found elevated levels of luteinizing hormone (LH), the former group with decreased plasma testosterone levels and the latter with raised testosterone. Some of Kolodny's subjects appeared to suffer from primary testicular dysfunction so that it is clear that the non-comparability of groups is one of the reasons for the generally confusing hormonal picture.

EXPLANATIONS

Introduction

The major explanations of the acquisition of homosexual behaviour will be considered successively in terms of the age at which the effects of biological influences or environmental events are said to occur, beginning with the view that homosexuality is genetically determined, and proceeding through intrauterine influences, early infantile experiences, to single-sex environments, specific sexual experiences, and population control. Typically the explanations are intended by their supporters to account for the homosexual behaviour of *all* homosexuals. Thus at one extreme are the proponents of a biological view, and at the other extreme of an environmental view. Occasionally there is a hint of a biology–environment interaction, but in the main the views may be characterized as: the homosexual behaviour of all persons behaving in this manner is environmental in origin, or is biological in origin. By contrast, my approach is that there are two broadly distinct groups of homosexual individuals – the primary and the secondary. In general, and very cautiously, I expect future research to indicate the greater importance of biological influences for the primary group and of social learning influences for the secondary group.

Genetic influences

The first, and still the largest, sample of twins studied with respect to homosexual behaviour was reported by Kallmann (1952a, b), who described the result of a study of 85 pairs of twins. Information on sexual behaviour was available for 37 of the 40 monozygotic (identical) pairs and 26 of the dizygotic (non-identical) pairs. Whereas all the monozygotic pairs were concordant (similar) for homosexuality, this was true for less than half of the dizygotic group. Despite the apparent conclusiveness of this finding Kallmann's own conclusion was rather cautious: 'On the whole, adaptational equilibrium between the potentialities of organic sex differentials and consequent patterns of psychosexual behaviour, seems to be so labile that the attainment of muturational balance may be displayed at different development stages by a variety of disturbing mechanisms.' Thus Kallman seems to be hinting strongly at the possibility of gene–environment interaction in the causation of homosexual behaviour. A year later, Kallmann (1953) considered the 100 per cent concordance between monozygotic twins obtained in his earlier study to be 'a statistical artefact'. In the same book he reported in the form of a footnote: 'A monozygotic pair, one of whom was both schizophrenic and homosexual, the other was neither' (p. 115).

Since this early work several authors (e.g. Rainer et al. 1960; Klintworth 1962; Parker 1964) have reported pairs of monozygotic twins *discordant* for sexual behaviour, one being homosexual and the other heterosexual. The report by Rainer et al. was concerned with two pairs of monozygotic twins, one female and one male, and in both cases the authors claim an early discrepancy in the maternal handling of the members of both pairs of twins. They emphasize the extent to which twins that cannot be easily distinguished induce maternal anxiety. The mother feels she needs to differentiate the twins. Consequently she accentuates, deliberately or otherwise, relatively small initial differences. A similar emphasis on differences in the way twins are handled was made by Parker in his report on three discordant homosexual pairs, two male and one female.

Heston and Shields (1968) report two sets of British data, the first being concerned with a family with a sibship of 14, which contained three pairs of male monozygotic twins. The second set of data consisted of all the twin pairs (12 in number) in the Maudsley Twin Register, which had been kept since 1948, in which at least one member of the pair had a 'diagnosis' of homosexuality. In the first set of data two of the three monozygotic twin pairs were concordant for homosexuality, and one for heterosexuality. All six individuals grew up in 'a severely disruptive environment'. Heston and Shields considered that both genetic and environmental factors were required to explain the aetiology of sexual behaviour in this family. Of the twelve male twins with a primary or secondary diagnosis of homosexuality five were monozygotic, and of these, three were concordant and two discordant (one of the latter two formed part of the series reported by Parker). Of the seven dizygotic twins only one was concordant and six were not.

Despite the reports of discordant pairs it seems that concordance for sexual behaviour is more frequent in identical than non-identical twins. This would be considered as supporting a genetic control of the behaviour in question. Nevertheless, so far as sexual behaviour, which is inevitably largely interpersonal, whether in overt behaviour or in feelings, is concerned, some doubts must remain. Twins raised in the same home may have their first sexual experience with each other. By definition, identical twins are of the same sex. Given both the possible relative importance of the first sexual experience for later orientation, and the well-known closeness of identical twins, concordance for homosexual behaviour might equally well have an environmental as a genetic basis. It follows that even for those reports in which identical twins are more frequently concordant for homosexual behaviour than non-identical twins, one cannot conclude with confidence that this had a genetic basis unless the twins were separated very early in life and were subsequently reared apart in environments in which heterosexual behaviour was equally encouraged, or equally discouraged. In a study comparing separated and non-separated identical and non-identical twins, the genetic view of causation would be supported if the concordance for non-separated identical twins were as great for separated ones, and if it were greater in both than for non-identical twins of the same sex, whether reared apart of not. The difficulties of securing a sizeable sample of identical-twin pairs reared apart are formidable and would be complicated by both the relative infrequency of the homosexual preference and the reluctance of homosexual individuals to identify themselves. An alternative research design, which would employ the powerful statistical techniques developed in psychogenetic work on animals (Jinks and Fulker 1970), might be possible using non-twin siblings, who would be much more easily obtainable.

MacCulloch et al. (1967) have described the case of a monozygotic twin pair *discordant* for sexual orientation, the homosexual twin being of the *primary* group. This appears to be one of the few reports in which there are sufficiently full data to assign the homosexual twin in a discordant pair confidently to either the primary or the secondary group. It is of interest that the homosexual twin of MacCulloch et al. was unaggressive and dependent as a child, in very marked contrast to his heterosexual co-twin. Because the twins were discordant a solely genetic explanation is ruled out, and an environmental contribution must be sought. The effects of the post-natal psychological environment provided by the twins' parents would have had to have been particularly powerful to produce such major generalized differences in behaviour between the members of the twin pair and the possibility was therefore raised that the source of the 'environmental' contribution determining the primary homosexuality of the MacCulloch et al. twin was the intrauterine hormone environment in which the babies spent their first nine months after conception (see MacCulloch and Feldman 1977). Of course, there does not have to be a sharp division between a genetic and an intrauterine view of the causation of primary homosexuality. It may be that there is a relative genetic predisposition, which then leads to differences in the intrauterine hormone environment of certain individuals: genetic predisposition does not have to be an all or none phenomenon. The evidence concerning pre-natal hormonal influences follows.

Pre-natal hormones

It has been established that sex dimorphic behaviour in subhuman mammals is organized early in development, either pre- or perinatally, by sex hormones (Money and Ehrhardt 1972). There are only a few studies in humans which relate to the effects of pre-natal hormones, but one significant work is that of Money and Ehrhardt (1971) who studied ten cases of androgen insensitivity, all of whom were homosexual in relation to their chromosomal sex although they were phenotypically female. It is not possible to partial out the effects of hormones and rearing in this and other similar studies, e.g. Money and Ogunro (1974).

However, there is a possible hormonal indicator of pre-natal androgen deficiency which can be used in the adult human male. This potentially promising line of enquiry was opened up by Dörner and his colleagues in East Germany, who have carried out a good deal of animal work concerned with the role of hormones in the general process of brain differentiation. An important finding which underlines the study which follows concerns the successive influence of androgen and oestrogen. When normal female rats (i.e. *not* exposed to high androgen levels at a critical period of differentiation – prior to birth) are injected as adults with oestrogen, the result is an increase in the production of luteinizing hormone (LH). The effect on normal male rats (exposed at around birth to male levels of androgen) is the opposite: a lowering of LH. This *positive oestrogen feedback effect* is thought to be due to sexual differentiation of the brain. It suggests another way in which there could be hormonal differences between some homosexuals and all heterosexuals:

differences in androgen levels could occur *in utero*, during the period of brain differentation. In this case the *adult* levels of sex hormones of either group of homosexual males would not be expected to differ reliably from those of heterosexual males. However, at least one important chemical effect of the early presence or absence of androgen should be detectable in adults: the effect of injected oestrogen would be the female pattern of response for both heterosexual females and male primary homosexuals (the positive oestrogen feedback effect) in distinct contrast to heterosexual males and secondary homosexuals who should not show the same feedback effect. Dörner et al. (1975) investigated 21 homosexual, 5 bisexual and 20 heterosexual males. The two former groups correspond roughly to the primary and secondary categories. Wheareas there was no difference in the serum testosterone levels of any of the three groups, there was a statistically significant difference in the oestrogen feedback effect between the 'primary' group and the combined heterosexual and 'secondary' groups.

Birke (1981) has criticized this study on three grounds. First, the oestrogen feedback effect has been demonstrated in males of primate species, suggesting that the effect is not anomalous. Second, while the Dörner results achieved statistical significance, they were obtained in only half the homosexual men and the feedback effect was very small indeed as compared to that in healthy human females – that is the *substantive* significance is very limited. Third, the homosexuals in the Dörner study were attending hospitals for venereal diseases and they may have been under stress – which in turn may have been responsible for the feedback effect. Much further doubt is raised by an unpublished attempt to replicate the Dörner results by Feldman et al. (1980). In this study the male homosexual sample was divided very carefully into primary and secondary individuals, as defined by Feldman and MacCulloch, and compared with the heterosexual group. No differences were found between any of the three male groups. All showed the characteristic male response. It seems that the oestrogen feedback effect may be yet another false trail in the long search for a biological basis for at least a proportion of homosexuals.

Finally, a fascinating opportunity for an ethically acceptable test of the effect of hormonal influences during pregnancy was available to Yalom et al. (1973). Mothers-to-be who suffer from diabetes are often given large doses of oestrogen to protect their unborn children from certain medical consequences of the diabetes. The authors compared the six-year-old sons of diabetic mothers who had been given oestrogen during pregnancy with the sons of mothers who did not suffer from diabetes, and hence did not receive oetstrogen. Differences were found on some measures of interest, namely for aggressive behaviour and athletic skills. However, the overlap between the groups was very considerable. Moreover, Yalom et al. failed to check the possibility that the diabetic mothers – who required special care during pregnancy – may have behaved more protectively by discouraging aggression etc. in their sons' early years than did the mothers with normal pregnancies. In order to test biological explanations fully the alternative, environmental explanation must always be borne in mind, and vice versa.

Child-rearing influences

The notion that the quality of the relationship between mother and young son is responsible for the kind of sexual relationship the boy is able to make in adulthood has its origin in the psychoanalytic theory of personality development, and specifically the Oedipal situation, homosexuality being seen as the result of an unresolved Oedipal conflict. The normal resolution for that conflict would be that the boy identified with his father, and the girl with her mother. In behavioural terms, both would then learn appropriate sex roles, which would include heterosexual behaviour. The prediction is that an unusually close and initimate relationship with the mother will hinder the development of heterosexual relationships during adolescence and adulthood, and so lead to homosexual behaviour by both boys and girls. The process will be assisted by the behaviour of the father being hostile and rejecting.

The studies which follow have almost all been retrospective in nature, the source of evidence concerning his/her childhood being the recollection of the adult male or female homosexual. Only those studies on non-patient groups and which have used a comparison group of other adults, presumed to be heterosexual, will be cited.

Evans (1969) used a 27-item questionnaire and administered it to a group of non-patient homosexual men and to a comparison group. Snortum et al. (1969) used a self-administered inventory of developmental experiences with a group of male homosexual subjects about to be exempted from military service and with control groups. Both sets of results confirm the significance of a close, binding mother and a rejecting, detached father in the aetiology of male homosexuality, but both studies are subject to the criticism that the answers to retrospective questions given by homosexuals may be influenced by their own acceptance of the theory in question.

Bene (1965a) compared 83 non-patient homosexuals with the same number of married (presumed heterosexual) males of roughly equivalent age and social class. Both groups were administered the Family Relations Test (Bene and Anthony 1962) in order to ascertain the nature of their child–parent relationships. The results showed that homosexual men recalled unsatisfactory relationships with their fathers more frequently than with their mothers. Manosevitz (1970) compared a sample of 28 non-patient homosexual and 22 heterosexual males, matched for educational socioeconomic levels. It was found that the parents of the homosexuals were more likely to be divorced or separated than were the parents of the heterosexuals at the time of testing. The conclusion was that homosexuals more frequently came from homes in which they experienced the effects of marital discord.

Apperson and McAdoo (1968) report that in their sample of 22 non-patient homosexuals and 22 heterosexual controls they found that the fathers of the homosexuals were more commonly reported as critical, impatient and rejecting and that the mothers were less restricting than the mothers of the heterosexual group. In contrast to the above studies, Greenblatt (1966) found no difference between homosexual and heterosexual men on semantic differential ratings of the attributes of mother and father. Fathers of both groups were rated as good, generous, pleasant, dominant and underprotective. Mothers were also rated as good and pleasant, as neither dominant or subordinate, as neither overprotective nor underprotective. Interestingly enough, Snortum et al. (1969, p. 770) concluded: 'The characteristics presently ascribed to the parents of homosexuals bear a striking resemblance to those that have been attributed to parents of schizophrenic patients.'

Bene (1965b), using a group of 37 non-patient female homosexuals and 18 married heterosexual controls, carried out a corresponding study to that with male heterosexuals described earlier. Her results suggested that although lesbians received less affection and felt more hostility towards their mothers than did the married controls, much more striking differences between the two groups were found in the feelings that were recalled about their fathers. The lesbian group were more often hostile towards and afraid of their fathers than were the married control subjects, and also felt that their fathers were weak and incompetent. In addition, Bene asked each subject whether her parents had wanted a boy when she was born. Significant differences emerged between the groups, which suggested that there might be a connection between the parents' wish for a son and the homosexuality of their daughter. Similar findings were also noted by Kenyon (1968), who carried out a postal questionnaire study of 123 non-patient female homosexuals and married controls. He found that three times as many homosexuals as heterosexual controls (28 per cent *versus* 10 per cent) thought that their parents would have preferred a boy to them. Kenyon also noted that poor relationships were recalled more frequently with both parents by the homosexual than by the control group. This finding was confounded to some extent by the higher neuroticism scores of the homosexual group.

Kolaszynska-Carr (1970) asked her subjects to describe the relationships they had with their mother and their father. The replies to these two questions were recorded verbatim and were rated by two independent judges into five major categories. When the overall ratings of the groups for relationships with the father were compared, only the two heterosexual groups were found to differ; the female group getting on less well with the father during childhood. The two female groups did not differ significantly from each other. The two male groups differed only in that more homosexual replies were placed in the 'not very well' category.

When the overall ratings of the four groups for their relationships with their mother were compared, differences were found only between the two homosexual groups; the female group getting on less well with the mother. The hypothesis concerning poor parental relationships for both male and female homosexuals received little support from this study. This is of some importance because Kolaszynska-Carr's study is probably the best designed and controlled yet reported.

What conclusions can we draw concerning the theory that inappropriate child–parent relationships predispose to adult homosexual behaviour? On the face of it, the majority of studies support the view that male homosexuals had more than usually close relationships with their mothers and less than usually close ones with their fathers. Female homosexuals tend to report a relationship with their father which was hostile and rejecting on the part of the latter. Before we can accept these conclusions at even a descriptive level we should note the higher scores obtained by Kenyon's (1968) homosexual group as compared with his heterosexual group on the Neuroticism Scale of the Maudsley Personality Inventory. The implication is that disturbed individuals seeking explanations for their present problems are most likely to 'blame' the way they were handled by their parents than are other individuals.

Another such report which casts doubt on the parental-relationship theory has been contributed by Siegelman (1974). He studies several hundred non-patient male homosexuals and heterosexuals and found that for the groups as a whole the homosexuals did describe less satisfactory family relations. However, when subgroups of those who scored low on a questionnaire measure of anxiety were compared, the differences in family relationships disappeared, suggesting that disturbed relationships are reported only by highly anxious homosexuals, and not by homosexuals in general.

Another problem is raised by the possibility that parental rejection, or over-closeness, even if it did occur, was in response to an existing feature of the child, rather than responsible for a later homosexual orientation in a child not otherwise predisposed. Bell (1968) has cited considerable evidence for the view that children serve as stimuli for their parents: a child unresponsive to parental stimulation will fail to reinforce parental attention, thus extinguishing that attention. For example, the apparent association of an 'autistic' child with 'cool, rejecting' parents suggests the conclusion that the parents have 'caused' the autism. The reverse is, at least, equally possible. Applying this analogy to the present context, it is possible that a father who hoped for a 'manly' son might reject an 'effeminate' one (I shall shortly suggest that the primary homosexual is likely to have been relatively 'effeminate' in childhood). Faced with this situation, the mother might protect the boy concerned. The parental behaviour is thus in response to the child, rather than the reverse. Similarly, parents who wished for a son, but instead were granted a daughter, might respond with rejection. The findings of Bene (1956b) and of Kenyon (1968), mentioned above, support this possibility. A different kind of response would be to treat a girl as if she were a boy, by strongly discouraging 'feminine' behaviour, including heterosexually oriented behaviour. The opposite case would be that parents who wanted a girl, but had a boy, might strongly discourage 'masculine' behaviour.

However, it would be wrong to go to the other extreme, and completely discount parental behaviour as initiating behaviour in the child, as well as responding to it. For example, parents who convey strong disapproval of heterosexual activities but fail to mention homosexual ones might, particularly in the context of a single-sex environment (see next section), inhibit the use of heterosexual outlets and increase the likelihood of homosexual ones. A particularly unpleasant father might lead a daughter to expect the worst from men in general, hence to believe that they are better avoided. Other examples could be given. What is clear is that retrospective studies are quite unsatisfactory as methods of testing any explanation where the evidence is obtained by self-report and consists of evaluations of earlier events. The only completely satisfactory method is that of the prospective study. My present conclusion is that parent–child relationships are certainly worthy of investigation, but that we should view the relationship as an interaction, rather than a one-way process.

However, a means of avoiding the effects of bias on retrospective studies of adult homosexuals is provided by the proposed primary–secondary dichotomy, if we can assume that neither group is more likely than the other to give biased retrospective accounts. Differences in parent–child relationships as reported by members of the two homosexual groups would then be of considerable interest. Unfortunately, the published reports to date of parent–child relationships do not allow the respondents to be divided into primaries and secondaries. In general, I would expect the nature of parent–child and parent–parent relationships to be largely irrelevant to the development of the primary homosexual. In contrast, an environment which inhibited the development of heterosexual behaviour, either through direct means or by poor parental modelling, would be more likely to be found in the childhood of secondary homosexuals than of both primary homosexuals and heterosexuals.

It is convenient to collect together at this point the occasional data on the childhood behaviour of homosexuals interviewed as adults. Once again, there should be no greater tendency for biased descriptions by primaries than by secondaries – in the sense of reporting childhood behaviour which suggested that they were 'inevitably' different. I expect primaries to report both sex-inappropriate behaviour and at least occasional expressions of a desire to be female, secondaries to report neither (or at least much less frequently than primary homosexuals and no more frequently than primary heterosexuals). Evans (1972) reported relationships between body-build, homosexual behaviour and self-reported childhood behaviour. As mentioned earlier he found homosexuals to be higher on linearity, being long in proportion to bulk, and lower on muscularity. Those males in the total group who were high on linearity and low on muscularity more often avoided physical fights, described themselves as frail and played with girls. Unfortunately, Evans did not compare his homosexual and heterosexual groups directly on the above childhood behaviours, let alone make separate comparisons for the two proposed homosexual groups, so that only an indirect inference is possible. However, these data do suggest a tendency towards childhood behavioural differences between some adult homosexuals and heterosexuals. A similar inference can be drawn from data collected by Carrier (1971) on Mexican homosexuals divided by self-description into anal-active and anal-passive subgroups on the basis of the role they preferred in anal intercourse. Whereas 88 per cent of the anal-active group reported heterosexual contacts, only 32 per cent of the anal-passive group did so, suggesting a very rough identification of the former as secondaries and the latter as primaries. Significantly more passive subjects reported playing with dolls and experimenting with female clothing as children, and as regarding themselves as effeminate, both as children and adults. Interestingly there were no differences between the groups in ratings of their parents on a scale of masculinity–femininity, suggesting that parental modelling was unlikely to account for the self-described effeminate behaviour of the anal-passive group. Finally, whereas none of the anal-active group experienced a desire to be female at least once, 83 per cent of the anal-passive group did so.

Green et al. (1972) compared the playroom toy preferences of 15 boys described by their parents as 'masculine' with those of 15 boys described as 'feminine', because of cross-dressing (i.e. in girls' clothing), preferring female playmates, and showing female gestures. Masculine boys played more with masculine toys, feminine boys played more with feminine toys. The 'feminine' group was considered to show the set of behaviours described by adult transsexuals as characterizing themselves in childhood. The authors refer to anecdotal evidence that adult homosexuals also report such childhood behaviour.

Single-sex environments

There is considerable evidence to link the isolation of animals from access to the opposite sex with disturbed heterosexual behaviour and occasional homosexual behaviour. Although, in natural surroundings, mammalian homosexual behaviour takes place when animals are sexually aroused, it usually does so only in addition to heterosexual behaviour. A copulatory preference for males in adult male rats can be induced by prolonged segregation from females (Jenkins 1928). A proportion of the sample who were isolated continued for an indefinite period to prefer homosexual behaviour, even when allowed access to females. Similarly, Rasmussen (1955) showed that male rats given an electric shock when they attempted to copulate with females were discouraged from further attempts at heterosexual behaviour.

The concept of imprinting at a critical period of development (Sluckin, 1970) has been used to account for such effects. The degree of reversibility of imprinted responses appears to be related to the level of the maturation of the organism. Harlow (1965) showed that adult monkeys separated from their mothers during the first six months of life were relatively incapable, either of sexual behaviour with the opposite sex or of appropriate maternal behaviour towards their own first-born offspring. However, there seemed to be some degree of recovery, because mating behaviour improved at a later age and their response to the second-born offspring was also normal.

Human infants and adolescents are rarely isolated completely, so that it is difficult to separate out the effects of isolation from the opportunites to copy other youngsters who are behaving in a homosexual manner, which they in turn might have acquired from a particular subculture. Membership of a single-sex subculture such as a boarding school, the norm in which was homosexual behaviour, would provide a powerful environment for the acquisition of homosexual behaviour through the imitation of models.

Unfortunately, there is very little evidence for or against such hypothesized increase in homosexual behaviour in single-sex environments, other than of an anecdotal or autobiographical kind (Lewis 1955). Schofield (1965), as a minor aspect of his survey of the heterosexual behaviour of adolescents, asked his subjects questions concerning their homosexual experiences. A very much higher proportion of those educated in single-sex boarding schools reported such experiences than those educated in day schools, whether co-educational or single-sex. However, Schofield did not question his subjects concerning their present preferred sexual orientation, and as his sample went up to the age of 19 years only, the persistence of the effects of school experience could not be assessed. West (1967) cites anecdotal evidence of the acquisition of homosexual behaviour by previously heterosexual males incarcerated in prisons or prisoner-of-war camps. He suggests that the post-confinement persistence of such homosexual behaviour is dependent upon whether it afforded a sexual outlet only or was associated also with emotional gratification, but reported no quantitative data concerning the post-confinement effect.

Kolaszynska-Carr (1970) found that the proportion of each of her four groups (see p. 26 above) who attended boarding school varied between 16 and 31 per cent. All intergroup differences were non-significant. However, certain significant differences were noted in the average length of time the subjects in each group attended boarding school. The average length of attendance for the male homosexuals was eight years, significantly longer than the average length of attendance (five years) of the male heterosexuals. The average length of attendance of the male homosexuals was also significantly longer than that (four years) of the female homosexuals. Other inter group differences were not significant. Hence the length of stay in a single-sex environment during adolescence may be of importance for the development of homosexual behaviour in males.

There is also an interesting speculation by Ruse (1981). The basis of this is a letter from a philosopher of science (Richard Alexander) to Suppe (one of the editorial board of the *Journal of Homosexuality*). Ruse cites Alexander as follows: We know that males masturbate more than females (both very likely are concomitants of more intense sexual competition). Moreover, male masturbation provides visual as well as tactual stimuli that are very similar to those involved in some homosexual activities. If one is stimulated sexually a great deal by seeing his own erect penis, then to be sexually stimulated by seeing someone else's is not such a great leap. Even if tactual and other stimuli are not greatly different between the sexes (and they may actually be) this great difference in visual feedback seems to be potentially quite significant (Ruse 1981, p. 14). Ruse suggests that 'because so many males must wait so long before they can have heterosexual experiences, their only sexual relief is masturbation. By the time heterosexual possibilites are available, it may be too late. The masturbating males prefer penises to vaginas. Thus, as a result of changes in society unrelated to sexuality, males are pushed towards homosexuality (Ruse 1981, p. 14).

Ruse notes the lack of evidence concerning this possibility – as indicated above there are some data on increased homosexuality in single-sex environments but none on the long-term consequences of such environments. He also points out the lack of data on adult sexual preference in societies which bar adolescent heterosexuality.

Early sexual experiences

Some indication of the relationship between the age of homosexual and heterosexual encounters and self-labelling as homosexual is provided in a report by Troiden and Goode (1980). They interviewed 150 homosexual males in three locations in the north-eastern United States, all aged between 20 and 40. Almost all interviews were conducted in the respondent's home.

The older the segment of the sample the older the age when the respondent first guessed that he might be gay, labelled his feelings as gay and had his first homosexual relationship. This suggests that as society is more tolerant of homosexual behaviour the more accurate and visible is the information available to young males to define themselves as gay. It ties in with the recent study by Shively and DeCecco (1978) at San Francisco State College, in which the percentage of exclusive homosexual males was much higher than in the Kinsey survey and the proportion of bisexual males much lower.

Other results indicated that the more high-school heterosexual experience, involving more than kissing, a respondent had, the older he was when he passed through the various stages of awareness of homosexuality listed above. Conversely, the more homosexual experience he had the earlier he did so. Troiden and Goode did not report the subjective consequences, pleasurable or otherwise, of these high-school sexual experiences.

In her British study Kolaszynska-Carr (1970) looked only at relationships with the opposite sex during adolescence and not at same-sex relationships, but she did consider some subjective aspects. Differences between the homosexual and control groups in the frequency of dating were not found up to the age of 15 but were found from the age of 15 onwards. Considerable differences between homosexual and heterosexual groups were found in the number of subjects who had wanted to go out with members of the opposite sex in the age periods 10 to 15 and 15 to 20. Far fewer of the two homosexual groups reported this desire. Whereas for the heterosexual groups there was a significant rise in the second age period over the first in the number who wanted to date members of the opposite sex, there was no such rise for the two homosexual groups. Thus while early differences existed they had been considerably amplified by the age of 20. Most of Kolaszynska-Carr's subjects who had experienced heterosexual attraction could recall clearly the first time they had felt sexually attracted to a member of the opposite sex. The mean ages at which the two groups of homosexual subjects had first experienced such attraction were significantly higher than the ages of the two heterosexual groups. In the cases of those homosexuals who had experienced heterosexual attraction, it had occurred less frequently, had been less strong, had more often ceased to exist, and had first occurred at a significantly later age, than among the heterosexuals. This finding may have considerable relevance to the explanation of homosexual behaviour. It seems that the secondary homosexuals begin their heterosexual life at a later age than do heterosexual individuals, perhaps because they have to overcome barriers against overt heterosexual behaviour learned in their home environments, as suggested earlier.

Significantly more of a lesbian group (40 per cent) than of a heterosexual group (25 per cent) remembered being frightened by the sexual behaviour of a man (Kenyon 1968). Gundlach and Riess (1968) noted a significantly higher incidence of rape below the age of 16 among a homosexual group than among a heterosexual one. What does not appear to have been done is a study of the feeling of adult homosexual individuals about their early heterosexual encounters in terms of the extent to which they felt that this had matched their expectations and hopes. It is the discrepancy between the expectation and the return in heterosexual, as opposed to homosexual, encounters that is of particular interest.

However, some data are available on the adolescent self-perceptions of adult British homosexuals (Kolaszynska-Carr 1970). No differences were detected between the homosexual and the heterosexual groups in the number who believed that they were unattractive to the opposite sex up to the age of 15 and from the age of 15 to the age of 20, nor were any differences found in the number of homosexuals and heterosexuals who had held the slightly more extreme belief that they would never be attractive to members of the opposite sex. The extent of feelings of rejection by the opposite sex because of personal unattractiveness appeared therefore to be very similar among all groups. However, the heterosexuals, both males and females, had met sexual interest from the opposite sex significantly more frequently than the homosexuals. Kolaszynska-Carr put forward two possible reasons for this difference: first, the homosexuals avoided the company of the opposite sex, thereby reducing the likelihood of such sexual situations developing; second, the opposite sex had perceived the sexual orientation of the homosexual person, consequently they did not show sexual interest or make physical advances as these were not likely to be reciprocated. A quarter of the male homosexuals and nearly half of the females had experienced successful heterosexual intercourse, as compared to almost all heterosexuals. More heterosexuals than homosexuals reported having attempted intercourse out of strong physical desire. Homosexuals, not surprisingly, often attempted intercourse to prove that they were not homosexual. Reports of impairment of performance or lack of responsiveness were common even from those homosexuals who had experienced successful heterosexual intercourse. For most heterosexuals it was an enjoyable and satisfying experience, to be repeated; for the homosexuals it had been less often enjoyable and was an activity which they did not desire to repeat. As compared to the female heterosexuals, the female homosexuals reacted to heterosexual intercourse with panic and disgust.

The possibility of a combination of relatively pleasant homosexual, and relatively unpleasant heterosexual, experiences in heterosexually arousable individuals is important for a social learning explanation of the secondary group of homosexuals. A relevant study has been carried out by Manosevitz (1970). He found that the total sexual activity before adolescence reported by his homosexual group (all interviewed as adults) was greater than for the heterosexual comparison group. Total sexual activity was not greater for homosexuals than heterosexuals during and after adolescence. He compared those homosexuals who had successful heterosexual relations leading to orgasm, with the heterosexual members of his sample. When asked how they felt about their first heterosexual intercourse experience the heterosexuals tended to rate it as very enjoyable, the homosexuals as only moderately pleasant. The groups were asked if they ever felt nervous, anxious or violent when sexually excited by females. Significant differences in the expected directions were obtained on all questions. Manosevitz considers that his findings suggest that the pre-homosexual child becomes sexually active earlier in his life than the pre-heterosexual individual. 'If a child's object choice is undifferentiated, that is, directed towards both males and females, and if he is sexually precocious while most of his social relations are with males, then it is possible that many of his early sexual experiences will be with same sexed partners. It is entirely possible that these early sexual experiences with males may affect the subsequent development and adult sexual preferences' (Manosevitz 1970, p. 401). Kinsey et al. (1948) also reported an earlier sexual development in homosexual than in heterosexual individuals.

Population control

This is a very different approach to any of the explanations reviewed above. It is concerned with the social behaviour of an entire society rather than with biological predispositions or the social experiences of specific individuals. It argues for the survival value of homosexuality in a world of scarce resources. Harris (1977) suggests that the high cost of rearing children in present-day United States is responsible not only for a lower birth rate but also for an increased attention to homosexuality.

The Etoro, who live in Papua, New Guinea, have beliefs which encourage the homosexual preference (Kelly 1974). Heterosexuality is thought to make crops wither and die and is allowed only on one-third of the days of the year and then only in the forest, never in a house or its vicinity. Conversely, homosexuality is thought to cause crops to 'flourish and yield bountifully'. The Etoro have a rather low birth rate for their region, possibly by as much as 15 per cent (Werner 1975). An examination of pro-natalist societies (abortion is virtually illegal) *versus* ante-natal ones indicates that homosexuality is permitted for at least a segment of the population in 60 per cent of the latter as against 25 per cent of the former (Werner 1979). In other words, Werner implicates homosexuality as a population-control device in addition to abortion. These results are interesting, but it should be noted that both legal abortion and legal homosexuality are features of liberal, relatively secular societies – both may result more from a greater emphasis on personal freedom than from the need for population control. A good test would be provided by present-day China, which is engaged in a very vigorous campaign to restrict population growth. Has this been accompanied by a relaxation of barriers against homosexuality?

A major recent study (Bell et al. 1981)

In 1969–70 researchers from the Kinsey Institute for Sex Research began the most important, thorough and well-designed study to date into the development of sexual preference in men and women. The total homosexual sample numbered nearly 1000 and was drawn from a range of sources but mainly gay bars, public advertising and personal contact. Inevitably it was not a fully generalizable sample of the total homosexual population even of the San Francisco Bay Area (where the study was conducted), let alone that of the entire USA. The heterosexual group was much smaller, about 500 in all, but was obtained by block sampling techniques and was matched with its homosexual counterpart for age, education and occupational levels.

The interview schedule was constructed with the care and thoroughness which has always characterized the work of the Kinsey Institute and included about 200 questions on all aspects of childhood and adolescence. The aim was to cover all areas relevant to current theories of the social development of sexual preference. Both closed and open-ended questions were included, all interviewing was carried out in respondents' homes and interviewers received considerable training. Careful checks, mainly by test–retest methods, were made to ensure reliability and the research group aimed for substantive, as well as merely statistical, significance. The latter was set at the 0.05 level and the former at 10 percentage points between the homosexual and heterosexual for difference measures and for correlations between a variable and sexual preference that accounted for at least 1 per cent of the variance. (It has to be said that the latter seems rather small and in the description of the results of major importance which follows only those which account for at least 10 per cent of the variance concerned are mentioned.) Finally, in tracing the complex sequence of the development of sexual preference, in which many detailed variables might be involved, the researchers employed path analysis. Essentially, this is a technique which enables detailed tracing of how independent variables separately and together influence the final dependent measure – in this case adult sexual preference – as well as each other along the way. It also indicates the relative importance of each independent variable.

The major results were as follows:

1. Little or no support was found for many traditional notions.

   (a) Psychoanalytic beliefs concerning parental relationships or traits. For example, boys who grew up with dominant mothers and weak fathers were scarcely more likely to become homosexual than those who grew up in 'ideal' family settings: the connection between boys' relationships with their mothers and later sexual preference was 'hardly worth mentioning'.

(b) The sociological model that attributes homosexuality to poor peer relationships. Isolation from peers relates to gender nonconformity rather than to homosexuality itself. Nor was labelling by others important. Differential labelling was instead the *result* of an emerging homosexual orientation.

(c) Certain social learning approaches. Homosexuals were no more likely than heterosexuals to have had traumatic negative experiences such as rape or parental punishment for sex play with children of the opposite sex; there was no support for the stereotype of 'seduction' of a boy by an older man or of a girl by an older woman.

2. The following were the major positive findings.

(a) By adolescence sexual preference is determined, even though sexual activity may not yet have started. Either there are strong learning effects or there is a strong 'propensity' which emerges almost irrespective of specific learning experiences. The first explanation may hold for some homosexuals, the second for others.

(b) Early homosexual 'feelings' rather than activities predict the later development of adult sexual preference, for both homosexuals and heterosexuals.

(c) Homosexual men and women do report pre-adult heterosexual experiences. The key difference with adult heterosexual men and women is that such experiences were much less likely to be enjoyed.

(d) For both homosexual men and women there is a powerful link between gender nonconformity and adult homosexual preference (gender nonconformity means a preference by boys for 'typical' girls' activities and vice versa for girls). However, there was a wide range, and many of the homosexual men and women conformed as children to their gender roles.

(e) For some homosexuals their preference may arise from a 'biological precursor'.

This theme was then examined by the authors in more detail. They conducted separate path analyses for the homosexual men who rated both their feelings and behaviours as 6 on the Kinsey scale (55 per cent of the total white sample) and for those rating themselves from 2 to 4 (8 per cent of the white sample). The main findings of this second analysis are as follows:

1. Men

(a) For the exclusively homosexual men there was a clear and strong path from homosexual feelings in childhood to homosexual preference in adulthood. In contrast, for bisexual men this did not appear in the path model. A bisexual's actual homosexual activities in adolescence are much more important, being directly connected to adult homosexual preference. Further, among the exclusively homosexual men the homosexuality was well established by age 19. Conversely, experiences after the age of 19 (as reported by the study) seem to have been more important for the bisexual men.

(b) Exclusive homosexuality tends to emerge from a 'deep-seated predisposition', while bisexuality is more subject to influence by social and sexual learning.

(c) For the effeminate males early homosexual feelings were the only predictor; for the non-effeminate men they were influenced by a combination of homosexual feelings and behaviours and a relative lack of heterosexual arousal.

2. Women

(a) For the 'masculine' homosexual women childhood gender nonconformity such as a preference for masculine activities strongly predicted adult homosexuality. It did not do so at all for the 'non-masculine' homosexual women.

(b) Non-masculine women were more likely to be influenced by homosexual activities in their youth. 'Masculine women may be destined to a particular sexual outcome before the age of 19' (p. 206).

(c) For the exclusively homosexual women childhood gender nonconformity was much more important than for the bisexuals.

(d) Again as for the males, the sexual preference of exclusively homosexual women was very well established by aged 19, that of the bisexual women became established at a later age.

It is very unfortunate that the Kinsey 6 group was not confined to those who had always been the Kinsey 6 rather than those currently so rated. Nevertheless certain tentative overall conclusions seem in order. First, early gender nonconformity is associated with early homosexual feelings and the two together lead, seemingly inevitably, to adult homosexual preference of the exclusive type, in both men and women. Second, positively rewarding homosexual experiences during adolescence or even later are the crucial factor for the adult homosexual preference of the bisexual kind.

Bell et al. conclude very cautiously: 'our findings are not unconnected with what one would expect to find, if indeed there were a biological basis for sexual preference' (p. 216). Further, if there is a biological basis for homosexuality, 'It probably accounts for gender non-conformity as well as sexual orientation' (p. 217). They go on to relate both outcomes to perinatal differentiation of the foetal brain and other biological events discussed earlier. Moreover, 'familial factors commonly thought to account for homosexuality may themselves be the *result* of a pre-homosexual son or daughter being "different" to begin with' (p. 218).

Concluding comment

There seems a reasonably close relationship between the results of the very large-scale study by Bell et al. (1981) and the Feldman–MacCulloch theory of sexual preference (1971). Both suggest that there are two broad groups of homosexuals. The first has been exclusively homosexual from the first sexual feelings and activities. Their sexual preference has a biological basis and this is true for both male and female primary homosexuals. It was suggested by the Feldman–MacCulloch theory that the biological basis for the primary group was provided by biochemical events occurring between conception and birth which affected the developing foetus. We do not yet have a satisfactory method of testing this explanation so it remains a speculation at present. The same theory laid much emphasis on negative heterosexual experiences in the development of secondary homosexual group. The results of Bell et al. (1981) now make this doubtful and it seems likely that positively reinforced (i.e. pleasant) homosexual experiences are much more important than negatively reinforced (i.e. unpleasant) heterosexual experiences.

This is as far as we can take the matter at the present time. With the exceptions noted in my critique of the Bell et al. study, the retrospective approach has been taken about as far as possible. The next research stage would be either an inevitably large-scale prospective study and/or a set of biochemical measures much superior to any yet devised.

REFERENCES

Achilles, Nancy (1967). The development of the homosexual bar as an institution. In J. H. Gagnon and W. Simon (eds), *Sexual Deviance*, New York: Harper & Row.

Apperson, L. B. and McAdoo, W. G. (1968). Parental factors in the childhood of homosexuals. *Journal of Abnormal and Social Psychology*, 73, 201–6.

Bell, A. P. (1975). Research on homosexuality: Back to the drawing board. *Archives of Sexual Behavior*, 4, 421–31.

Bell, A. P., and Weinberg, M. S. (1978). *Homosexualities: A Study of Diversities among Men and Women*, New York: Simon & Schuster.

Bell, A. P., Weinberg, M. S., and Hammersmith, S. K. (1981). *Sexual Preference*

London: Mitchell Beazley.

Bell, R. A. (1968). A reinterpretation of the direction of effect in studies of socialization. *Psychological Review*, 75, 81–95.

Bene, E. (1965a). On the genesis of male homosexuality: an attempt at clarifying the role of the parents. *British Journal of Psychiatry*, III, 803–13.

Bene, E. (1965b). On the genesis of female homosexuality. *British Journal of Psychiatry*, III, 815–21.

Bene, E., and Anthony, J. (1962). *Bene–Anthony Family Relations Test*, London: NFER.

Birke, L. I. A. (1981). Is homosexuality hormonally determined? *Journal of Homosexuality*, 6, 35–50.

Bullough, V. L. (1974). Homosexuality and the medical model. *Journal of Homosexuality*, I, 99.

Carrier, J. M. (1971). Participants in urban American male homosexual encounters. *Archives of Sexual Behavior*, I, 279–93.

Ct.App. (1978). Brief for the Government in Seal *v*. Middendorf, U.S. Ct. of Appeals, 9th Cir. No. 77–2461.

Ct.Cl. (1969). Schlegel *v*. United States, 416F, 2d, 1372. 1373.

D. C.Cir. (1963). 317F. 2d, 582

Dean, R. B., and Richardson, H. (1964). Analysis of MMPI profiles of forty college-educated overt male homosexuals. *Journal of Consulting Psychology*, 28, 483–6.

Doerr, P., Kockott, G., Vogt, H. J., Pirke, K. M., and Dittmar, F. (1973). Plasma testosterone, estradiol and semen analysis in male homosexuals. *Archives of General Psychiatry*, 29, 829–33.

Doerr, P., Pirke, K. M., Kockott, G., and Dittmar, F. (1976). Further studies on sex hormones in male homosexuals. *Archives of General Psychiatry*, 33, 611–14.

Dörner, G., Rohde, W., Stahl, F., Krell, L., and Masius, W. G. (1975). A neuro-endocrine predisposition for homosexuality in men. *Archives of Sexual Behavior*, 4, 1–8.

Evans, R. B. (1969). Childhood parental relationships of homosexual men. *Journal of Consulting and Clinical Psychology*, 33, 129–35.

Evans, R. B. (1972). Physical and biochemical characteristics of homosexual men. *Journal of Consulting and Clinical Psychology*, 39, 140–7.

Feldman, M. P., and MacCulloch, M. J. (1971). *Homosexual Behaviour: Therapy and Assessment*, Oxford: Pergamon.

Feldman, M. P., McGivern, M. A., Shaw, R. W., and Butt, W. R. (1980). Oestrogen feedback effects in homosexual males. Unpublished study, Departments of Psychology and Clinical Endocrinology, University of Birmingham.

Gagnon, J. H., and Simon, W. (1967). Introduction: Deviant behaviour and sexual deviance. In J. H. Gagnon and W. Simon (eds), *Sexual Deviance*, I, New York: Harper & Row.

Green, R., Fuller, M., Rutley, B. R., and Hendler, J. (1972). Playroom toy preferences of fifteen masculine and fifteen feminine boys. *Behaviour Therapy*, 3, 425–29.

Greenblatt, D. R. (1966). Semantic differential analysis of the triangular system hypothesis in adjusted overt male homosexuals. Unpublished doctoral thesis. University of California.

Gundlach, R. H., and Riess, B. F. (1968). Self and sexual identity in the female: A study of female homosexuals. In A. J. Riess Jr (ed.), *New Directions in Mental Health*, New York: Grune & Stratton.

Harlow, H. (1965). Sexual behavior in the rhesus monkey. In F. A. Beach (ed.), *Sex and Behavior*, New York: Wiley.

Harris, M. (1977). *Cannibals and Kings: The Origins of Cultures*, New York: Random House.

Hays, S. (1978). Unpublished M.Sc. thesis, Department of Psychology, University of Birmingham.

Heller, C. G., and Maddock, W. O. (1947). The clinical uses of testosterone in the male. *Vitamins and Hormones*, 5, 393–432.

Heston, L. L., and Shields, J. (1968). Homosexuality in twins. *Archives of General Psychiatry*, 18, 149.

Hooker, E. (1967). The homosexual community. In J. H. Gagnon and W. Simon (eds), *Sexual Deviance*, New York: Harper & Row.

Jenkins, M. (1928). The effect of segregation on the sex behaviour of the white rat. *Genetic Psychology Monographs*, 3, 461–471.

Jinks, L., and Fulker, D. W. (1970). Comparison of the biometrical genetical MAVA and classical approaches to the analysis of human behaviour. *Psychological Bulletin*, 73, 311–349.

Kallman, F. J. (1952a). Comparative twin study of the genetic aspects of male homosexuality. *Journal of Nervous and Mental Disease*, 115, 283–298.

Kallman, F. J. (1952b). Twin sibships and the study of male homosexuality. *American Journal of Human Genetics*, 4, 136–146.

Kallman, F. J. (1953). *Heredity in Health and Mental Disorder*, New York: Norton.

Kelly, R. (1974). *Etoro Social Structure: A Study in Structural Contradictions*. Unpublished doctoral dissertation, University of Michigan.

Kenyon, F. E. (1968). Studies in female homosexuality, IV. Social and psychiatric aspect. *British Journal of Psychiatry*, 114, 1337–1343.

Kinsey, A. C., Pomeroy, W. B., and Martin, C. E. (1948). *Sexual Behavior in the Human Male*, Philadelphia: Saunders.

Kinsey, A. C., Pomeroy, W. B., Martin, C. E., and Gebhard, P. H. (1953). *Sexual Behavior in the Human Female*, Philadelphia: Saunders.

Klintworth, G. K. (1962). A pair of male monozygotic twins discordant for homosexuality. *Journal of Nervous and Mental Disease*, 135, 113–118.

Knutson, D. C. (1980). Introduction. *Journal of Homosexuality*, 5, 5–24 (special double issue: Homosexuality and the Law).

Kolaszynska-Carr, A. (1970). Unpublished thesis, University of Birmingham.

Kolodny, R. C., Jacobs, L. S., Masters, W. H., Torro, G., and Daughaday, W. H. (1972). Plasma gonadotrophins and prolactin in male homosexuals. *Lancet*, II (7766) 18–20.

Kolodny, R. C., Masters, W. H., Hendry, J., and Torro, G. (1971). Plasma testosterone and semen analysis in male homosexuals. *New England Journal of Medicine*, 285, 1170–4.

(La: 1975) People *v.* Lindsey, 310 So. 2d 89.

Levine, M. (1979). Gay ghetto. *Journal of Homosexuality*, 4, 363–78.

Levitt, E. E., and Klassen, A. D. (1974). Public attitudes towards homosexuality: part of the 1970 national survey by the Institute for Sexual Research. *Journal of Homosexuality*, 1, 29–30.

Lewis, C. S. (1955). *Surprised by Joy: The Shape of My Early Life*, London: Bles.

Loraine, J. A., Adamopoulos, D. A., Kirkham, K. E., Ismail, A. A. A., and Dove, G. A., (1971). Patterns of hormone excretion in male and female homosexuals. *Nature*, 234, 552–5.

MacCulloch, M. J., and Feldman, M. P. (1977). On the aetiology of homosexuality. *Revista Latino Americana de Psicologica*, 9, 101–15.

MacCulloch, M. J., Feldman, M. P., and Emery, A. E. (1967). The treatment by aversion therapy of an identical twin discordant for homosexuality. Unpublished manuscript, Crumpsall Hospital, Manchester.

Manosevitz, M. (1970). Early sexual behaviour in adult homosexual and heterosexual males. *Journal of Abnormal Psychology*, 76, 396–402.

Margolese, M. S. (1970). Homosexuality: A new endocrine correlate. *Hormones and Behaviour*, 1, 151–5.

Meyer-Bahlburg, H. F. L. (1977). Sex hormones and male homosexuality in comparative perspective. *Archives of Sexual Behavior*, 6: 4, 297–326.

Money, J., and Ehrhardt, A. A. (1971). Fetal hormones and the brain: effect on sexual dimorphism of behavior – a review. *Archives of Sexual Behavior*, 1, 241–62.

Money, J. and Ehrhardt, A. A. (1972). *Man and Woman, Boy and Girl*, Baltimore: John Hopkins Press.

Money, J., and Ogunro, C. (1974). Behavioral sexology: ten cases of genetic male intersexuality with impaired prenatal and pubertal androgenization. *Archives of Sexual Behavior*, 3, 181–205.

(9th Cir. 1973). McKeand v. Laird, 490 F. 2d 1262.

Parker, N. (1964). Twins: a psychiatric study of a neurotic group. *Medical Journal of Australia*, 2, 735–40.

Parks, G. A., Korth-Schutz, S., Penny, R., Hilding, R. F., Dumanrs K. W., Frasier, S. D., and New, M. I. (1974). Variation in pituitary-gonadal function in adolescent male homosexuals and heterosexuals. *Journal of Clinical Endocrinology and Metabolism*, 39, 796–801.

Pillard, R. C., Rose, R. M., and Sherwood, M. (1974). Plasma testosterone levels in homosexual men. *Archives of Sexual Behavior*, 3, 453–8.

Rainer, J. D., Mesnikoff, A., Kolb, L. C., and Carr, A. (1960). Homosexuality and heterosexuality in identical twins. *Psychosomatic medicine*, 22, 251–9.

Ramsay, R. W., and van Velzen, V. (1968). Behaviour therapy for sexual perversions. *Behaviour Research and Therapy*, 6, 233.

Rasmussen, E. W. (1955). Experimental homosexual behaviour in male albino rats. *Acta Psychologica*, 11, 303–34.

Ruse, M. (1981). Are there gay genes? Sociobiology and homosexuality. *Journal of Homosexuality*, 6, 5–34.

Schofield, M. (1965). *The Sexual Behaviour of Young People*, London: Longmans.

Shively, M. G., and DeCecco, J. P. (1978). Sexual orientation survey of students on the San Francisco State University Campus. *Journal of Homosexuality*, 4, 29–40.

Siegelman, M. (1974). Parental background of homosexual and heterosexual women. *British Journal of Psychiatry*, 124, 14–21.

Slukin, W. (1970). *Early Learning in Man and Animal*, London: Allen & Unwin.

Snortum, J. R., Gillespie, N. F., Marshall, J. E., McLaughlin, J. P., and Mosberg, L., (1969). Family dynamics and homosexuality. *Psychological Reports*, 24, 763–70.

Suppe, F. (1981). The Bell and Weinberg study: Future priorities for research on homosexuality. *Journal of Homosexuality*, 6, 69–97.

Tanner, J. M. (1951). Current advances in the study of physique. Photogrammetric anthropometry and an androgyny scale. *Lancet*, 1, 574–7.

Troiden, R. R., and Goode, E. (1980). Variables related to the acquisition of a gay identity. *Journal of Homosexuality*, 383–92.

(Wash. 1977) Gaylord *v.* Tacoma School Dist., 559 P. 2d 1340.

Werner, D. (1975). On the societal acceptance or rejection of male homosexuality. Unpublished MA thesis, Hunter College.

Werner, D. (1979). A cross-cultural perspective on theory and research on male homosexuality. *Journal of Homosexuality*, 4, 345–62.

West, D. J. (1967). *Homosexuality* (3rd edn). London: Duckworth.

Yalom, I. D., Green, R., and Fisk, N. (1973). Prenatal exposure to female hormones. *Archives of General Psychiatry*, 28, 554–61.

2

Homosexual Behaviour in Animals

P. A. Tyler

INTRODUCTION

The history of the study of animal homosexuality has provided a useful illustration of the problems encountered by comparative psychologists who have emphasized a human-oriented approach to animal behaviour. Under the influence of the predominant psychoanalytic belief in the basic bisexuality of human males and females in the first half of this century, comparative psychologists came to emphasize the ease with which sexual behaviour patterns characteristic of the opposite sex may appear in animals (see review by Goy and Goldfoot 1975). As the popularity of stimulus-response theories increased, attention turned to the idea that sexual stimuli can elicit behaviour patterns typical of the other sex, even when displayed to members of the same sex (Beach 1965, 1979). Now after some years of relatively low ebb, the fortunes of the animal-modelling approach have been revived by recent discoveries about pre-natal and early post-natal determination of sex in mammals. These discoveries have encouraged renewed speculation that human homosexuality has a discoverable physiological genesis in development, which may be clarified by further work in animals (Dörner 1976).

Human homosexuals are frequently caricatured by the news and arts media as effeminate men or masculine women, even though most are indistinguishable from the 'straight' majority until their sexual preferences can be determined. Masculinity or feminity are not useful predictors of sexual preference in either sex. (For an alternative view on this issue see chapter 1.) Yet animal modellers frequently use heterotypical sexual behaviour as the primary or only criterion of homosexuality. Further, it is generally agreed that human homosexual preference is the outcome of a constellation of social and environmental causes unique to humans, acting during development. This observation is not intended to deny the importance of biological factors, but to emphasize their interaction with the social environment. It has also been pointed out, in criticism of recent comparative approaches, that homosexuality is taken as a phenomenon, a problem to be explained, at a time when psychiatry and clinical psychology are retreating from the view of homosexuality as a mental illness (e.g. Birke 1981).

If traditional comparative approaches present a distorted view of both animal and human homosexual behaviour, it is justifiable to ask how students of animal behaviour can contribute to knowledge in this area. The answer is that human and animal homosexual behaviour can be placed within the broader context of the evolution of sexual diversity, encouraging greater understanding of the crucial roles of genotype and environment in the normal development of different sexual behaviour patterns. Comparison among species, including consideration of the prevalence of heterotypical behaviour in natural populations, and of the ease with which such behaviour may be induced experimentally, are important. References to relatively few, often anecdotal, animal studies are frequent in the human literature (e.g. West 1977), so there is a clearly felt need for continuity in this area. Unfortunately the evidence, although perhaps more extensive than seems to be recognized by most psychologists, is patchy and incomplete. In particular, there are large gaps in the important observations needed to relate sexual diversity to ecological variables. Nonetheless, it is to be hoped that this review can provide a background for understanding the nature of the information that still needs to be gathered.

OBSERVATION AND DESCRIPTION

Problems of definition

Sexual reproduction, which is the normal state in vertebrates, was accompanied early in its evolution by differentiation of animal species into two sexes. The causes of the success of sexual reproduction at the expense of asexual processes are still a matter for debate and controversy in reproductive biology (see Maynard Smith 1978). Differentiation is thought to have occurred first at the level of the gamete, with the consequence that fertilization results in a union between a large, nutritious immobile egg and a small, active but non-nutritious spermatozoan. In most species of animals evolution has subsequently produced a set of sex-related behavioural characteristics which enable the egg-bearing female to signal her receptiveness or otherwise to males, and the sperm-bearing male to seek out and signal the value of his potential genetic contribution to the receptive female. Sexual behaviour in both male and female animals has universally evolved to serve the function of sexual reproduction, and the different behaviour patterns of the two sexes have come under the influence of their different physiological and hormonal constitutions. It is usually assumed by biologists therefore that heterosexually directed acts are the inevitable outcome of natural selection, and that any deviation from this condition is the maladaptive consequence of developmental accidents of the kind perhaps that produce genetic disorders such as Down's syndrome or dwarfism. The logical corollary of this position is that normal sex-related activities will only be performed in the presence of a potentially receptive member of the other sex, all homosexual acts being defined as deviant.

Yet evolutionary theory does not require such a narrow view, congenial as it may be to the more puritanical in our society. Males of many species are known to be rather non-discriminating in their displays and attempts to mate. Receptive female mammals may mount and be mounted by other females as well as by males. The ability of both sexes to display some of the behaviour patterns more characteristic of the opposite sex is normal and has already been noted. In some species the time needed to discriminate the sex of one's partner might be better spent initiating courtship and mating, especially if there are eager rivals nearby ready to step in if the process is moving too slowly. Considerations such as these clearly provide a problem for the definition of homo- and heterosexuality. Many animals which are primarily heterosexual may engage in some homosexual acts, either as part of the process of sexual discrimination or in the absence of a preferred stimulus. This fact has given rise to statements in the literature to the effect that 'homosexuality is widespread in animals' (e.g. Kenyon 1974). On the other hand, there still appears to be little evidence of permanent or exclusive homosexual preferences becoming established in natural mixed-sex populations of any animal species, so that statements that 'homosexuality is rare in animals' also appear in the ethological literature.

Further problems of definition are raised, ironically, by experimental attempts to understand the causal foundations of homosexuality in humans. Successful physiological manipulations can make it possible to rear a genetically male or female foetus to behave like a member of the other sex. Such experiments have usually been done with rats, but both birds and other mammals have also been studied. Although such experiments are important and interesting and demonstrate the dependence of sex-related behaviours on hormonal constitution and on the nature of early experience, they do raise a question about their relevance to homosexuality, especially human homosexuality. If a genetic male is changed into a behaving female, who then mates with a male, can either partner really be considered a homosexual? They are after all merely displaying the behaviour appropriate to their present sex.

All problems of definition derive mainly from the layman's rather simplistic view of sexuality, in which genetic sex, sex of rearing and sexual response are all concordant. If biological sex is clearly identifiable, but discordant from sexual response, homosexuality is assumed. Other combinations and gradations of response cannot be handled within such a bimodal scheme. These problems of definition are well known and frequently discussed by students of human homosexuality (e.g. Freund 1974; West 1977). If anything the problem is reduced for the animal psychologist, because one can concentrate on behaviour and ignore the problems of emotional attachment, unconscious wishes, social pressures and rest of the complex processes of human personality. This chapter will initially adopt a rather inclusive definition of animal homosexuality in order to obtain some understanding of the biological significance of such relationships in the animal world.

RESEARCH METHODS

Before looking for causes underlying homosexual behaviour in animals, it is reasonable to ask about its incidence and distribution across species. There is however very little information on this question. In the early days of the study of human homosexuality, Kinsey and his colleagues (1948, 1953) carried out their well-known investigation of prevalence by asking penetrating questions in a structured individual interview. Such a method is not open to ethologists, who are limited to methods of direct observation. Since few investigations have been directed primarily at the question of the prevalence of homosexuality in any non-human species, the most likely source of data would seem to be the few major field studies which have tried to catalogue all behaviour of a group of animals over an extended period of time. The studies by Goodall (1971) on chimps, by Schaller on gorillas (1963) and lions (1972), and by DeVore (1965), the Altmanns (1970), Struhsaker (1967), Kummer (1968) and others on various species of monkeys all fall into this category; all report few if any observations of homosexuality. Indeed, Goodall (1971) stated categorically that she did not observe homosexual behaviour in the Gombe chimpanzees.

Although there are reasons to think that primates and social carnivores are among the more likely orders of mammals to develop some homosexual behaviour patterns (Goy and Goldfoot 1975), there are several possible reasons why such patterns are not among those observed in large field studies:

1 Homosexuality does not occur in natural populations.
2 It occurs, but too infrequently to be observed reliably.
3 It occurs frequently, but out of sight of the observer.
4 It occurs frequently and is seen but misinterpreted by the observer.

Many ethologists have indicated their belief that homosexuality does not occur in natural populations (e.g. Wickler 1972), but heterosexual behaviour is not frequently observed either. Schaller, for example, only noted a few observations of mating in mountain gorillas. Wilson (1975) has commented on the need for large numbers of hours of observation before such rare events as intraspecific killing are seen in natural populations. The problem is compounded if the rare event is one which can occur quietly and is likely to happen out of sight of the main group or of the dominant individuals in the group.

These conditions may hold if homosexuality in primate troops occurs mainly between young adult males, who are sexually active but have reduced access to females. Finally, apparently overt sexual acts like mounting same-sex companions are frequently noted in the field studies, but these are normally interpreted as non-sexual behaviours which contribute to group maintenance and the dominance structure (e.g. see Marler 1965). The possibility must be considered, however, that the ethologist, in his desire to see all naturally occurring behaviour as adaptive, is predisposed not to see homosexual acts but to reinterpret them as having a more acceptable and adaptive communicative function. Of course the opposite bias is also a potential danger.

An alternative approach to that of following animals around in their natural environment in the hope of seeing something interesting is the much easier one of keeping them penned in. Confined populations include both zoo animals and farmyard and domestic species. Most of our comparative data on animal homosexuality have been obtained from such populations. Before describing some of these observations in the next section, the well-known disadvantages of studying animals in captivity should be mentioned. The lack of freedom and the artifical environment can give rise to behavioural disturbances which encompass sexual behaviour. Some species are notoriously difficult to breed in captivity (including most primates) because of reduced sexuality, while others show an excess of sexual display (Zuckerman 1932). Stereotyped and repetitive acts, which may include autoerotic behaviour, are well known too. Under these circumstances, it is understandably difficult to interpret observations of homosexuality, especially as the observations themselves are frequently anecdotal or non-systematic. It is not possible to obtain any estimate of prevalence from such studies, but the possibility that sexual preference may vary can be noted for any species.

SURVEY OF REPORTED OBSERVATIONS

Invertebrates

Most investigators interested in using animal models to study the causes of homosexual behaviour have concentrated on the rat (Beach 1979; Dörner 1976), but in fact some form of heterotypical sexuality has been observed in a wide variety of different species, not all of which can be discussed here. In this context it is worth mentioning that the majority of invertebrate species do not conform to the vertebrate pattern of sexual differentiation. For example, many of the Mollusca (e.g. snails) and the Annelida (earthworm) are hermaphrodites, having reproductive organs of both sexes in the same body. Other invertebrate forms may reproduce parthenogenetically, daughters being produced from the germ cells of the mother without the intervention of a male. Forms of hermaphroditism and parthenogenesis have arisen secondarily in vertebrates, and can give the appearance of homosexuality, as will be seen.

The most interesting group of invertebrates from the present standpoint are the insects, which normally do show the vertebrate pattern of a genetically based differentiation into two sexes. Extensive early work revealed a variety of sex-determining mechanisms: for example in Diptera, the flies, as in humans, males are normally XY (heterogametic), while females are XX (homogametic); but whereas in mammals the occasional XXY individual is male, indicating that the Y chromosome is male-determining, in Drosophila flies the XXY genotype gives rise to a normal female (Bridges 1925). In Lepidoptera, butterflies and moths, the sex chromosomes are reversed, with the female usually being the heterogametic sex (often indicated as ZW) while males are homogametic (ZZ).

An early theory of the genetic basis of human homosexuality derived, curiously, from the work on sex determination in moths (Suarez and Przybeck 1980). Goldschmidt (1934; and see Wigglesworth 1965) found that it was possible to obtain heterogametic males and homogametic females, atypically, in the gypsy moth, *Lymantria dispar*. In addition many intersexual forms were found. He explained the results by suggesting that Z chromosomes contained a male-determining factor, and that all gametes of maternal origin contained a female-determining factor transmitted non-genetically. The sex factors could vary in 'strength', or the extent to which they influenced development, so that a moth with a male, ZZ, genotype could develop into a female if the strength of the female factor outweighed that of the two male factors. Although Goldschmidt's theory was later shown to be incorrect, it was influential (see Wigglesworth 1965) and the idea that 'strong' or 'weak' male and female factors could combine in the human genotype was attractive. Lang (1940) used these ideas to derive his theory that male homosexuality could result from the differentiation of a female genotype into a phenotypic male. The theory was wrong in all its particulars – human male homosexuals have a male karyotype – and is only of historical interest, but it does provide a useful illustration of the hazards of comparative generalization. Firstly, biological mechanisms of sex-determination are not constant even within the class Insecta of the phylum Arthropoda, nor within the class Mammalia of the phylum Chordata, so generalization across phyla does not make evolutionary sense. Secondly, there was no suggestion by the entomologists that ZW male moths had homosexual tendencies. The apparent anomaly of the atypical sex chromosome karyotype was later resolved by showing that genetic sex-determination is more complex than first thought, depending as in other insect orders on several genetic loci.

Behaviour which more closely resembles homosexuality has been investigated recently in Drosophila fruit flies. *D. melanogaster* males are vigorous in their courtship of virgin females, less so when confronted with a mated female, and are normally unmoved by other males. Hall's group (e.g. Tompkins et al.

1980) have found that virgin females emit a pheromone which stimulates males to courtship, whereas mated females and mature males produce different, courtship-inhibiting pheromones. There are a number of mutant genes which can produce homosexual courtship in mature male flies. Males with the fruitless (*fru*) mutation appear to produce a pheromone which stimulates courtship in normal (wild-type) males, and they in return court normal males (Gill 1963; Hall 1978). Males with the *olf C* mutation fail to respond to inhibitory male sex pheromones and court each other vigorously. Unlike *fru* males they are not courted by normal males, but they do court normal males. Unlike normal flies *olf C* males were not inhibited in their courtship of virgin females in the presence of male extract, but their courtship was inhibited by the presence of mated female extract. Normal mature males will also court each other more vigorously in the presence of compounds extracted from virgin females (Tompkins and Hall 1981), and they will vigorously court young males less than 12 hours old (Jallon and Hotta 1979).

The insect work illustrates the importance of gender-appropriate stimuli to the performance of sexual behaviour in invertebrates. Learning of appropriate responses to those stimuli would be too slow and wasteful in these short-lived animals. Nevertheless, in the Drosophila studies, the responses themselves are not necessarily inappropriate. Males give homotypical responses in the presence of pheromonal stimuli indicating 'femaleness' (even when in fact emanating from males), or in the absence of stimuli indicating 'maleness'. If two sources of information are in conflict, the chemical sense is dominant over the visual.

Birds

In birds, homosexual pairings between females have been observed in the Western gull colonies of Santa Barbara Island, California (Hunt and Hunt 1977). As in other species of gulls, males normally establish and defend breeding territories to which they attract females, and where courtship, mating and nesting, followed by egg-laying and incubation, occur. In a significant minority of cases, the entire process is carried out by pairs of female Western gulls, including occasionally mounting and copulation attempts. The homosexual pairs, which may exist for several years, also produce and incubate clutches with as many as six eggs (Wingfield et al. 1982). Because sex dimorphism is slight in these gulls, the sex of the birds was confirmed by capturing them and performing a laparotomy, which also revealed the condition of the reproductive system. Homosexuality is infrequently reported in birds, but has also been observed in male greylag geese (Lorenz 1966), male mallard ducks (Schutz 1965) and turkeys. Female turkeys, after being mated by a male, may then court other females with the male display. If the courted female is receptive she may be mounted, and copulatory movements can be carried to the point where the stimulation produced by these movements terminates her receptivity (Hale and Schein 1962). Scott (1942) observed similar behaviour in female sage grouse.

Domestic mammals

Homosexual behaviour is well known in domestic animals, and can be put to advantage by farmers, as well as proving an occasional economic hazard. Bulls will mount and attempt copulation with other males (bulls or steers) as readily as with oestrous cows, a trait which is used to relieve them of semen for artificial insemination (Craig 1981). Semen is also collected from bulls, boars, stallions and rams using wooden dummies; male domestic ungulates are fortunately not discriminating about their choice of mating partner. Young bulls, boars and rams kept in all-male groups often develop patterns of male–male mounting and attempted copulations, with subordinates usually taking the passive role (e.g. Geist 1971, for sheep in natural habitats). In confined groups of young boars for example Jakway and Sumption (unpublished, cited by Craig 1981) found that homosexual pair relationships formed which persisted even when the males were mating with females. One member of the pair would stand quietly while the other achieved anal intromission and ejaculation. Difficulties can arise when a form of bullying known as 'bulling' occurs. In large groups of steers one individual may be repeatedly mounted by the others, until it collapses from injuries or exhaustion. The incidence of bulling appears to be increasing, and may be related to the introduction of modern management techniques, including oestrogen implants for growth, rapid turnover of animals on feed lots and crowded conditions (Pierson et al. 1976). Hafez and Scott (1962) reported that in Russia impotence due to homosexuality in young rams was treated by a form of behaviour therapy, involving gradual introduction of ewes.

Cows, like the females of a number of ungulate species, display homosexual mounting. When a cow (or a female antelope) is in oestrus, she is mounted by other females in the group, and less commonly she may mount them in turn. The behaviour is used by farmers to indicate when a cow is in heat and is therefore ready for artificial insemination. Hurnik et al. (1975) found that by 24-hour time-lapse video-recording every ovulation in a herd of cows could be detected by the mounting activity, whereas herdsmen missed 35 per cent of the cows in heat when they relied on the normal procedure of checking twice daily. Two-thirds of the mounts occurred late in the evening or in the early morning, when they were missed by human observers. In a more natural setting, Buechner and Schloeth (1965) noted that several female Uganda kob visited a mating arena and herded females within a territory with striking male-like displays. One fought with territorial males even though she had no horns. The hormonal state of these females was not investigated.

Pet owners and breeders are also familiar with homosexuality. Young male dogs raised together frequently engage in mutual sexual activity, with a subordinate taking the female role (Fuller and DuBuis 1962). King (1954) found that young male Basenjis vigorously approached and mounted strange males, often terminating with ejaculation. As they became older the approach to strangers turned to aggression. Young or adult females were much less likely to mount another, and when mounting occurred it was rudimentary and brief. Young male cats will also attempt to copulate with another male if a female is not present (Rosenblatt and Schneirla 1962). If the partner crouches, he usually does not adopt the full female behaviour pattern, but Green et al. (1957) observed one young male which exhibited the full female pattern including vigorous treading and a typical female post-copulatory reaction. The active male may also show the full male mating pattern, including occasional ejaculation (Aronson 1949). Female –female mounting is observed less frequently. The mounted female can show the full female sexual pattern even if the partner's male-like perform-ance is abbreviated.

Primates

Primate species are commonly thought to be extensively bisexual, with both sexes displaying the 'presenting' response characteristic of female proceptive behaviour and the mounting and thrusting characteristic of the male mating pattern. Early reports suggested that male homosexuality was frequent in Hamadryas baboons (Zuckerman 1932; Maslow 1936) and in rhesus monkeys (Carpenter 1942), but these reports did not make it clear whether the monkeys were in fact sexually aroused. Later commentators emphasized that the perfunctory presenting and mounting displayed towards same-sex companions in primates is merely a form of social communication derived from the sexual act and not a form of homosexuality (e.g. Wickler 1967). More recently, homosexual preference with mutual arousal and anal penetration has been demonstrated in a pair of male rhesus monkeys by Erwin and Maple (1976). Female homosexuality has been reported by Goy and Goldfoot (1975) to be less frequent in rhesus than that between males, but it has been analysed in some detail in a mixed-sex natural population by Michael et al. (1974) and Akers and Conaway (1979). The females concerned showed strong partner preference but the relationship is not fully reciprocal. The mounted female is usually in the receptive, ovulatory phase of the oestrous cycle, and both also engage in heterosexual activity. Akers and Conaway observed a total of 1561 female–female mounts involving seven of the eight females in a six-month period; during the same period, 113 heterosexual copulations to ejaculation were noted. Some information is available for other species of macaque, particularly the stumptail macaque (Chevalier-Skolnikoff 1974, 1976). Adult male stumptails will mount juvenile males and achieve anal intromission, and oral sex is quite common. Females which take the 'male' role in female – female sexual contacts appear to achieve an orgasm which is masculine in its form. Watching heterosexual activity was a strong stimulus for homosexual mounting, but there was little relationship in this species to the female oestrous cycle. Other species of old-world (Catarrhine) monkeys in which female homosexuality has been observed include pigtail macaques (Tokuda et al. 1968), Japanese macaques (Hanby and Brown 1974) and langurs (Hrdy 1977), while only males were observed to engage in homosexual mounting in vervets (Struhsaker 1967).

A survey of the sexual behaviour patterns of non-human primates has emphasized both the diversity of the known behaviour patterns and the paucity of information about the forest-dwelling species, particularly those from South America (Mitchell 1979). Not all monkeys show the rhesus pattern of solicitation and mounting, or the clear-cut sexual dimorphism of the baboons and macaques. In Patas monkeys, for example, although they are sexually dimorphic, ground-dwelling African monkeys, related to the baboons and macaques, females do not solicit males with the presenting pattern. Carpenter, who was so struck by the bisexuality of rhesus on Cayo Santiago, saw no sign of homosexuality in howler monkeys (Maslow 1940). Talmage-Riggs and Anschel (1973) observed that homosexual mounting in a group of four female squirrel monkeys appeared after they were separated from males for a year, and suggested that homosexual contact was a substitute for heterosexual mating. Akers and Conaway (1979) reported an earlier unpublished observation that high levels of homosexual activity did occur in squirrel monkeys during the breeding season. In talapoins, a pair-bonding species which normally showed low levels of sexual activity, high-ranking females were observed to initiate homosexual activity, sometimes as mounter, occasionally as mountee.

Unfortunately for comparisons with our own species, there is very little information on the great apes. Female mounting was reported in early studies of chimpanzees by Bingham (1928) and Yerkes (1939; also see Zuckerman 1932), and Mitchell (1979) noted that both males and females may mount others of the same sex. Van Hooff (1973) reportedly observed a young male mounting another's head and thrusting into its face. Savage and Bakeman (1976; cited by Mitchell 1979) observed female–female thrusting bouts with visible clitoral erection and with copulation gestures and vocalizations in the pygmy chimpanzee. In free-ranging mountain gorillas, Schaller (1963) noted no homosexual mounting by either sex. Harcourt et al.

(1981) saw ten incidents of female homosexuality in captive mountain gorillas; in seven of them one partner was in oestrus. They considered these occurrences to be rare.

Conclusions

A number of tentative conclusions may be drawn from this broad, but not exhaustive, survey of observations on animal homosexuality. There is clearly considerable variability among species, both in the prevalence of homosexuality and in the ease with which it may be observed, but the lack of reported observation does not necessarily reflect lack of behavioural incidence. Nevertheless there are a number of widely accepted generalizations that must be challenged. For example, Beach believed that bisexuality is universal in mammals, and that it increases as brain size and plasticity increases, but that exclusive homosexuality does not exist in animals. These rules are supported by reference to very few species of laboratory animals, including rats, hamsters, guinea pigs, dogs and rhesus monkeys, and there is too little information about a range of species under natural conditions to provide support for any of them. Certainly the observations I have reviewed, taken together with the difficulty of culling out a few examples of homosexuality from the vast number of studies of heterosexual behaviour, would not lead to any of these conclusions.

The common belief that animals merely respond to opposite sex stimulation with occasional heterotypical behaviour, and therefore do not display exclusive homosexual affectional bonds, seems to be simply wrong, an oversimplified application of the behaviouristic approach. No doubt it is true of Drosophilid flies, and perhaps of laboratory rodents, but long-term exclusive homosexual preferences have been reviewed in species ranging from gulls to geese, and from boars to pigtail macaques. Goy and Goldfoot (1975) suggested that for developmental reasons, bisexuality would tend to characterize one sex much more strongly than the other. That may be the case, but they follow Beach in citing cats and dogs as species where the female, not the male, is bisexual, whereas others (Fuller and DuBuis 1962; Rosenblatt and Schneirla 1962) had noted a greater incidence of homosexuality in males. The only species where the male was the 'bisexual' sex was the rhesus monkey where, as has been noted, females show more homosexual behaviour than do females of most other species. The correlation with brain size is also suspect: the animals with the largest and most flexible brains, the primates, do not seem to exhibit much homosexuality under natural conditions, and in confinement sexual behaviour becomes bizarre more often than heterotypical (Maple 1977).

RELATIONSHIP WITH OTHER BEHAVIOUR

Heterosexual behaviour

In most species which show seasonal or regular phases of sexual activity homosexual acts tend to parallel heterosexual ones. Female mammals, whether cows or bitches, in heat stimulate both male and female companions to sexual activity, as Beach has noted. In some species, including cattle and some primates, the oestrous female, especially if dominant, may prefer to do the mounting. In some cases, as in the turkey, this behaviour may have the adaptive function of reducing the receptivity or the access to males of a subordinate. In the case of males too, if mating behaviour is seasonal, overt homosexual acts tend to occur during the mating season. There is also evidence that the nearby presence of a receptive, but non-cooperative, female may excite a male to a homosexual act (e.g. Kruuk 1972 for hyenas; macaques) and male monkeys sometimes masturbate in the presence of an oestrous female. On the whole those animals which have long-term bonds are also less affected by seasonal hormonal cycles (e.g. stumptail macaques).

Dominance

There have been a number of references to the relative dominance of animals in this review, and it should be recognized that dominance is a nebulous concept: different measures often fail to give consistent results (e.g. Rowell 1974; Gartlan 1968). In primates particularly, participation in a dyadic relationship as mounter or mountee may make a major contribution to the measure of relative dominance, so the frequently noted fact that the mounter is the dominant partner may be tautologous. Zuckerman (1932) long ago proposed a close relationship between dominance and homosexuality in primates, such that species like baboons which have strong dominance-rank structures should exhibit the greatest amount of homosexuality. In fact later ethologists like Wickler and Marler were probably right to suggest that much of the behaviour that Zuckerman and his contemporaries observed was not homosexuality, but social communication and appeasement behaviour. The indications are that the actual relationships between homosexuality and dominance are more complex and are still to be worked out for most species.

Social structure of species

Although no major attempt has yet been made to relate variations in homosexual behaviour to social structure across many species, it seems likely that such a relationship should exist. Three major factors thought to contribute to variation in social structure are the role of the male in parental care, feeding ecology and degree of predation. In the majority of mammalian species no paternal care is needed and young males form separate bands. Large mature males compete for females during the mating season, either defending harems for short periods (red deer) or extended ones (horses) or, rarely, defending a territory to which females are attracted (kob, wildebeeste) or more commonly mating promiscuously. Sexual selection both by inter-male competition and by female choice produces the normal mammalian pattern of larger, stronger and later maturing males. This common pattern provides the opportunity and incentive for both male and female homosexuality. Young adult males are rejected by their parents and thrown together for security. Attempts at heterosexuality are highly risky as they involve challenging older, larger animals, yet young males are subject to the same seasonal internal stimulation as their elders. Other young males are available, also aroused but familiar and non-threatening. Females too are frequently grouped together for protection, or for access to males in the mating season. Although sexually active their access to partners for mating may be restricted by the activities of a dominant or harem-holding male.

If biparental care is obligatory for optimal survival of young, as in most species of birds and in a number of mammals (Kleiman 1977), an alternative social structure centred on the pair-bonded family unit may exist. In such cases long and elaborate courtship rituals and greeting ceremonies ensure compatibility and assure each partner of the continuing fidelity of the other. The behaviour patterns associated with such rituals emerge during development and are practised in play with immature companions. If animals which normally form heterosexual pair bonds are raised exclusively with like-sexed companions, it appears that at least some of them will develop preferences for homosexual relationships. It therefore seems likely from a consideration of the social structure of species in the light of the observations reviewed that homosexuality has distinctly different origins: one associated with the greater availability of same-sex peers at a time of sexual arousal, the other with development of long-term partner preferences. The first describes the rather promiscuous opportunistic homosexuality of cattle, and indeed most observed instances of homosexuality when females are in heat; the second the rarer but more interesting cases of specific homosexual preference in birds and a few mammals.

THEORIES OF ANIMAL HOMOSEXUALITY

Early experience

The main goal of most recent theories of homosexuality in animals has been to explain the origins of such behaviour in humans. Thus the weight of interest in the few reported instances of homosexual imprinting in ducks and geese (Hess 1959; Lorenz 1966; Schütz 1965) has far exceeded their capacity to bear it. The notes by Lorenz on geese and Hess on mallards are mere anecdotes, while Schütz found that in mallards only the males imprint sexually, and that under certain circumstances they could imprint on, and later attempt to mate with, other males. Curiously, despite a recent resurgence of interest in sexual imprinting by ethologists, there appears to be no recent work on homosexual imprinting. Nevertheless the early findings have been taken as a model for the development of homosexual preferences in humans (e.g. Money 1981). Because there are similarities in social structure, in the formation of pair bonds and the existence of biparental families, such comparisons may be less far-fetched than first appears from the phylogenetic disparity. More information about the role of an imprinting-like process in the development of homosexual preferences could come from the study of mammalian species which normally form extended heterosexual pair bonds. These include members of the dog family, such as jackals, a few primates such as the marmoset, and the gibbons, which are of great interest but relatively unknown.

Hormones and physiology

Most of the current interest in animal models of homosexuality centres on the implications of recent discoveries about the sexual differentiation of the brain. The work has been reviewed comprehensively and critically by Goy and Goldfoot (1975), Meyer-Bahlburg (1977) and Goy and McEwen (1980). Simply stated, the idea is that the mammalian brain differentiates sexually at about the time of birth under the influence of testicular hormones. In the presence of such perinatal androgens the animal becomes, neurally and behaviourally, a male, responsive to androgens and unresponsive to oestrogens when mature. In their absence, a 'female' brain develops which will later control the cycle characteristic of female receptivity. The above description is oversimplified and does not, for example, include the emerging role of histocompatibility antigens associated with the Y chromosome in the early differentiation of the male gonads (Jost 1979). Nor is it yet clear that the sexual differentiation of primates follows the same pattern as that established for rodents (Goy 1979).

It has proved possible, by following the established model, to produce 'homosexual' behaviour at will in rodents. Neonatally castrated male rats, primed with oestrogen when mature, adopt the normal, female behaviour pattern and induce other males to mount and attempt copulation. Homosexuality in rats is defined by Dörner (1976) as the adoption of the lordosis (receptive female) posture by genetic males. In an apparently logical extension of the model to humans, Dörner has gone on to suggest that male homosexuality is the result of a feminine pattern of brain differentiation. Doubts about the validity of Dörner's model have been expressed at the beginning of the chapter. It would, however, be useful to have more information about the naturally occurring individual differences in homosexual preferences of rats, correlated hormonal differences, and the extent to which they can be manipulated by genetic techniques of cross-breeding and selection.

Alternative developmental strategies

Classical instinct theory (Tinbergen 1951) was developed within the traditional biological paradigm of buffered developmental systems. Natural selection was presumed to ensure that adaptively important behaviour like courtship and mating did not deviate from the species norm either between or within individuals. By contrast, recent evolutionary theory recognizes that variant behavioural strategies may be adaptive. In Maynard Smith's (1976) well-known model based on games theory, if everyone in a population of animals is a 'dove', then a 'hawk' will be at an advantage (and vice versa). The outcome of such models is that alternative strategies must normally coexist in a population. A case in point is the 'sneaky' male stickleback. Morris (1952) originally noticed that small, dull non-territorial males often slip into the territory of breeding male sticklebacks, acting like females. As indicated in the title of his paper, he thought that they were homosexuals. It is now recognized that they were adopting the alternative sexual strategy of attempting to 'sneak' fertilizations by mating with a female on another male's territory while the latter's attention was distracted, perhaps by a territorial dispute. Could it be that true homosexuality is also an alternative developmental strategy, advantageous to the minority as long as the majority remain heterosexual? The difficulty with such a theory lies in identifying the possible selective advantage of homosexuality.

Sociobiological models

Interest in the evolutionary aspects of homosexuality has increased since the popularization of sociobiology with the publication of Wilson's 'new synthesis'

(1975). Homosexuality is of particular interest because of its resemblance to altruism in the questions it raises: how can a behaviour become established in a population when it clearly does not contribute to the reproductive success of the individual? A number of hypotheses have been suggested (Ruse 1982). Firstly, homosexuals might benefit kin (parents or siblings), either by direct assistance or indirectly by not competing for mates or other resources. If the altruistic homosexual is unlikely to reproduce successfully anyway by virtue of lower age or status, the benefit of becoming openly non-reproductive may outweigh the cost of not reproducing oneself by more than the reciprocal of the coefficient of relatedness as required by Hamilton's theory (1964). Secondly, it may be beneficial to the parents for some of their offspring to refrain from reproduction, to the benefit of the others, so that homosexuality is imposed by parental manipulation (Alexander 1974). A less credible possibility is that homosexuality is the consequence of single recessive genes, maintained in the population by heterozygote superiority.

Homosexuality would seem to be especially likely to develop if their is 'local mate competition' (Alexander and Sherman 1977). The existence of locally high concentrations of closely related males and females leads to high effective breeding ratios (many females per breeding male). Under these conditions, overt male homosexuality would reduce competition among relatives for mates. There is no evidence that any of the similar sociobiological hypotheses account for the evolution of homosexuality in animals or humans, but they do seem to make some testable predictions. For example, relatives of homosexuals should have more surviving offspring than the population norm; more social species should have a higher incidence of homosexuality than their more dispersive relatives. It would be interesting to compare the colony-forming Norway rat with the relatively solitary house mouse, or the more cohesive dog family with the dispersive cats. In general, however, the sociobiological hypotheses seem not to be especially helpful for understanding the studies reviewed earlier.

SUMMARY AND CONCLUSIONS

The excitement engendered by the discovery of the developmental mechanisms of sex-determination in rodents, with its resulting potential for experimental manipulation of the sexual response of adult animals, has tended to distort our view of animal and human sexuality. One particularly worrying consequence of such a distortion is the belief that 'deviant' sexual preference can be treated by purely medical means. Hormone replacement therapy, based on the unfounded belief that homosexuals produce insufficient testosterone, is probably fairly harmless, if ineffective (Meyer-Bahlburg

1977). Far more distressing is the approach of Roeder and Muller in West Germany who have been performing 'psychosurgery' or destruction of parts of the brain for the purpose of altering sexual behaviour since the 1960s. Part of the hypothalamus is defined, largely on the basis of animal experiments, as a 'mating centre' and, with a totally unjustifiable logical leap, thought of as a control centre for human sexual feelings (Rieber and Sigusch 1979). About 70 men have had this part of the brain removed, some merely to reverse a homosexual preference. Both the psychological counselling before the operations and evaluation of their subsequent effects seem to have been quite inadequate.

This chapter has attempted to broaden the psychologist's view of animal including human, homosexuality, and place it within the context of the evolution of sexuality. It has been seen that homosexual preference is only meaningful in bisexual species where heterosexual mating preference normally occurs. A number of hypotheses were presented which attempt to account for the development and the evolution of homosexuality, but none has yet attracted much empirical support. In view of the apparently large variation between species in the frequency with which observations of homosexual behaviour are reported, one of the more productive future directions would seem to be a search for correlations with social structure and ecology. Thus a species whose members benefit from the formation of long-lasting pair bonds based on early learning, like one which 'falls in love' at adolescence, may have evolved a mechanism which allows occasional extended bonds between members of the same sex.

In conclusion, the work surveyed in this chapter indicates that evidence relating to animal homosexual behaviour, and its causes, is far from complete. The many hazards of simple comparative generalizations from animals to humans need to be borne in mind by those attempting to understand homosexuality in humans.

REFERENCES

Akers, J. S., and Conaway, C. H. (1979). Female homosexual behavior in *Macaca mulatta. Archives of Sexual Behavior*, 8, 63–80.

Alexander, R. D. (1974). The evolution of social behavior. *Annual Review of Ecology and Systematics*, 5, 325–83.

Alexander, R. D., and Sherman, P. W. (1977). Local mate competition and parental investment in social insects. *Science*, 196, 494–500.

Altmann, S. A., and Altmann, J. (1970). *Baboon Ecology: African Field Research*, Chicago: University of Chicago Press.

Aronson, L. R. (1949). Behavior resembling spontaneous emissions in the domestic cat. *Journal of Comparative and Physiological Psychology*, 42, 226–7.

Beach, F. A. (ed.) (1965). *Sex and Behavior*, New York: Wiley.

Beach, F. A. (1979). Animal models for human sexuality. In R. Porter and J. Whelan (eds), *Sex, Hormones and Behaviour*, Amsterdam: Excerpta Medica.

Bingham, H. C. (1928). Sex development in apes. *Comparative Psychology Monograph*, 5, 1.

Birke, L. I. A. (1981). Is homosexuality hormonally determined? *Journal of Homosexuality*, 6, 35–49.

Bridges, C. B. (1925). Sex in relation to chromosomes and genes. *American Naturalist*, 59, 127–37.

Buechner, H. K., and Schloeth, R. (1965). Ceremonial mating behavior in Uganda kob (*Adenota kob thomasi* Neumann). *Zeitschrift für Tierpsychologie*, 22, 209–25.

Carpenter, C. R. (1942). Sexual behavior of free-ranging rhesus monkeys (*Macaca mulatta*): II. Periodicity of estrus, homosexual, autoerotic and non-conformist behavior. *Journal of Comparative Psychology*, 33, 143–62.

Chevalier-Skolnikoff, S. (1974). Male–female, female–female and male–male behavior in the stumptail monkey, with special attention to the female orgasm. *Archives of Sexual Behavior*, 3, 95–115.

Chevalier-Skolnikoff, S. (1976). Homosexual behavior in a laboratory group of stumptail monkeys (*Macaca arctoides*): forms, contexts, and possible social functions. *Archives of Sexual Behavior*, 5, 511–27.

Craig, J. V. (1981). *Domestic Animal Behavior: Causes and Implications for Animal Care and Management*, Englewood-Cliffs, NJ: Prentice-Hall.

Devore, I. (1965). Male dominance and mating behaviour in baboons. In F. A. Beach (ed.), *Sex and Behavior*, New York: Wiley.

Dörner, G. (1976). *Hormones and Brain Differentiation*, Amsterdam: Elsevier.

Erwin, J., and Maple, T. (1976). Ambisexual behaviour with male–male anal penetration in male rhesus monkeys. *Archives of Sexual Behavior*, 5, 9–14.

Freund, K. (1974). Male homosexuality: An analysis of the pattern. In J. A. Loraine (ed.), *Understanding Homosexuality: Its Biological and Psychological Bases*, Lancaster: Medical and Technical Publishing.

Fuller, J. L., and DuBuis, E. M. (1962). The behaviour of dogs. In E. S. E. Hafez (ed.), *The Behaviour of Domestic Animals*, London: Bailliere, Tindall & Cox.

Gartlan, J. S. (1968). Structure and function in primate society. *Folia primatologica*, 8, 89–120.

Geist, V. (1971). *Mountain Sheep*. Chicago: University of Chicago Press.

Gill, K. S. (1963). A mutation causing abnormal courtship and mating behaviour in males of *Drosophila melanogaster*. *American Zoologist*, 3, 507 (abst.)

Goldschmidt, R. (1934). Lymantria. *Bibliographia Genetica*, 11, 1–86.

Goodall, J. Van L. (1971). *In the Shadow of Man*, Boston: Houghton Mifflin.

Goy, R. W. (1979). Sexual compatibility in rhesus monkeys: Predicting sexual performance of oppositely sexed pairs of adults. In R. Porter and J. Whelan (eds), *Sex, Hormones and Behaviour*, Amsterdam: Excerpta Medica.

Goy, R. W., and Goldfoot, D. (1975). Neuroendocrinology: Animal models and problems of human sexuality. *Archives of Sexual Behavior*, 4, 405–20.

Goy, R. W., and McEwen, B. S. (1980). *Sexual Differentiation of the Brain*, Cambridge, Mass.: MIT Press.

Green, J. D., Clemente, C. D., and De Groot, J. (1957). Rhinencephalic lesions and behavior in cats. *Journal of Comparative Neurology*, 108, 505–45.

Hafez, E. S. E., and Scott, J. P. (1962). The behaviour of sheep and goats. In E. S. E. Hafez (ed.), *The Behaviour of Domestic Animals*, London: Bailliere, Tindall & Cox.

Hale, E. B., and Schein, M. W. (1962). The behaviour of turkeys. In E. S. E. Hafez (ed.), *The Behaviour of Domestic Animals*, London: Bailliere, Tindall & Cox,

Hall, J. C. (1978). Courtship among males due to a male-sterile mutation in *Drosophila melanogaster. Behavior Genetics*, 8, 125–41.

Hamilton, W. D. (1964). The genetical evolution of social behavior, I and II. *Journal of Theoretical Biology*, 7, 1–52.

Hanby, J. P., and Brown, C. E. (1974). Development of sociosexual behaviors in Japanese macaques, *Macaca fuscata. Behaviour*, 49, 152–96.

Harcourt, A. H., Stewart, K. J., and Fossey, D. (1981). Gorilla reproduction in the wild. In C. E. Graham (ed.), *Reproductive Biology of the Great Apes: Comparative and Biomedical Perspectives*, London: Academic Press.

Hess, E. H. (1959). Imprinting. *Science*, 130, 133–41.

Hooff, J. A. R. A. M. van. (1973). A structural analysis of the social behaviour of a semi-captive group of chimpanzees. In M. von Cranach and I. Vine (eds), *Social Communication and Movement*, London: Academic Press.

Hrdy, S. B. (1977). *The Langurs of Abu*, Cambridge, Mass.: Harvard Univeristy Press.

Hunt, G. L., and Hunt, M. W. (1977). Female–female pairing in western gulls (*Larus occidentalis*) in Southern California. *Science*, 196, 1466–7.

Hurnik, J. F., King, G. J., and Robertson, H. A. (1975). Estrous and related behaviour in postpartum Holstein cows. *Applied Animal Ethology*, 2, 55–68.

Jallon, J.-M., and Hotta, Y. (1979). Genetic and behavioral studies of Drosophila female sex appeal. *Behavior Genetics*, 9, 257–75.

Jost, A. (1979). Basic sexual trends in the development of vertebrates. In R. Porter and J. Whelan (eds), *Sex, Hormones and Behaviour*, Amsterdam: Excerpta Medica.

Kenyon, F. E. (1974). Female homosexuality. In J. A. Loraine (ed.), *Understanding Homosexuality: Its Biological and Psychological Bases*, Lancaster: Medical and Technical Publishing.

King, J. A. (1954). Closed social groups among domestic dogs. *Proceedings of the American Philosophical Society*, 98, 327–36.

Kinsey, A. C., Pomeroy, W. B., and Martin, C. E. (1948). *Sexual Behavior in the Human Male*, Philadelphia: Saunders.

Kinsey, A. C., Pomeroy, W. B., Martin, C. E., and Gebhard, P. H. (1953). *Behavior in the Human Female*, Philadelphia: Saunders.

Kleiman, D. G. (1977). Monogamy in mammals. *Quarterly Review of Biology*, 52, 39–69.

Kruuk, H. (1972). *The Spotted Hyena*, Chicago: University of Chicago Press.

Kummer, H. (1968). *Social Organization of Hamadryas Baboons*, Chicago: University of Chicago Press.

Lang, T. (1940). Studies on the genetic determination of homosexuality. *Journal of Nervous and Mental Disorders*, 92, 55–64.

Lorenz, K. (1966). *On Aggression*, New York: Harcourt, Brace & World.

Maple, T. (1977). Unusual sexual behavior of nonhuman primates. In J. Money and H.

Musaph (eds), *Handbook of Sexology*, Amsterdam: Elsevier.

Marler, P. (1965). Communication in monkeys and apes. In I. Devore (ed.), *Primate Behavior*, New York: Holt, Rinehart & Winston.

Maslow, A. H. (1936). The role of dominance in the social and sexual behavior of infrahuman primates. *Journal of Genetic Psychology*, 48, 261–338.

Maslow, A. H. (1940). Dominance quality and social behavior in infra-human primates. *Journal of Social Psychology*, 11, 313–24.

Maynard Smith, J. (1976). Evolution and the theory of games. *American Scientist*, 64, 41–5.

Maynard Smith, J. (1978). *The Evolution of Sex*, Cambridge: Cambridge University Press.

Meyer-Bahlburg, H. F. L. (1977). Sex hormones and male homosexuality in comparative perspective. *Archives of Sexual Behavior*, 6, 297–325.

Michael, R. P., Wilson, M. I., and Zumpe, D. (1974). The bisexual behavior of female rhesus monkeys. In R. C. Friedman, R. M. Richart and R. L. Vandewiele (eds), *Sex Differences in Behavior*, New York: Wiley.

Mitchell, G. (1979). *Behavioral Sex Differences in Nonhuman Primates*, New York: Van Nostrand Reinhold.

Money, J. (1981). The development of sexuality and eroticism in humankind. *Quarterly Review of Biology*, 56, 379–404.

Morris, D. (1952). Homosexuality in the ten-spined stickleback (*Pygosteus pungitius* L.). *Behaviour*, 4, 233–61.

Pierson, R. E., Jensen, R., Braddy, P. M., Horton, D. P., and Christie, R. M. (1976). Bulling among yearling feedlot steers. *Journal of the American Veterinary Medical Association*, 169, 521–3.

Rieber, I., and Sigusch, V. (1979). Psychosurgery on sex offenders and sexual 'deviants' in West Germany. *Archives of Sexual Behavior*, 8, 523–7.

Rosenblatt, J. S., and Schneirla, T. C. (1962). The behaviour of cats. In E. S. E. Hafez (ed.), *The Behaviour of Domestic Animals*, London: Bailliere, Tindall & Cox.

Rowell, T. E. (1974). The concept of social dominance. *Behavioral Biology*, 11, 131–54.

Ruse, M. (1982). Are there gay genes? Sociobiology and homosexuality. *Journal of Homosexuality*, 6, 5–34.

Schaller, G. B. (1963). *The Mountain Gorilla: Ecology and Behavior*. Chicago: University of Chicago Press.

Schaller, G. B. (1972). *The Serengeti Lion: A Study of Predator–Prey Relations*. Chicago: University of Chicago Press.

Schütz, F. (1965). Homosexualität und Pragung. Eine experimentelle Untersuchung an Enten. *Psychologische Forschung*, 28, 439–63.

Scott, J. W. (1942). Mating behavior of the sage grouse. *Auk*, 59, 477–98.

Struhsaker, T. (1967). Behavior of vervet monkeys (*Cercopithecus aethiops*). *University of California Publications in Zoology*, 82, 1–74.

Suarez, B. K., and Przybeck, T. R. (1980). Sibling sex ratio and male homosexuality. *Archives of Sexual Behavior*, 9, 1–12.

Talmage-Riggs, G., and Anschel, S. (1973). Homosexual behavior and dominance hierarchy in a group of captive female squirrel monkeys (*Saimiri sciurens*). *Folia Primatologica*, 19, 61–72.

Tinbergen, N. (1951). *The Study of Instinct*, Oxford: Clarendon Press.

Tokuda, K., Simons, R. C., and Jensen, G. D. (1968). Sexual behavior in a captive group of pigtailed monkeys (*Macaca nemestrina*). *Primates*, 9, 283–94.

Tompkins, L., and Hall, J. C. (1981). *Drosophila* males produce a pheromone which inhibits courtship. *Zeitschrift für Naturforschung*, 36c, 694–6.

Tompkins, L., Hall, J. C., and Hall, L. (1980). Courtship stimulating volatile compounds from normal and mutant Drosophila. *Journal of Insect Physiology*, 26, 689–97.

West, D. J. (1977). *Homosexuality reexamined* (4th edn), London: Duckworth.

Wickler, W. (1967). Socio-sexual signals and their intraspecific imitation among primates. In D. Morris (ed.), *Primate Ethology*, London: Weidenfeld & Nicholson.

Wickler, W. (1972). *The Sexual Code*. Garden City, NY: Doubleday.

Wigglesworth, V. B. (1965). *The Principles of Insect Physiology*, London: Methuen.

Wilson, E. O. (1975). *Sociobiology: The New Synthesis*, Cambridge, Mass.: Harvard University Press.

Wingfield, J. C., Newman, A. L., Hunt, G. L., and Farner, D. S. (1982). Endocrine aspects of female–female pairing in the Western gull (*Larus occidentalis wymani*). *Animal Behaviour*, 30, 9–22.

Yerkes, R. M. (1939). Social dominance and sexual status in the chimpanzee. *Quarterly Review of Biology*, 14, 115–36.

Zuckerman, S. (1932). *Social Life of Monkeys and Apes*, London: Kegan Paul.

3
Gender Identity and Sexual Behaviour

Harry Brierley

This chapter discusses sexual diversity, and associated concepts such as 'deviance', both in general terms and with specific reference to variations in gender identity, gender role and related sexual behaviours. I shall focus first on some of the problems of definition of terms which exist. I shall then discuss the concept of 'deviant' sexual behaviour and describe the sorts of models of sexual deviance that exist in the literature. This leads me to put forward my own model, which attempts to integrate the important psychological processes involved. This model will be applied, in particular, to fetishism, transvestism and transsexualism and to general variation in gender role and gender identity.

PROBLEMS OF DEFINITION

In common parlance the terms 'sex' and 'gender' are virtually synonymous. However, it is necessary to make a distinction between them if we are to understand sexual behaviour of differing varieties. 'Sex' itself is a concept capable of very wide meanings from, for instance, psychoanalytic polymorphous and latent sexuality, to the narrow euphemistic sense of 'having sex'. Sex is, of course, the distinction between man and woman, and an individual is ascribed male or female sexuality. This is fairly clearly and indelibly stated on the birth certificate. It is determined by the doctor attending the birth, in almost all cases no doubt by a fairly cursory examination of the physical organs of reproduction. The assumption is made that these organs represent appropriate internal structures and reproductive instincts. The diagnosis of sex is, therefore, relatively crude but almost irrevocable.

Behaviour connected with the physical organs and reproductive mechanisms, especially with a physiological erotic arousal, is sexual behaviour. Courtship may be called sexual behaviour; putting the shot, spitting and coal-mining in most cultures are characteristic of one sex rather than the other but are not sexual behaviour.

Behaviours which are not sexual in this sense but are associated with one sex rather than the other are genderal. That is to say, needlework and flower-arrangement are feminine occupations, whilst rugby football and gambling are masculine. This is not to say that females do not gamble but only that when they do so in this culture they are exhibiting genderal behaviour which is masculine. The only implication is that genderal behaviours are those which are most commonly found amongst men or women in a particular culture. At first sight this appears obvious, and a woman who spits may well be doing something regarded as masculine or unfeminine but certainly not sexual. However, we cannot understand sexual variations without appreciating that there is an area of confusion. If a man seeks a feminine occupation or dresses in a feminine manner a dissonance occurs which results in the interpretation of the behaviour as sexual when it may well be entirely genderal.

The origins of sex and gender are not, of course, unconnected, even though a female may be masculine and a male feminine. Their origins do involve morphological sex to a considerable degree. Thus when we meet a stranger in the street we note certain badges of gender: hair length, adornments, cosmetics, and so on. We make confident predictions about the way the stranger will behave in terms of norms of masculine and feminine behaviour. We note also body features, breasts, arm length, waist, hip width, beard and other more subtle factors like smell and we make confident predictions about the individual's sexual instincts and the possession of reproductive sexual organs. One does not predict the other only in a hazardous way. If a woman chooses to wear trousers and drive a bus there may be a confused response and she may be identified not simply as a female enjoying a masculine occupation but as one who is sexually different from the norm. If a transvestite chooses to wear the clothes of the opposite sex, he or she is perceived as a sexual threat and provokes a call for legal sanctions.

Looked at in these broad terms the meanings of sex and gender ought to be clear and rational, but the consensus is not solid and usage continues to be confused. The gender concept owes a great deal to the work of Money (Money et al. 1957) and his colleagues. However, Money's meaning tends to be confused by the way his argument has developed. It has been necessary for him to look at two components of gender: 'role' and 'identity'. Identity in Money's view is established in the early years of life and role is fixed later. In reality it is clear that there is no such dichotomy; it can only be some components of gender which are acquired earlier than others. Nevertheless Money does give what he calls the 'Official definitions' (Money and Ehrhardt 1972):

Gender Identity: The sameness, unity, and persistence of one's individuality as male, female, or ambivalent, in greater or lesser degree, especially as it is experienced in self awareness and behaviour; gender identity is the private experience of gender role, and gender role is the public expression of gender identity.

Gender Role: Everything that a person says and does, to indicate to others or to the self the degree that one is either male, or female, or ambivalent; it includes but is not restricted to sexual arousal and response.

Complex though these definitions are they do not seem consistent with Money's general thesis. For example, how, if gender identity is 'the private experience of gender role', does it become fixed, as Money asserts, by the age of two to three years whereas gender role is not fixed until much later? Why also does Money include sexual arousal as an aspect of gender role?

Stoller (1968) has a rather more simple approach:

Gender is a term that has psychological and cultural rather than biological connotations; if the proper terms for sex are 'male' and 'female', the proper terms for gender are 'masculine' and 'feminine'; these latter may be quite independent of (biological) sex. Gender is the amount of masculinity or femininity found in a person, and, obviously, while there are mixtures of both in many humans, the normal male has a preponderance of masculinity and the normal female a preponderance of femininity.

The latter fact is actuarial rather than biological, of course, and some would prefer the use of 'average' rather than 'normal'.

Oakley (1972) comments on the fact that in different cultures the same distinctions prevail between the sexes but there are great variations in gender roles. She points out that where 'intersex' cases have been studied they may be just as masculine or feminine as those who are biologically normal. She concludes, 'If proof is needed that sex and gender are two separate entities then this is it.'

'DEVIANT' SEXUAL BEHAVIOUR

Research in sexual behaviour is difficult because, on the one hand, of the private nature of sexual instincts and, on the other, of social pressures. Sexual responsiveness, being 'sexy' or even promiscuous, carries a social value – although some groups affect to deny this. Vague beliefs of normality in sexual behaviour exist, e.g. frequency of intercourse, and 'sex' at an early age being an indicator of normality. Such themes, although belonging more to folklore than fact, become foci for the neurotic anxieties of some people. These social pressures to conform to what is decreed as 'normal' are immense and must necessarily influence behaviour. An individual's erotic fantasies and sexual behaviour are liable to be classified as 'abnormal' or 'deviant', because society has not recognized the normality of a wide variation of sexual behaviours.

Arbitrary lines are drawn, as exemplified by the well-known scale of homosexuality devised by Kinsey; but who is deviant on such a scale? A fetishist earns the title if there is a belief, usually on the part of a doctor, that the individual is dependent on his fetish to obtain orgasm – an unlikely limitation. There is evidence that fetishism is the norm rather than the deviation, and indeed social norms have changed somewhat over the last 20 years. It seems that a fetish for black nighties has become a part of normal sexual behaviour but a fetish for black plastic macs has not. The inconsistency is remarkable.

In the final analysis an individual's sexual behaviour becomes 'deviant' when he seeks help, usually medical, allowing his discomfort to be attributed to his sexual behaviour. The exchange between Green and Bancroft (Crown 1979) puts this succinctly in reference to homosexuality: 'Green: Homosexuality may be the sole condition which is a mental disorder only if you go to a psychiatrist for it! Bancroft: The treatment then is to get rid of all psychiatrists.' Unfortunately Green understates the situation since much the same is true of many aspects of sexual behaviour.

MODELS OF SEXUAL DEVIANCE

Vast changes in social awareness of sexual behaviour have occurred since the second world war, exposing its complexity. To avoid pejorative terms like 'deviance', the term 'variation' can be used (or 'diversity' – see Introduction). A number of models of sexual variation are in use. All these, however, minimize the wholeness of human behaviour and depict the variant as variant only in his biological sexuality and the consequent behaviour. The principal models are as follows:

The classificatory model

The traditional medical approach has been to gather together parcels of behaviour into diagnostic categories. Symptoms are linked together, often on tenuous grounds; importance is attached to a diagnosis; then a 'treatment of choice' is assumed to follow. Discussion of the symptoms of, say, transsexualism are copious in the literature. To such workers it seems important to resolve what constitutes the 'true transsexual'. Whether he stands or sits to urinate are matters for solemn evaluation (Wallinder 1975). In reality it is usually, if not always, the case that there are no obvious reliable sequelae from such diagnoses (Laub and Fisk 1974). Such diagnostic categories appear as discrete paragraphs both in text-books and in the International Classification of Diseases.

Criticism of this approach usually evokes the comment that 'the medical model has not been properly understood'. While this may be so, it seems rarely to have been properly explained. It must surely stand on more than a grouping together of behaviours which seem related. A proper model should have implications for action, provide an identification of origins and dynamics and have some reliable basis for predictions.

There are a very large number of such categories of sexual variation as postulated diagnoses. Cross-dressing alone provides 56 at a conservative estimate (Brierley 1979).

The psychodynamic model

The psychodynamic approach conceives of sexual variations as perversions. Normal sexual urges are channelled into unusual forms by the accidents of nurture and experience. Perversion in this context, as with much psychoanalytic usage, does not have quite the same meaning as in day-to-day usage. Within a psychodynamic framework, diagnostic categories are inappropriate because of the individuality of the process. The dynamics of a specific case are seen as appropriate to that case only and the dynamics of the case may well not be those of similar behaviour in others. In fact, many analytical writers are seduced, presumably by the medical model, into making general applications of the dynamics of single cases, as if dealing with diagnostic categories. Fenichel's (1930) analysis of a case which included transvestite behaviour of a fetishistic kind concluded that the dynamics elicited in analysis did not account for the transvestite behaviour. Moreover, he confessed that similar dynamics were to be found in many different kinds of sexual behaviour. Nevertheless Fenichel's analysis has quite commonly been taken as an authoritative explanation of all cross-dressing behaviour – and quite wrongly so.

Freud based his thinking on the concept of infantile polymorphous sexuality, which became channelled into individual forms in maturity. Psychotherapy is thus directed towards initiating a rechannelling of the sexual urges. 'Change therapy' is often used as a derogatory term for such a general approach, implying that society directs the therapist to guide the change towards some 'socially desirable' goal. Whilst this ought not to be so, it is sometimes not clear that this has been grasped by the therapist. This is sometimes true of behaviour therapy, where concentration on the symptom avoids an analysis of the goals which the therapist may be inferring in the client.

Hypotheses such as that of McGuire et al. (1965) that sexual behaviour patterns are learned by contiguous masturbation have a close similarity to those of psychoanalysis. Based loosely on learning principles, McGuire's suggestion is that patterns of sexual behaviour are shaped around fantasies and objects by the concomitant erotic reinforcement in masturbation. This assumes, as did Freud, a polymorphic sexuality constrained by learning.

The biological model

The biological approach contests the notion of undifferentiated sexuality at birth (e.g. Diamond 1965). From this viewpoint, animal studies are interpreted as showing that sexual behaviour is not dependent on post-natal learning. Thus sexual behaviour is seen as a product of physiological and genetic influences which can be adjusted by physical methods such as hormone therapy, brain surgery, and reassignment of sex.

The sociological model

This approach regards sexual diversity as a matter primarily of statistical variation. From this viewpoint it is stressed that all societies breed members with widely differing sexual behaviour, sometimes approved in one society, honoured in another and despised in a third. This being so, it is argued that the ideal society is not one in which the sexual behaviour of all is closely similar but one which can cater for, and value, a wide range of sexual variation. Western society is clearly not such a society, struggling as it does to contain sexual variations by exclusion, imprisonment, hospitalization, ghettos, etc. Glover (1960) expresses this view in respect of homosexuality: 'the answer to this problem, if it be a problem, is in the development of greater tolerance amongst sections of the community which at present tend to make a scapegoat of homosexuality. In this sense the treatment of homosexuality as a whole should be directed as much at the "diseased" prejudices of society as at the "diseased" propensities of the individual homosexual.'

The human rights model

The minority groups look at the problems of sexual variation from a different perspective. Like sociologists, members of such groups may point to the occurrence and acceptance of the same 'deviant' sexual variations in other cultures and at other times. They argue that the problem is thus of society's creation and that it is society which violates the rights of the minorities. From this viewpoint, the failure of a society to tolerate those who differ in their sexual behaviour is a mark of its fundamental unjust nature.

The value of the models

I suggest that none of these ways of thinking about sexual variation does a great deal to further the understanding of human sexual behaviour. The major obstacles are the attention to biological sex alone and the misconception of some behaviours as solely sexual. Thus the homosexual becomes for Money (1970) a person with a propensity for same-sex copulation, without reference to the mass of non-sexual qualities which seem to characterize the total person who is homosexual (Willmott and Brierley 1983). Even more marked is the assumption that all cross-dressing and cross-gender behaviour is sexual. Nowhere can this be more farcically expressed than in Karpman (1947), who says that all cross-dressing is fetishistic in that it is followed in the next few hours by masturbation – or urination, which is the psychic equivalent!

Goode (1981) is one of the many who have entered the debate about whether homosexuality should be defined as a role or as a form of sexual behaviour. Essentially the debate is abortive since it assumes the homogeneity of the homosexual role, ignoring the fact that there are as many roles as there are homosexuals.

I contend that it is essential to look at the total personality organization of the individual to understand his or her sexual behaviour, not just to examine the person's biological needs. Freud in 1905 recognized this full well and wrote in his 'Three essays on sexuality' of the impossibility of understanding homosexuality on the basis of physical sex alone and turned to some concept of 'mental sex', which seems, at least, to have elements which foreshadow the concept of gender as Stoller defines it.

The gender concept has its origins in the work of Money and the Hampsons (1955 and 1957). They found that where sex at birth was in some doubt in hermaphrodite children, the 'sex' of rearing was almost always adopted. The rearing pattern appeared to transcend the biological factors. A child who should be regarded as female according to, say, chromosomal criteria but who was reared as a boy would acquire a belief that she/he was masculine like other boys. She/he would acquire the usual cultural characteristics of a boy. Moreover if an attempt was made to reverse the rearing pattern after two or three years it would not succeed and a masculine gender identity would be retained. Thus it seemed that the gender identity or sense of 'I am a boy' became established in this early critical period whilst the acquisition of the gender role, or style of behaving like a boy, would follow on.

Clearly such issues of gender identity and role are vastly important in understanding the gender dysphorias, transvestism, transsexualism and homosexuality. It seems clear that the transsexual's claim is 'I am feminine (or masculine) but my body is male (or female) – change my body and I will be a coherent whole.'

A MODEL OF SEXUAL BEHAVIOUR

Bancroft (1972) proposed a model of the functional aspects of sexual behaviour in terms of cognitive consistency principles. Figure 3.1 is an attempt to elaborate on Bancroft's model using personal construct theory. The figure has three main parts. Firstly, the personal construct system, covering the range of self concepts or elements, exemplified by 'Me as I really am', 'Me as I wish I was', and 'Me as others would see the real me'. In personal construct terms it is hypothesized that the individual's construct system, which is highly personalized and can only be loosely described, as it is in this example, serves as the structure on which the individual can best perceive his world as secure and predictable. Personal constructs are tools which allow the individual to anticipate events reliably.

In ideal circumstances, and in the well-integrated personality, separate elements of the type shown in figure 3.1 would be closely related. The individual would construe his real self very much as he construes the way others see him, and how he would like to be. The example illustrates, of course, a highly dissonant personality whose perception of his role relationships would be very complex and uncertain. He would be fundamentally insecure because of his inability to make general confident predictions about his world, an important aspect of which would be his sexual roles. Kelly suggests that it is the need to make sound predictions of events which primarily reinforces behaviour rather than pleasure *per se*.

Secondly, in the area of interpersonal perceptions gender role is, like other roles, not a self concept as much as a persistent pattern of behaviour which arises from the expectations of how those about the individual will construe him. Thus the role is played without great dependency on cues. The gender identity, on the other hand, is a core role and is determined by the most firmly established and least flexible constructs. It goes without saying that both role and identity are expectations of how the individual will be seen by others, not necessarily of how he is actually seen by them.

The sex object is the person, or perhaps object, on whom sexual arousal is centred in the broad sense. In this model, the sex object, as perceived by the individual, is adopted by the application of his personal construct system to reality, that is, the person seeks the best realistic fit to maximize the predictive capacity of his construct system, in a sexual sense. It will be increasingly difficult to determine an adequate sex object the more disparate the set of self concepts becomes. The sex object would need to be construed in terms of the individual's true self as much as in terms of the way others are predicted to construe him or her.

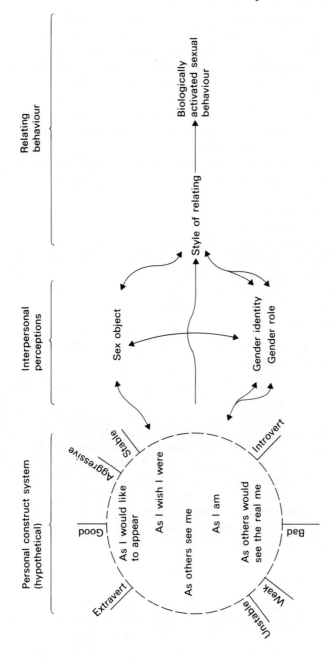

Figure 3.1   Model – origins of sexual behaviour

The sex object must clearly be in a relationship with the gender identity and role. This relationship is described as the 'style of relating', which is, in effect, the behavioural solution to the maintenance of an equilibrium in the system. This style of relating, when biologically activated, gives rise to the individual's style of sexual behaviour and forms the third part of the system.

The separate elements of the system are in a state of homeostatic balance. That is to say, the system adjusts as far as possible to maintain stability and to oppose external constraints. Core constructs and gender identity are themselves resistant to change and the sex object appears moderately so. The style of relating is fairly fluid and, as is implicit in personal construct theory, the construct system itself, is in a constant state of modification and testing, to maximize its predictive efficiency. The system functions as a whole to maintain the best working compromise and determines the style of relating and consequently sexual behaviour itself.

The model represents only the psychological aspect of the system. Other forces produce constraints on this system. The law and social conventions in particular limit the resultant sexual behaviour. Biological and endocrine factors play some part, it seems, in determining gender. Family structures, occupational roles and environmental issues are similarly involved in determining the construct system itself.

Implications of the model

The immediate implication of such a model is the unacceptability of conceptualizing sexual variations as discrete entities. It may be possible to say that an individual conforms to some degree to some hypothetical concept of, say, a homosexual or a heterosexual but not that he or she belongs to a distinct group of people with a common circumscribed behaviour pattern. Rationally one can make sense of sex-related patterns of behaviour only as varying modes of adaptation within a fairly delicately balanced system.

An obstacle to change in such a system may well be that, unlike the neuroses, which are essentially maladaptive, sexual patterns may be adaptive and valued by the individual. It is often only the secondary factors, like law or social disapproval, which cause pain and motivate change.

The model applied to cross-dressing

A consideration of cross-dressing behaviour illustrates some points about the model and its implications for all aspects of the individual's functioning. It is possible, using this model, to see the relationship between three conditions, fetishism, transvestism and transsexualism, a relationship which undoubtedly exists despite the usual assumption that the three are separate 'syndromes'.

Conventionally fetishism is seen as the use of an inanimate object for sexual gratification. One large class of fetishistic objects is clothing of the opposite sex, often of a bizarre kind, such as rubber or leather garments. In one form of fetishism a heterosexual partner may wear the fetishistic article. Indeed clothing fashion often seems to involve elements of common fetishes. Alternatively the fetishism may be autosexual and the individual handles, fantasizes or wears the garment himself, promoting erotic arousal centred upon his own body. Not infrequently the fetishistic transvestite examines himself in a mirror and is aroused by the fantasy of being the sort of person he sees there. More often than not his cross-dressing is unconvincing as a portrayal of a person of the opposite sex, deliberately dressed as he is in unusual, garish articles. Fetishism of this kind is rarely exclusive, and is usually private, outside an otherwise heterosexual existence – even if he sometimes attempts to involve a partner in the fetish. There are thus two alternative sex objects to which the individual relates and, hypothetically, the two are related to different aspects of his self concept. The heterosexual object is associated with how he would hope to be perceived, and the image he sees in the mirror with how he really experiences himself.

Asexual transvestism represents a partial resolution of this situation. Transvestism is often misunderstood as being solely fetishistic – a confusion of a gender problem with a purely sexual one. Many transvestites report a development from a fetishistic phase, although by no means all clothing fetishists develop to the transvestite position. The fetishistic element declines until the individual finds the cross gender role rewarding in its own right, and is then no longer materially involved in an erotic experience. Instead of the fantasy relationship with the second sex-object, he incorporates that object and modifies his own gender identity. The asexual transvestite often describes his two selves as 'my brother and sister', feeling that they are different people with different characteristics. Still the 'brother' seems to maintain an ordinary heterosexual existence. Occasionally the 'sister' experiments with alternative sex objects, but they almost invariably prove unsatisfactory. However, the 'sister' role resolves difficulties by providing a means of sporadic flight into an idealized world where there are no sexual obligations and all is just 'lace curtains, tea cups, and feminine chat'.

Like many of the 'minorities', transsexuals find themselves in a position where they must conform to the concept of a distinct disease entity to press their point. Thus almost invariably they strenuously deny the previous existence of any fetishistic or transvestite phase. Nevertheless, the idea of the transsexual as a person with a fixed cross-gender identity from the earliest days of consciousness rarely fits the individual in reality. The path of the development of a conviction that life in a cross-sex role is necessary is usually clear and more often than not passes through transvestite or homosexual phases. The solution is, therefore, not unlike that adopted by the transvestite, except that the demands of the strongly atypical gender identity require a more radical assumption of a whole-time cross-gender role. In fact he takes refuge in the new role and, as Stoller (1968) points out, the situation is eased by the obliteration of his sexual drives resulting from oestrogen therapy. He may attempt to create a new form of sex object in relation to his idealized new role but, of course, this attempt is weakly motivated at a sexual level.

These three patterns of sexual behaviour are, therefore, three modes of adaptation or states of equilibrium within the system the model attempts to outline. They are solutions for the individual rather than fixed prescribed roles to which the individual conforms. To place, for instance, the transsexual (defined only in terms of his wish for reassignment) in such a hypothetical strait-jacket as a condition for meeting his demands is clearly putting the cart before the horse.

GENDER ROLE AND IDENTITY

Gender is perhaps the most contentious part of the model just described. It has to be admitted that in Money's concept of gender identity as immutable after the early years of life it hardly seems appropriate to a homeostatic system at all. Despite Money's later denials, it seems fairly clear that he initially thought of gender as wholly or almost wholly learned. At one stage (Money 1970) he argued for the imprinting of gender. The argument has been put forward that gender is genetically and physiologically determined, hence equally immutable. Hutt (1972) seems inclined to this view and sums up her assessment of Money's work by saying, 'the evidence to date has made such a view untenable.' It is therefore important to look at the question of gender development and assess the extent to which it needs to be involved in a consideration of sexual variations.

Bancroft (1972) remarks, 'as far as gender identity is concerned, it is how the individual sees himself rather than how others see him that is most important.' This is implicit in the model, but few researches have endeavoured to link self concepts of gender with biological factors. In Money's own work so little seems to have been done to determine gender identity in an objective manner that his conclusions are laid open to much doubt and criticism. Evidence is at best tenuously inferred from studies of the gender dysphorias and animal studies of copulatory behaviour.

Order seems to dictate that strict sexual dimorphism be the rule. There should be male and female: the remainder are 'errors' or 'experiments of nature'. In a High Court judgement in 1983 Mr Justice Parker declared that this was 'a matter of common sense'. However, it does seem beyond biological science to define sex in clear-cut, unarguable terms, and the law has to resort to an operational definition that sex is simply what is written on the birth certificate, despite any evidence to the contrary. It could be said that the sex-differentiation process is such that 'errors' are a direct and predictable result, and therefore not errors at all but part of the normal pattern of things.

Polani (1972) lists four 'components of sex'. The first three are reasonably clear physical issues: gonads, hormones and internal genital tracts, and external genitalia. The fourth is simply 'a variety of attributes'; some are anatomical and physiological, like skin texture, whilst others are 'cultural and socio-psychological attributes not specifically sexual'. Admitting, or finding it necessary to include such a diverse group of attributes as part of a definition of sex immediately suggests that a concept of distinct groups of males and females is indeed no matter of common sense but considerably idealized.

CHROMOSOMAL ASPECTS

The sex chromosome complex, male XY and female XX, has become an accepted key to sexual differentiation. There are, however, a substantial number of individuals showing sex chromosome complexes which do not conform. They are the first of two categories of unusual sex-determination. Hutt (1972) stresses the rarity of these cases, but, rare or not, they represent a real part of humanity which does not fit in with the dimorphic model. In addition we have those sexually intermediate states which result from the process of intrauterine differentiation itself.

In its initial stages the human foetus is female in form, and only at about the third month do male features begin to appear. This differentiation from female form is believed to be associated with the presence of the Y chromosome characterizing the male.

Perhaps the major anomaly in this process is that of the XX male who is born 'masculinized' in anatomy with testes and yet does not appear to possess a Y chromosome. More common are the Klinefelter syndrome cases whose genetic make-up is of the XXY type, but XXXY and XXYY also occur. The Klinefelter cases are sterile, possess small male genitalia, weak secondary hair and sometimes small breasts. As with many of the genetic 'errors' it is not clear why these cases are regarded as male with an extra X chromosome rather than female with a Y. This could be a curious convention or predisposition to ascribe to people the benefits of being male if at all possible! The Klinefelter has been quoted in older textbooks as sometimes transvestite, fetishistic and sometimes homosexual. Of course, such sexual behaviours are likely to be sought out in the examination of individuals seen at the outset as having sexual problems and they merit no wide generalization. Certainly they do not indicate a genetic basis to the gender dysphorias.

There are many other genetic patterns including the 'mosaics' who possess body cells of both XX and XY types. Armstrong and Marshall (1964) published a report on a case of this kind who lived as a female, had a male appearance but possessed both ovaries and testes. Some chromosome patterns like the triple X female seem to be of no consequence, the individual being a seemingly normal female.

Studies of chromosome structures, therefore, throw up intermediate states or hermaphrodites classified as male or female to fit the birth certificate and convention but who are effectively sexually indeterminate. Looked at from the other angle no studies of gender dysphorias, homosexuality or transsexuality give any indication of genetic 'errors' being relevant.

Curious results have occurred in the study of inheritance in homosexual groups. Brother/sister ratios have been found to be atypical. In the general population the ratio of brothers to sisters of male probands is 106:100. Darke (1948) found a similar ratio for male homosexuals but Kallman (1952) found a ratio of 125:100 in a highly regarded study. Lang (1940) found a ratio of 121:100 rising to 128:100 amongst homosexuals over 25 years. Of course such patterns are as likely to be related to rearing patterns as they are to inheritance.

More complex family patterns were shown by Martensen-Larsen (1957). Again more brothers than expected were found and the male homosexuals came more frequently from the younger third of the family. Slater (1958, 1962) confirmed this and the rather obvious corollary that homosexuals tend to have older mothers. This, for Martensen-Larsen, seemed to indicate that the important variable was that of rearing, but he strengthened the inheritance hypothesis when he found a preponderance of males in the sibs of fathers and grandfathers whilst there was a preponderance of sisters amongst mothers and grandmothers. Lesbians on the other hand had a preponderance of female sibs. More recent studies have tended not to confirm many of the older findings about the family relationships of homosexuals (e.g. Siegelman 1981) but it does appear that the more recent studies involve more heterogeneous populations and it is hard to dismiss replicated previous findings.

Kallman's (1952) studies of twins showed virtually 100 per cent concordance for homosexuality in monozygotic twins but a concordance rate for dizygotics in line with Kinsey's findings for the incidence of homosexual behaviour in the general population. However, too much has, perhaps, been made of Kallman's study and he himself was at pains to point out in his original paper the grave limitations imposed on his work by prevailing social and legal forces.

If the Y chromosome initiates the differentiation process, a male child may not result for a number of other reasons. Also, the absence of a Y chromosome may not result in a strictly female child. A male foetus castrated *in utero* will be born with external genitalia which appear female. The effect has been produced experimentally in animals only but the administration of hormones which suppress androgens during pregnancy may produce the same result. Despite the apparent external female organs in the genetic male, the female internal organs would not be present and there would be testes.

Analogues in humans are found in the testicular feminization syndrome and the 5–α reductase deficiency. In these cases genetic XY males appear female at birth as a result, in the former, of a foetal insensitivity to androgen and, in the latter, of an absence of an enzyme responsible for the production of an androgen derivative. These cases are often unrecognized at birth and are reared as females until there are problems at adolescence in the failure to menstruate, masculinization, or other features which bring them to medical attention. The conventional approach has been to feminize the individual by oestrogens, removing the undescended testes, and perhaps to carry out some surgical modification. These 'girls' are reported to be strongly feminine in appearance with emphatically female psychosexual orientation and strong maternal feelings. However, such cases have rarely been examined in any depth psychologically and the cases described at the end of this chapter conflict with this view. There is always a tendency for clinical judgement of matters as difficult to determine as gender identity to support the medical course already chosen.

In genetic females the adrenogenital syndrome produces male-like development in the foetus. In these cases there is a high secretion of androgens in the absence of a Y chromosome in the foetus, which develops a penis but no testes and has female ovaries. There is no vagina. A similar phenomenon has been found in the children of mothers treated with hormones to prevent miscarriages. The medical convention has been to carry out surgery to remove the internal female organs and to administer androgens to masculinize the individual further. The few studies that exist report male appearance and psychosexual disposition.

Ehrhardt and his colleagues (1967, 1968) examined cases of adrenogenital syndrome where the masculinization had been corrected soon after birth. He reported that they were tomboyish, chose boys' games, rejected dolls, did not have homosexual feelings but were uninterested in the male sex. Here it seems that there were no remaining male features of a physical kind to affect the post-natal learning of masculine gender roles or to suppress the feminine behaviour.

DÖRNER'S WORK

Dörner (1979) presents a complex series of investigations purporting to demonstrate a relationship between physiological processes and gender. His fundamental hypothesis is of a closed-loop endocrine system. Changes in the environment, external and internal, affect neurotransmitter metabolism. In turn the neurotransmitters affect fundamental processes of reproduction and metabolism as well as information processing. In turn the cycle is completed by the environment being affected. Usually such a loop is reversible but Dörner suggests that this is not so at critical periods of sex-differentiation of the foetus.

One aspect of sex-differentiation is the gonadotrophin secretion mechanism. Neurotransmitters influence the hypothalamus to secrete a gonadotrophin-release hormone and under this influence the pituitary secretes gonadotrophins. Sex hormones exert either a male inhibitory or female stimulatory influence on the secretion and this sex difference is a feature of foetal differentiation (Dörner et al. 1976). Animal studies support this argument and Dörner claimed that the higher the androgen level during sex-differentiation at the stage of foetal differentiation the more masculine the sexual behaviour of both sexes. On this basis he argues that hyposexuality, bisexuality and homosexuality represent the influence of increasing androgen deficiency at the foetal differentiation of males and androgen excess for females.

Many workers seem to have failed to find evidence of hormonal differences between heterosexuals and homosexuals but Dörner claimed to find that 'effeminate homosexuals' and 'transsexuals' showed raised luteinizing hormone and follicle-stimulating hormone as well as low free plasma testosterone. In two papers (1972 and – with his colleagues – 1975) Dörner examined the feedback associated with the administration of oestrogens in homosexuals and transsexuals. He claimed to have found female patterns of +ve feedback, i.e. increased gonadotrophin levels. His conclusion was that these groups 'possess at least in part a predominantly female differentiated brain'.

Some support comes from Seyler et al. (1978) who found that the gonadotrophin release in female to male transsexuals and lesbians was more typical of males than females. Otherwise attempts to replicate this part of Dörner's work seems to have been unfruitful. Haslam (personal communication, 1982) reports a continuing attempt to examine the feedback response to conjugated oestrogens in male transsexuals. Some preliminary results showed a female pattern in some transsexuals, though a fair proportion of control subjects showed the same result.

There are many weak points in Dörner's work. For Dörner, environmental influences refer to very fundamental processes such as the effects of bottle-feeding. His concept of 'effeminacy' appears very vague and is dependent on superficial cultural factors such as adornments. He nevertheless gives it a crucial position in his argument. He does not seem to appreciate the radical difference between 'effeminacy' and 'femininity'. Most importantly, the statistical appraisal of his results seems, at best, vague.

Of great concern are Dörner's enthusiastic extrapolation of his findings to suggest monitoring the amniotic fluid so as to detect 'potential permanent disorders of mating and non-mating behaviour' and his hopes for intervention. He cites Roeder and Muller (1969) and their effective suppression of homosexual behaviour by the use of stereotaxic lesions of the hypothalamic ventromedial nucleus. The suggestion is as naive as it is abhorrent but it is by no means without precedent. Lukianowicz (1959) expressed a similar notion: 'all the horrors of the reassignment of transsexuals can be avoided by a simple brain operation'! The view is based on the false assumption that homosexuals and transsexuals 'suffer'. It is of importance in the context of work like Dörner's to realize that such 'suffering', if it exists at all, is imposed solely by society. In particular, transsexuals, even more than homosexuals, uniformly reject attempts to coerce them into an acceptance of their genetic sex. Furthermore it is facile to assume that suppression of sexual behaviour in a homosexual constitutes the 'normalization' of the whole person – it may simply create an impotent homosexual.

Dörner's stance is clearly one in which sex and gender are determined largely by biological processes and partly by elementary environmental ones which have gross physiological consequences of a particular kind. Research by Imperator-McGinley and co-workers (1974, 1979) and the report by Savage et al. (1980) on 5–α reductase deficiency appear to conflict with important aspects of both Money's and Dörner's work, which both envisage the establishment of a fixed gender identity.

Imperator-McGinley investigated a village community in the Dominican Republic. Thirty-eight cases were studied intensively. These people were diagnosed as suffering from the 5-α reductase enzyme deficiency. The function of the enzyme is to promote the conversion of testosterone into dihydrotestosterone during the period of foetal sex-differentiation. Testosterone and dihydrotestosterone have different functions. Testosterone is believed to effect the development of male internal structures whilst dihydrotestosterone governs the external organ development. At puberty testosterone governs voice changes, muscle mass, and increases in phallic size, whilst dihydrotestosterone governs prostate growth, facial hair and recession of hair-line, as well as acne. The cases studied were genetic males born with apparently female genitalia who were reared as girls until puberty. At that time there was a spontaneous morphological change with testicles appearing and penile development. Imperator-McGinley reports that, in addition, the initially acquired feminine gender identity was relinquished and a masculine identity adopted. Imperator-McGinley was quickly taken to task in letters to the *New England Medical Journal* by supporters of the school regarding learning as the major source of gender identity. It seemed that the reversal of gender at puberty indicated that learning played little part. However, Imperator-McGinley responded by pointing out that the acquisition of an early feminine identity was strong support for the learning hypothesis, although the reversal of the learned role suggested that it could be overridden by the androgen influence. Such is the ambiguity of much of the existing biological evidence.

SOCIAL LEARNING EFFECTS AND GENDER ROLE

It seems fair to say that some aspects of gender identity are learned, even though they may be less crucial aspects. Money does seem to have modified his stance over the years in favour of a greater contribution from biological influences. If gender identity is the sense of belonging to one group, boy or girl, there can be little doubt that simple cognitive components can be acquired by learning. The biological fact of morphological differences is also relevant. Thus at this simple level it must be the case that gender is determined by a biological predisposition and a process of learning. The extent to which the finer attributes of gender are acquired by learning or biological predisposition is more uncertain. The biological influences may well be a great deal more subtle than the influence of simple morphology but it is necessary to appreciate that there is no exact one-to-one relationship between sex and gender. The lack of such relationship is shown by transsexuals and probably by homosexuals. As Bancroft (1972) says 'the homosexual, if he is to achieve stability, usually needs to produce a special type of gender identity – "I am a homosexual".'

There is also evidence from other cultures. Mead (1950) gives a classic account of how the masculine and feminine models of gender differ dramatically in different cultures. Although males usually acquire in all cultures the gender identity appropriate to their sex, what being a male or being a female amounts to in terms of, say, aggression, child-care, adornment and styles of courtship behaviour is infinitely variable. Such variety can hardly be attributable to biological processes alone.

Biological differences can underlie learning of course. It has been suggested that birth is more traumatic for boys on purely physical grounds and this alone may lead to differences in nursing. To this the greater irritability of boys has been attributed. They respond less to stress but relax less easily, they cry more and sleep less, even in very early days of life. The maternal respondent behaviour follows suit. Moss (1970) showed that at three weeks mothers held male babies half an hour longer in each eight-hour period than girls. Mothers respond to children according to what they believe is the sex of the child and, if misled, will behave inappropriately. Mother's soothing of the boy gives way to toleration. She expects him to oppose her and to assert himself against her. The girl she regards as an extension of herself, sharing in the things she does and being in emotional harmony with her.

Hartley (1966) classified such parental actions under four principal headings. A mother manipulates the female child a great deal, she examines her closely, combs her hair at length, dresses her attentively and continually praises her looks. Parents canalize the child's play by presenting toys and regulating play by approval and disapproval so that it is appropriate to the child's sex. They prescribe for the children boxing-gloves, tea-sets, guns and doll's houses, which foreshadow what they expect of the child in later life. Both parents employ specific verbal appellations, e.g. 'big strong boy' or 'pretty little girl'. The fact that in some dialects there is a pronounced difference between masculine and feminine speech suggests that parental speech style to boy and girl might also differ. In the speech-training of transsexuals it is usually more important to modify the speech rhythm, inflections and usages than the pitch. Finally, the child is exposed to real-life activities which are again gender-appropriate. The boy is encouraged to help dad with the car and the girl to lay tables and bake cakes with mum. Of course, such parental actions are almost entirely culturally determined but it is significant that on the whole it is easier for the girl to respond than the boy. A young girl can realistically help in the home whilst a boy of the same age can do very little to assist repairing the car. Admiration of the girl is easily accepted by her but counter-balanced by the challenges to the boy to be bigger and stronger.

Between three and eight years children become quite clear about the toys appropriate to their sex but it is curious that their choices are more emphatic when observed than when playing alone. If the children deviate from appropriate play forms they are constrained; boys especially are ridiculed as 'soft' or 'sissy'.

Institutions, be they 'bonny baby' competitions or schools, propagate gender stereotypes. Sexton (1970) emphasizes the feminizing effect of education conducted mostly by female teachers. Male teachers for boys and female teachers for girls was a cause espoused by a whole teachers' union. However, the argument is simplistic since the acquisition of gender is not simple global imitation of whole figures. Freud (1933) recognized that the child finds its models not just in single individuals but in the functions exercised by many individuals around him. The child's model of father will include the extent to which mother also exerts a paternal role.

Bandura (1963) and others have shown the importance of resource control in identifying the degree to which a child imitates one parent or another. Grinder and Judith (1965) also found that boys tended to see fathers as resource controllers and that girls saw mothers in that role. Again Bandura comments on the complexity of the gender models: 'Children are not simply junior-sized replicas of one or the other model – rather they exhibit a relatively novel amalgam of elements from both . . . parents' response repertoires.'

There is evidence too of the relationship between parent's rearing behaviour and the child's gender. Thus highly masculine males see their fathers as more punitive but also more caring than less masculine males do. Maternal dominance tends to be associated with more feminine and non-aggressive boys on the one hand and aggressive girls on the other.

In adolescence and later life society enforces very many genderal features quite rigidly. The badges of gender may change but the gender line is kept starkly defined. A young man may wear two ear-rings in one ear and demonstrate his aggressive masculinity but also assert with conviction that he would look 'a bloody fool' with one ear-ring in each ear. A male may not wear clothing of certain colours or certain classes of perfume without becoming genderally suspect. He may not stand in a particular way or make particular gestures or he may be labelled with some contempt. At all costs he must keep his voice in a low register. He must profess high aspirations and climb mountains 'just because they are there'. He must demonstrate financial success and independence.

These qualities are reflected in parental expectations. Aberle and Naegele (1952) showed that American middle-class fathers became concerned if their sons did not take responsibility and if they lacked initiative. They needed to have athletic prowess and academic achievement from them. The fathers were most concerned if their sons were over-conforming, excitable, fearful or showed what they believed to be homosexual traits. On the other hand girls were expected to marry and to be affectionate and 'sweet', but their roles were less emphatically laid down.

In adult life roles are enforced by ridicule and law. Professions and occupations are either closed to genderally non-conforming males or else society classes as 'queer' the man in an occupation which is seen as not conforming to the masculine role. Women appear to be less restricted, although feminist movements deny this. Obstructions to women in genderally atypical roles may be very positive but they do not contain the same ruthless sanctions of ridicule and, in the extreme, fear. Lesbians are not, it seems, 'security risks' as male homosexuals are accused of being. The male teacher who is convicted of a sexual offence is by law reported to the Department of Education and 'black- listed' whether or not his offence is related to children. The male 'streaker' is prosecuted and heavily fined on the basis one supposes of a presumed sexual motivation. The female 'streaker' becomes something of a television personality as a sort of liberated feminist!

ILLUSTRATIVE CASE

In the following case the identities of the two women concerned are of course disguised, owing to the delicate nature of their problem. The relevant facts are nonetheless substantially correct.

Anne was an 18-year-old member of the sixth form of a girl's public school. She attended a routine medical examination and without explanation was referred by the doctor to an endocrinologist. Naturally the matter of the referral was discussed by the family and her older sister Beverly, aged 20, a law student, went to see her general practitioner asking that she could be similarly referred.

Both girls were intellectually bright and excelled in sports. The younger was a member of a girl's football team whilst the older played squash for her county. Both were outgoing, sociable and popular. Both had good health records. They had casual boyfriends but neither had had any heterosexual relationships of any intensity. They gave the impression of being substantially unaware of sexual feelings.

Physically they were tall, almost six feet. They had large hands and noticeably long arms. Their body contours and faces were rounded. Their skins were clear, with no unusual hair growth apparent. However, they had male proportions in rather wide shoulders, little or no waist and smaller hips than one would expect of women. Their voices were rather deep by female standards but soft with feminine intonation. Their mannerisms were neither distinctly masculine nor feminine.

They were the only children of parents in early middle age when they were born. The family was a close-knit group and the home life was happy and stable. The parents were proud of their children and they stated categorically that they were unaware of any medical problems which Anne and Beverly might have. They did not know of any family history of health problems. They were surprised by the mysterious referral of Anne and by Beverly's initiative but they were placid people and accepted that, whatever it was about, the medical attention was for the best. Questioning of the parents revealed no abnormality in the rearing pattern of the girls and their sex had never been in question as far as family and friends were concerned. Neither had their success in sport at a fairly high level been seen as unusual.

The endocrinologist who examined the girls reported that they were both masculine, so much so that he had difficulty in treating them as female. He felt they were like men dressed up. This seemed strikingly at variance with their general acceptance as girls. The psychiatrist found Anne but not Beverly to be very masculine. I, on the other hand, who spent considerable time with both girls, found Anne to be quite attractively feminine, despite being aware of her rather male body-build. I found Beverly less feminine, but not outstandingly masculine, and attributed this to her much more assertive manner and obvious achievement needs. It seemed possible that the different impressions were determined by the orientation and attitudes which the three professions brought to the problem.

The school doctor had noted three features in the examination of Anne: little or no breast development, failure to menstruate, and a somewhat enlarged clitoris. Beverly also showed these features when examined. The endocrinological investigations showed that both were genetic males with the positive symptoms of 5–α reductase deficiency, but it should be noted that there was no evidence of gross spontaneous masculinization, which has been reported particularly in more recent literature, and certainly no changes of gender.

The principal results of the psychological investigations were as follows: Terman-Miles Attitude Interest Test (see Brierley 1979): Anne scored −27 and Beverly −22. Both these suggest normal femininity of attitudes. The responses were remarkably similar. On six of the seven subtests they did not differ by more than two points. On the seventh they differed by seven points on 105 items. This subtest emphasizes strong emotional reactions, fear, anger, etc., and here Beverly had the higher score.

Cattell 16 PF Questionnaire: The same striking similarity was found here. Beverly was more tense and less emotionally stable to a minor degree. Anne was rather more guarded and suspicious but had less self-conflict. The small differences could be attributed to age: Beverly had had to deal with her problems for longer and had reached a level of doubt and discouragement. Both girls were bright and practically minded with strong social needs. There were no features which might have suggested that they were other than perfectly normal females.

Repertory grid (details of this particular application of the technique are given in Brierley 1979): Beverly's grid showed that she construed herself as quite removed from all other elements including 'the person I would most like to be'. She could not see herself becoming like other people, only as becoming increasingly sensitive and submissive. Anne's grid was more complex; she saw herself as gathering qualities which were more masculine. Both girls construed themselves as tense, insecure and rather ill-controlled. They wanted to acquire stability and self-confidence.

Personal Questionnaire (PQRST – Mulhall 1976): This technique, based on interview, evaluates the relative strength of the patients' problem areas. Anne showed that her major dissatisfactions were to do with her body, especially in so far as she was physically different, which isolated her from other girls so that she had to lie about her periods and obscure her lack of breast development. This distressed her a great deal. She expressed pleasure in her 'feminine feelings'. Beverly was very unhappy about her body which she felt was 'freakish'. She was discontented about feeling like 'a boy gone wrong' and being 'tomboyish'. Instinctively her athletic and sporting ability was enjoyable but at the same time she regretted it as unfeminine. She was very much concerned that she could not get 'a straight answer' (although she never asked the question!) and she very much disliked discussing her problems.

Discussion by a multidisciplinary gender dysphoria committee became centred around the objectives of hormonal and surgical procedures and subsequent counselling. The core issue from which no escape seemed possible was that of whether the girls should be treated in a way to make them conform better to the male or female stereotype. It seemed impossible to maintain the view that they would never adequately conform to either. The impasse can be illustrated by the fact that a prolonged discussion ended with the resolution to leave counselling to a female psychiatrist who was neither present nor had any previous experience in counselling people with gender problems! In the event continued semi-ignorance seemed to be the best policy. Anne was informed that she suffered from a malformation of her internal reproductive organs. This information distressed her a great deal. Beverly had a similar explanation but an operation to remove her 'ovaries' was carried out whilst in reality her testes were removed.

The two girls exemplified a clear and continued acceptance of a feminine gender identity and role. Neither expressed any desire to be more masculine in any way; in fact they were apparently rather guilty about their tomboyishness. Certainly neither would readily have adopted a male role. This was clear in early tentative counselling. Indeed to attempt to initiate a gender-role change would have been socially disastrous to both. Their problems were in no way resolved and it is clear that they were trapped by a social, and to some extent medical, demand that they conform to one of the two proper sexes. They were neither men nor women but this was a fact that they themselves would have found hard to accept and society would have refused to accept. It is questionable whether several years of medical intervention left them any happier.

CONCLUSIONS

I began by pointing out the way in which concepts of 'sexual deviance' tend to be framed in terms of a diseased sexuality. This approach does not lead to an understanding of sexual variations. I then attempted to define what is meant by sex and gender. Some variations in what are often regarded as sexual behaviour, such as transsexualism, are more correctly variations in gender identity.

I have argued that sex itself is not as clearly defined as the convention of a sexual dichotomy assumes. Apart from the small but not insignificant group who do not conform biologically but are nevertheless assigned to male and female groups, there seems to be a need to include non-biological characteristics in the concept of sex which considerably confuse the issue of what is labelled male and female.

The biological investigations of the basis of sex and gender do not produce other than ambiguous answers. Rather, they blur the male–female dichotomy. However, there can be no doubt that both biology and learning are important in the development of gender identity. It thus seems important to appreciate that, in the understanding of sexual behaviour, an adherence to strict dichotomies of male/female and masculine/feminine is obstructive. Sex, gender and sexual behaviour are highly individual matters.

Kessler and McKenna (1978) describe experiments which lead them to conclude that the prime concept is gender and that it is a social concept at that. Sex, they argue, is simply the accumulation of social and scientific data which support a social dichotomy of gender. The present argument is not so extreme but emphasizes that both sex and gender are not as well defined and distinct as social 'common sense' dictates.

The study of two 'sisters' with a hermaphrodite condition shows clearly the adoption of a strong feminine gender identity in genetic males. This was strongly in conflict with their awareness of masculine physical characteristics. Difficulty in dealing with such a problem lies in the intensity of the social demand for conformity to the male–female dichotomy. Society finds it hard to accept that some people simply do not conform to these hypothetical and ubiquitous sex stereotypes.

REFERENCES

Aberle, D. F., and Naegele, K. D. (1952). Middle-class fathers' occupational role and attitudes toward children. *American Journal of Orthopsychiatry*, 22, 366–78.
Armstrong, C. N., and Marshall, A. J. (1964). *Intersexuality*, London: Academic Press.
Bancroft, J. (1972). The relationship between gender identity and sexual behaviour. In C. Ounsted and D. C. Taylor (eds), *Gender Differences*, Edinburgh: Churchill Livingstone.
Bandura, A., Ross, D., and Ross, S. A. (1963). A comparative test of the status envy, social power, and secondary reinforcement theories of identification learning. *Journal of Abnormal and Social Psychology*, 67, 6, 527–34.
Brierley, H. (1979). *Transvestism: A Handbook*. London: Pergamon.
Crown, S. (1979). Male homosexuality: perversion, deviation or variant? In *Ciba Foundation Symposium 62*, New York: Excerpta Medica.
Darke, R. A. (1948). Heredity as an etiological factor in homosexuality. *Journal of Nervous and Mental Disease*, 107, 251–68.

Diamond, M. (1965). A critical evaluation of the ontogeny of human sexual behaviour. *Quarterly Review of Biology*, 40, 147–75.

Dörner, G. (1972). Auslösung eines positiven Östrogenfeedback-Effect bei homosexuellen Männern. *Endokrinologie*, 60, 297–301.

Dörner, G. (1979). Hormones and sexual differentiation of the brain. In *Ciba Foundation Symposium* 62, New York: Excerpta Medica.

Dörner, G., Hecht, K., and Hinz, G. (1976). Teratopsychogenic effect apparently produced by non-physiological neurotransmettir concentrations during brain differentiation. *Endokrinologie*, 68, 1–5.

Dörner, G., Rohde, W., Stahl, F., Krell, L., and Masius, W. (1975). Neurendocrine conditioned predisposition for homosexuality in men. *Archives of Sexual Behaviour*, 4, 1–8.

Ehrhardt, A. A., Evers, K., and Money, J. (1968). Influence of androgen and some aspects of sexually dimorphic behaviour in women with late treated adrenogenital syndrome. *Johns Hopkins Medical Journal*, 123, 115–22.

Ehrhardt, A. A., and Money, J. (1967). Projestin-induced hermaphroditism: I.Q. and psychosexual identity in a study of ten girls. *Journal of Sex Research*, 3, 83–100.

Fenichel, O. (1930). The psychology of transvestism. *International Journal of Psycho-Analysis*, 11, 211.

Freud, S. (1905). Three essays on the theory of sexuality. The sexual aberrations. In *Complete Works of Sigmund Freud*, London: Hogarth.

Freud, S. (1933). *New Introductory Lectures on Psychoanalysis*, London: Hogarth.

Glover, E. (1960). The problem of male homosexuality. In *The Roots of Crime*, London: Imago.

Goode, E. (1981). Comments on the homosexual role. *Journal of Sex Research*, 17, 1, 54–65.

Grinder, R. E., and Judith, C. S. (1965). Sex differences in adolescents' perceptions of parental resource control. *Journal of Genetic Psychology*, 106, 337–44.

Hartley, R. E. (1966). A developmental view of female sex-role identification. In B. J. Biddle and E. J. Thomas (eds), *Role Theory*, New York: Wiley.

Hutt, C. (1972). *Males and Females*. Harmondsworth: Penguin.

Imperator-McGinley, J., Guerrero, L., Gautier, T. and Peterson, R. E. (1974). Steroid 5α-reductase deficiency in man. An inherited form of male pseudohermaphroditism. *Science*, 186, 1213–15.

Imperator-McGinley, J., Peterson, R. E., Gautier, T., and Sturla, E. (1979). Androgens and the evolution of male gender identity among male pseudohermaphrodites with 5α-reductase deficiency. *New England Medical Journal*, 300, 22, 1232–7.

Kallman, F. J. (1952). A comparative twin study on the genetic aspects of male homosexuality. *Journal of Nervous and Mental Disease*, 115, 283–9.

Karpman, B. J. (1947). Dream life in a case of transvestism. *Journal of Nervous and Mental Disease*, 106, 292.

Kessler, S. J., and McKenna, W. (1978). Gender: an ethnomethodological approach. New York: Wiley.

Lang, W. (1940). Studies on the genetic determination of homosexuality. *Journal of Nervous and Mental Disease*, 92, 55–64.

Laub, D. R., and Fisk, N. (1974). A rehabilitation program for gender dysphoria syndrome by surgical sex change. *Plastic Reconstructive Surgery*, 53, 388–403.

Lukianowicz, N. (1959). Survey of various aspects of transvestism in the light of our present knowledge. *Journal of Nervous and Mental Disease*, 128, 36–64.

McGuire, R. J., Carlisle, J. M., and Young, B. G. (1965). Sexual deviation as conditioned behaviour. *Behaviour Research and Therapy*, 2, 185–90.

Martensen-Larsen, O. (1957). The family constellation and homosexualism. *Acta Genetica et Statistica Medica*, 7, 445–6.

Mead, M. (1950). *Male and Female*. Harmondsworth: Penguin.

Money, J. (1970). Sexual dimorphism and homosexual gender identity. *Psychological Bulletin*, 74, 425–40.

Money, J., and Ehrhardt, A. (1972). Man and Woman, Boy and Girl, Baltimore: Johns Hopkins University Press.

Money, J., Hampson, J. G., and Hampson, J. L. (1955). An examination of some basic sexual concepts. The evidence of hermaphroditism. *Bulletin of Johns Hopkins Hospital*, 97, 301–57.

Money, J., Hampson, J. G., and Hampson, J. L. (1957). Imprinting and the establishment of the gender role. *A.M.A. Archives of Neurological Psychiatry*, 77, 333–6.

Moss, H. A. (1970). Sex, age and state as determinants of mother–infant interaction. In K. Danziger, (ed.), *Readings in Child Socialisation*, Oxford: Pergamon.

Mulhall, D. J. (1976). Systematic self-assessment by PQRST (Personal Questionnaire Rapid Scaling Technique), *Psychological Medicine*, 6, 591–7.

Oakley, A. (1972). *Sex, Gender and Society*, London: Temple Smith.

Polani, P. E. (1972). Errors of sex determinance and sex chromosome anomalies. In C. Ounsted and D. C. Taylor (eds), *Gender Differences*, Edinburgh: Churchill Livingstone.

Roeder, F., and Muller, D. (1969). Zur stereotaktischen Heilung der pädophilen Homosexualität. *Deutsch Medizinisch Wochenschrift*, 94, 409–15.

Savage, M. O., Preece, M. A., Jeffcoate, S. L., Ransley, P. G., Rumsby, G., Mansfield, M. D., and Williams, D. I. (1980). Familial male pseudohermaphroditism due to deficiency of 5α-reductase. *Clinical Endocrinology*, 12, 397–406.

Sexton, P. (1970). *Feminised Male: Classrooms, White Collars and the Decline of Manliness*, New York: Random.

Seyler, L. E., Canalis, E., Spare, S., and Reichlin, S. (1978). Abnormal gonadotrophin secretory responses to LRH in transsexual women after diethyl stlboestrol priming. *Journal of Clinical Endocrinology and Metabolism*, 47, 176–83.

Siegelman, M. (1981). Parental background of homosexual and heterosexual men: a cross-national replication. *Archives of Sexual Behavior*, 10, 6, 505–13.

Slater, E. (1958). The sibs and children of homosexuals. In D. R. Smith and W. A. Davidson (eds), *Symposium on Nuclear Sex*, London: Heineman.

Slater, E. (1962). Birth order and maternal age of homosexuals. *Lancet*, 1, 69–71.

Stoller, R. J. (1968). *Sex and Gender*. London: Hogarth.

Wallinder, J. (1975). *A Social-Psychiatric Follow-up Study of 24 Sex-reassigned Transsexuals*, Goteburg: Scandinavian University Books.

Willmott, M., and Brierley, H. (1984). Cognitive characteristics and homosexuality. *Archives of Sexual Behavior*, in press.

4
Fetishism, Sadomasochism and Related Behaviours

Chris Gosselin and Glenn Wilson

This chapter deals primarily with two forms of statistically unusual but behaviourally related sex behaviour, namely fetishism and sadomasochism. Emphasis is placed upon those variables which might provide clues as to why a proportion of males (for these behaviours virtually always concern males) take so fervently to sexual patterns which appear inappropriate to the propagation of the species. We pay relatively little attention to the clinical literature, since the clinical subject represents only about 10 per cent of those with these sexually variant patterns (Gosselin 1979; Spengler 1977) and is usually under legal or social pressure, feels excessive guilt, suffers marital discord and generally finds his sexual pattern a burden rather than merely a fact of life or a source of enjoyment. He is consequently unrepresentative of the variant population as a whole.

Nevertheless clinical material cannot be entirely disregarded. Much of the fundamental work on sexual variation is inevitably clinical. Sadly, however, most of it is unstructured and devoid of controlled experimentation. Even today, such uncontrolled studies are still being published: for example, Angelini and Maccio (1980) report from their study of only fourteen female and six male homosexuals seen for therapy in a psychiatric clinic or in jail that 'sadomasochism prevails in exclusively homosexual cases'. The fact that the sample was very small, was not compared with any control group and was observed in a special situation (prison or psychiatric clinic) seems to have escaped the attention of the authors when interpreting their findings. Despite such limitations, viewpoints based on years of experience cannot be lightly dismissed because of an absence of scientific methodology. Such material must therefore form part of the background in the study of sexual variation, neither to be accepted unreservedly nor to be dismissed out of hand.

DEFINITIONS

Fetishism may be defined as a form of behaviour wherein sexual activity or sexual fantasy focuses to an unusual extent upon a body part or an inanimate object rather than on a person as a whole. The question as to when such behaviour should be regarded as pathological has occupied classical writers on the subject but today seems largely irrelevant, for that point is more likely to be decided by the individual concerned himself, by upset relatives or marriage partners, or by the courts, probationary services or other judicial authorities rather than by the clinician to whom the person is referred. Chalkley and Powell's (1983) study points out that referral is in fact rarely brought about because of the practical limitations or inconveniences of having a fetish, but usually because of broader personal or social difficulties associated with it. And yet, like so many definitions in psychology, weaknesses appear if the definition given is examined in detail. Some of these were spotlighted many years ago by Binet (1891).

Binet claimed that the fetish object does not necessarily give sexual gratification in the genital sense, so such gratification cannot be used as an exclusive criterion by which a fetishism is identified. Instead, Binet speaks of a kind of adoration, a wish to possess or unite with, to appreciate with all the senses, to overvalue the fetish object in a way that might be associated with primitive religion rather than with straightforward arousal, with *agape* rather than with *eros*. Conversation with some of the subjects used in our own more recent research (Gosselin and Wilson 1980) revealed – somewhat to our surprise – that for at least some subjects, close contact with their preferred fetish material produced *relaxation rather than arousal*. This is reminiscent of the two types of transvestite spoken of by Benjamin (1966) and confirmed empirically by Buhrich and McConaghy (1977), one of which is sexually aroused by cross-dressing whilst the others becomes more relaxed.

We nevertheless suggest that the definition of fetishism should retain the idea that sexual arousal ensues from contact with the fetish object either in fact or in fantasy, for any broader concept introduces (and indeed has already introduced) unimaginable confusions. The child's clinging to his teddy bear, the young girl's treasuring of a pop star's silk scarf, Bartholomew's (1973) autohaemofetishism – 'pleasure almost like an orgasm' when the drug-user draws blood from a vein – the religious person's veneration of an icon, the lucky charm which autosuggestively gives extra sexual potency to the wearer, Cooper's (1980) 'colonial fetishism . . . justifying the power of a ruling class by infusing these positions with a sacred character' – all these are examples of the strong investment of affect that humans place at times in inanimate objects.

None of these, however, would seem to bear much resemblance to fetishism as portrayed in adult bookshops and strip clubs.

Certain psychodynamicists, seeking perhaps to demonstrate sexuality in a 'polymorphically perverse' form, appear to have taken Winnicott's (1953) concept of the transitional object and equated it to a fetish. A transitional object is something chosen and carried about by many very young children, representing something familiar in a world of anxiety-provoking novelty and probably serving as a comforter or anxiety-reducer. Winnicott regards the transitional object as the first 'not-me' article possessed by the child, containing me-odours and mother-odours, breast softness and body softness, which comes to symbolize in the end án ideal mother even when the real mother is absent. Freud (1927) and Hadfield (1967), on the other hand, have both in their own way equated adult fetishes with mother-symbols, so it is hardly surprising that the two have become confused. Yahalom (1967), for example, states that the disturbed child feels 'that all experience is unsafe, and desperately settles for a fetish, a perversion or a transitional object', as if the three were interchangeable. True, there are similarities. As Greenacre (1969, 1970) has pointed out, both are inanimate objects apparently adopted and utilized to maintain a 'psychophysical' balance in conditions of stress. There nevertheless seem more differences between them than there are similarities: the transitional object is virtually ubiquitous, is used by both sexes, appears in and belongs to infancy, and is relinquished when infancy gives way to childhood. The fetish object, on the other hand, is adopted by a minority of people, virtually all of whom are males, and is used by them as a preferential or necessary adjunct to adequate sexual performance in adult life: without very concerted treatment, it is retained for life. We therefore think it best to treat the two concepts as separate.

Sadomasochism is probably in much need of redefinition. A parallel definition to that of fetishism is usually given, classifying sadomasochism as sexual behaviour which focuses to an unusual extent on coercion and the giving or experiencing of pain, humiliation or restriction. Once more, the behaviour could be regarded as pathological when it produces excessive guilt feelings in the individual or when concentration on such matters is the only means of sexual gratification. It has nevertheless long been realized that this is a very inadequate definition, if only because many acts of sadomasochism involve no real elements of pain, humiliation or restriction. 'How can it be called "domination" when my client is a huge six-footer and I'm about half the size?' remarked a specialist prostitute to whom we spoke. Clearly, a great deal of the effect is dependent upon fantasy. Smirnoff (1969) and Kamel (1980) have pointed out from their very different viewpoints that the classic definition may be somewhat meaningless in reality, because neither party in a sadomasochistic partnership really regards the agreed form of pain as anything more than arousal, humiliation as anything more than the joyous right to adore or be adored, and restriction as anything more than permission to be still, to give in or even to release aggression without fear of hurting anyone. (There will of course be psychopathic exceptions to this admittedly generous appraisal of sadomasochistic activity: there are a few for whom the infliction of real pain, mutilation and death without reference to the victim is the ultimate excitement. The typical sadomasochistic relationship, however, has – as far as we have been able to make out – nothing of such horrors about it, for all the high-powered pornography that the participants might enjoy.)

Smirnoff analyses Leopold Sacher-Masoch's classic book *Venus in Furs* and points out that for all her apparent cruelty towards the masochistic hero, the heroine does nothing but what the hero has asked her to do. Meanwhile, Kamel (1980) finds that among gay sadomasochists the relevant behaviour is institutionalized to the extent that particular acts of dominance and submission are more common than others and that most of these acts involve no pain whatsoever. Kamel's information-gathering technique is unusual and could possibly produce an understanding of the subject denied to more 'pure' researchers: he took employment in an adult bookshop, established rapport with relevant homosexual customers, taped interviews with them and for three years gained information through informal conversation while in the role of potential participant in gay sadomasochistic activities. His paper consequently sets out in helpful detail the well-defined set of norms that appear to govern the growth, the course and even the demise of such relationships.

It might therefore be preferable to define sadomasochism in terms of a mutually agreed sexual relationship of unbalanced power (even if only with a fantasy partner) rather than a defined set of behaviours. Such a concept has been espoused by Sack and Miller (1975) and by Panken (1967), who sees the variation in terms of 'interacting or relational reciprocities, wherein the underlying motivation and intrapsychic dynamics differ for each partner'. This emphasizes the situation frequently stressed by sadomasochistic partnerships that, even if they have a preferred orientation towards sadism *or* masochism, they can empathize into and act out the opposite role in order to promote interaction and introduce novelty. Avery (1977) also infers that relationship is all-important, stating that 'sadomasochism is conducted under strict rules; both parties know precisely what the bursting point is.'

Other writers have produced alternative definitions of masochism, in particular by postulating that the phenomenon has symbolic meaning or a symbolic reason for its existence. Thus Lenzer (1975) sees the variation as representing maternal punishment for the sin of desiring the mother sexually (a symbolism which presumably becomes even more complex in a gay sadomasochistic relationship). Stolorow (1975) covers a number of eventualities to little effect by stating that masochistic activities may be attributed to 'sexual-aggressive instincts which have undergone specific vicissitudes at various phases of drive organisation, or to the (functioning of the) superego . . . *or* to the ego's mode of relating to external or internal objects, thus warding off dreaded object relationships'. Noting from an examination of case-history material that masochists have 'a fear of dissolution of the self-image' (whilst Socarides 1974 says that the sadists have a pre-Oedipal fear of merging and fusing with the mother), Stolorow goes on to state that 'the function of masochistic activities is to restore the self-image by experiencing pain and thus acquiring a spurious feeling of being alive.' Such convoluted and untestable premises are unfortunately thickly spread thoughout the literature on sexual variation. It is for this reason that we prefer the following definition of the most prevalent form of sadomasochism:

> A relationship giving rise to the sexual interaction of two or more people via a ritual whose outward appearance involves coercion, pain, restriction or suffering of some kind but which has been agreed upon, tacitly or overtly, between the parties concerned and may in reality involve none of these constraints.

STUDIES OF FETISHISTS AND SADOMASOCHISTS

The foregoing attempts to arrive at definitions of fetishism and sadomasochism demonstrate the almost inevitable need to make those definitions cognitive in approach rather than operational. The diversity of behaviour, for example, which under certain circumstances may be subsumed under the term sadomasochism, coupled with the need to take into account not only the conditions under which that behaviour may be regarded as sadomasochistic by the perpetrator but also the meaning which he places on that behaviour, render operational definitions almost impossible. A man pulling a garden roller round his lawn would not be thought of as exhibiting sadomasochistic behaviour by an empirical observer, unless the latter knew that his subject's concurrent fantasy was that of a slave drawing his sexually provocative mistress's chariot in a procession of conquest. Studies of variant behaviour *per se*, therefore, may do little but reinforce the conclusion drawn by Bell (1974) in the context of homosexuality, that differences within the experimental group are greater than those between that group and the control group. Many individual case-histories have been provided by Krafft-Ebing (1886), Freud (1927), Hirschfeld (1925), Ellis (1913) and Stekel (1971) in the classical mode, whilst Aarons (1974), North (1970), Lihn (1970), Abraham (1967), Cath and Cohen (1967), Bethell (1974) and Bemporad et al. (1976) provide a group of more modern examples which illustrate the breadth of behaviour associated with fetishism alone. However, the general 'common behaviour' in each group may be summed up under the following headings.

Fetishistic pattern

Nowadays, fetishism directed towards parts of the body (with the possible exception of the foot) or to objects which are not items of clothing have become limited to rare clinical presentations, whilst a focus on 'sexy' underwear and a speciality range of garments in leather, rubber and vinyl has occurred. Arousal occurs when the fetishist dresses in fact or in fantasy in such garments, and/or has his partner dress (again, in fact or in fantasy) in them. This can be a public display if the result does not look too ludicrous by the passing standards of fashion and if the partner is tolerant of such display, but will more often be in the privacy of home or garden. Sometimes this manner of dressing will be all that is necessary in order to effect arousal: if the fetishist's behaviour is more compulsive, however, it is less likely that a real partner will be involved. If alone, the more intensive fetishist will generally show a far greater association with the preferred garment or material. The underwear fetishist will make collections of underwear, either the real thing or in photographic form. He will sometimes steal these off clothes lines or out of linen baskets, and may wear them under his own masculine outer clothes (a form of transvestism distinct from 'femmiphilic' or gender dysphoric transvestism, where the cross-dressing is usually complete and carried out because the subject desires to 'be' a woman for some period of time). The fabric fetishist will dress at intervals in his favourite material, the covering often being from head to toe, frequently multi-layered, seeking a state where no part of himself is left uncovered by the material that arouses him: the result will almost certainly be restrictive and thus begin to take on a masochistic element into the bargain. He will at this point almost certainly be alone in his excitation, since his costume usually looks somewhat bizarre or effeminate (leather or vinyl garments are nearly always masculine or unisex in design; rubber garments are more often feminine in appearance) and is therefore seldom attractive to a female partner. Orgasm will eventually be brought on either by direct masturbation or by spontaneous emission as a result of visualizing powerful erotic fantasies, but in many cases this climax will be delayed for a considerable time. If a partner *is* present, lovemaking will probably occur in one form or another – the term 'lovemaking' being used rather than intercourse because little more than kissing or cuddling may take place.

Sadomasochism

Here the behaviour pattern is more complex, involving any one or more of a number of activities. Typical of these are direct beating with the hand or with a wide variety of instruments (paddle, shoe, belt, whip or cane being the most popular) the administration of pain by other methods such as pricking, burning, etc., restriction by tying up, gagging, blindfolding or immobilization in stocks and pillories, besides the more general category of forcing someone to do something which in theory they should not wish to do or accepting what under other circumstances might be regarded as 'unpleasant' actions. Allied to these physical activities is the more mental technique of humiliation, which may be either purely verbal and carried out by pouring scorn or abuse on the partner, or situational, in which the 'victim' is dressed in a belittling costume before performing degrading tasks. Alternatively, and perhaps more understandably by those unfamiliar with this form of behaviour, no physical or mental derogation or attack is carried out: instead, lovemaking is carried out via a stylized ritual of commands and obeisances in which the enjoyment of one partner is at least in theory assured because he or she gets exactly what is desired, whilst the other partner achieves pleasure through fulfilling those desires.

Empirical studies of fetishists and sadomasochists as a whole are comparatively rare, although general descriptions of the personalities involved are given in Epstein (1969) and North (1970). In recent years, however, one or two important studies of the phenomenology of these sexual patterns have appeared, and the findings of these will now be summarized.

SPENGLER'S STUDY OF SADOMASOCHISTS

In 1977, West German sexologist Andreas Spengler reported a study of 245 active sadomasochistic men located as placers of SM contact advertisements or as members of SM clubs. An anonymous questionnaire concerning sexual behaviour and psychosocial problems was sent out to 877 men and the sample studied represented a response rate of 28 per cent (roughly the same for the contact ads and clubs). Thirty per cent were exclusively heterosexual, 31 per cent bisexual and 38 per cent homosexually oriented, proportions which roughly paralleled the sex orientations revealed in contact ads themselves. The age range of subjects was 20 to 50+ with a mode in the 30–40 decade, and they were typically quite well educated and of high social status. Spengler suggests that subcultural realization of the deviance could be easier for people having more disposable time and money and that the better educated could have been more motivated to co-operate in the study.

Most of the men in the sample kept their interest secret from the outside world. Two-thirds claimed their mother, father and siblings did not know about it, and wives, friends and colleagues were only slightly better informed. Divorce rates were higher than average for the culture at large, being 16 per cent among the heterosexuals, 12 per cent among bisexuals and 5 per cent among homosexuals. Partners were sought (and obtained) primarily through contact ads, the typical ad yielding between one and ten answers. Other partners were found through personal contacts, bars, parks, clubs, parties and prostitution. Twenty per cent of the heterosexuals and 4 per cent of homosexuals had 'no partner at all' for SM sex. Participation in the SM subculture (special parties, correspondence, etc.) was variable, but usually more marked in the case of the homosexuals. Most of the sample purchased SM literature and magazines fairly regularly.

The frequency of active SM experiences appeared to be fairly low in the sample: only one in five were having weekly meetings with like-minded persons, and 15 per cent were having none at all. The median frequency of experiences per year was only five, which was hardly any higher than the median number of partners (4.5). From this it was concluded that SM sexual behaviour is characterized by low frequency and a high turnover of different partners. Comparisons across the sex-orientation groups showed that the homosexuals and bisexuals were about twice as active as the heterosexuals. Questions concerning the nature of relationships revealed that loose partnerships predominated over firm ones, particularly among homosexuals, and that prostitution was only a significant factor in passive SM experiences with women.

Levels of self-acceptance were generally quite high, positive evaluations like 'it's perfectly normal' or 'it was fun' predominating over negative ones like 'it's sick' or 'I've got to get out of this'. Most would want to be sadomasochists even if they 'could decide freely about it' and very few had ever sought medical help or contemplated suicide. There were indications that those who had stronger roots within the subculture and greater success in behavioural realization enjoyed the most positive self-acceptance.

Only a minority of the sample were oriented in an exclusively active (sadistic) or passive (masochistic) direction. More than two-thirds were versatile to some extent, and this applied to both homosexuals and heterosexuals. Overall, the active and passive roles were enjoyed about equally, but a greater proportion of heterosexuals than homosexuals were exclusively masochistic (25 per cent against 13 per cent). Of course, it could be argued that the active role is so 'normal' for a heterosexual that there would be no need for subcultural support for such a preference (however much the feminists may dislike this state of affairs).

Subjects varied with respect to how dependent they were on the SM element for sexual functioning. An exclusive SM preference was reported by 16 per cent and a similar number could not achieve orgasm without SM activity. Those who were passively inclined and those who were less versatile as regards the active/passive dimension were also more dependent upon SM in their sex lives. Another 32 per cent liked to have sex predominantly with SM and 59 per cent needed at least SM fantasies before obtaining sexual climax. The rest of the sample expressed various lesser degrees of fixation.

The frequency of masturbation was similar to that of 'common homosexuals' in West Germany (once a week or more being typical). This activity could not be regarded as substitute gratification because those who had the most experience with partners were also the most frequent masturbators. A number of autoerotic SM activities were also declared: 28 per cent reported self-bondage, self-beating, torture of nipples with clamps, and suchlike during masturbation.

The most popular items of equipment were whips, canes and bonds (utilized by about 60 per cent). Next in order of frequency came torture apparatus (27 per cent), clothes-pins and clamps (7 per cent), glowing objects (7 per cent), needles (6 per cent), knives and razor-blades (4 per cent). Apart from beating and bondage, anal manipulation and nipple torture were the most common practices. About one-third of the sample had definite fetishistic fixations, but this group was not otherwise distinguishable from the remaining sadomasochists. Leather and boots were the most common fetish objects (50 per cent each), followed by jeans (19 per cent), uniforms (16 per cent), women's clothing (14 per cent), rubber (12 per cent), 'strafhose' (11 per cent), urolagnia (10 per cent) and coprophilia (5 per cent).

The first awareness of SM tendencies was quite late among many subjects: 43 per cent experienced it only after the age of 19 years and 11 per cent after the age of 30. Heterosexuals were more likely to have been aware of their special inclination from an early age than homosexuals or bisexuals (11 per cent recalling it before the age of 10). The homosexuals frequently 'came out' as gay some time before getting involved in SM practices.

Spengler notes in conclusion that the big difference between the homosexual and heterosexual sadomasochist lies in the difficulty the latter has in finding similarly enthusiastic female partners. His almost sole hope of realization is with prostitutes and it may be necessary for him to indulge in the fiction that they are genuine sadists. The result is that the prospect for subcultural meetings in homosexually oriented groups is far better and variety in partners more obtainable.

Furthermore, as Kamel (1980) points out, the existence of a gay SM subculture makes it possible to screen out the more extreme and dangerous practitioners. Within the 'leatherman' set it is important to acquire and maintain a reputation for 'stability' – for understanding the norms and limits set by the subculture. Heterosexual SM, according to Kamel, lacks these self-imposed restraints to a large extent and therefore more often surfaces to public view in cases of violent sexual acts involving unwilling victims. Kamel's study will not be dealt with in any detail here because it is impressionistic rather than strictly empirical; nevertheless, it may be read with profit by anyone interested in the workings and language of the gay SM subculture in the US.

PRINCE AND BENTLER'S STUDY OF TRANSVESTITES

Virginia Prince (himself an active transvestite) and Peter Bentler (of the University of California, Los Angeles) reported in 1972 on the characteristics of 504 male cross-dressers subscribing to the magazine *Transvestia*. This sample appeared to be predominantly heterosexual (89 per cent classifying themselves as such) and only 28 per cent admitted to having had homosexual experience. Eighty-six per cent claimed an average or above-average interest in women. A minority did, however, have transsexual tendencies – 14 per cent were interested in having a sex-change operation and 5 per cent were currently taking female hormones.

With respect to social background, the striking thing was how normal the group seemed to be. Eighty-two per cent came from an intact home, 72 per cent reported that their father presented a good masculine image, and 51 per cent said the father was the dominant partner in their parents' marriage. The majority were married men themselves with children of their own and good jobs. Although 83 per cent were treated just as a boy in childhood, cross-dressing frequently began at a young age (54 per cent before the age of ten).

Dressing patterns were variable, but 85 per cent liked to assume a complete woman's costume and 34 per cent had appeared so dressed in public. Thirty-two per cent wore lingerie and 27 per cent wore a woman's nightgown during intercourse. Most tried to keep their predilection secret from friends and colleagues, yet only 20 per cent of the wives were unaware of their husband's cross-dressing. Of the 80 per cent of wives who were aware of their husband's habit, about equal proportions were perceived as accepting and antagonistic respectively. Sadomasochistic interests were declared by only 15 per cent of the sample; this impulse usually took the form of being tied up or humiliated while dressed as a woman.

Only 24 per cent had ever sought psychiatric help and of these more than half felt it had been unhelpful. Questionnaires with smaller subsamples confirmed low levels of psychopathology. As regards personality and symptoms of mental disorder there was little to distinguish the transvestites from the general population.

GOSSELIN AND WILSON'S STUDY OF FETISHISTS, SADO-MASOCHISTS AND TRANSVESTITES

A survey of sexually variant men in Britain was reported on by Gosselin and Wilson (1980). The sample included 87 members of the 'Mackintosh

Society' for rubber fetishists, 38 members of the 'Atomage' correspondence club for leatherites, 133 sadomasochist club members and 285 members of the 'Beaumont Society' for transvestites and transsexuals. Questionnaires included details of social background, sexual behaviour and fantasies, and personality and psychopathology. Smaller numbers of these groups were interviewed in depth to round out the quantitative picture provided by the objective questionnaires.

One major finding to emerge from the study was that of considerable overlap among the various groups with respect to their sexual preferences and activities. This is illustrated in figure 4.1, which shows the extent to which each self-nominated group shared a significant interest in the other two major predilections. To a great extent the common elements among the three variations seem to be enjoyment of impersonal sex objects such as clothing and materials and a desire to take the submissive role in sexual encounters. Items in the Sex Behaviour Inventory such as 'being forced to do something', 'being whipped or spanked', 'being tied up', 'wearing clothes of the opposite sex' and 'being excited by material or clothing' were rated higher than control males by all the variant male groups. To a large extent, then, it seems that the choice of membership of the particular groups is arbitrary – many individuals might feel

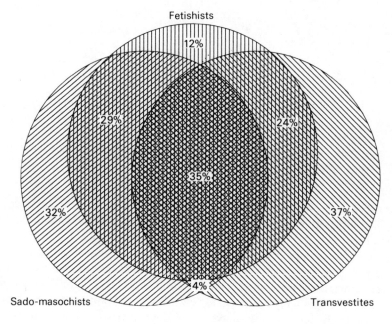

Figure 4.1   The extent of overlap in the interests of three major groups of variants
Source: Gosselin and Wilson 1980

equally at home in one of the other groups. However, as can be seen from figure 4.1, fetishism overlaps more with sadomasochism and transvestism than the latter two do with each other. Thus fetishism would appear more basic or 'prototypic' – sadomasochism and transvestism could be interpreted as alternative directions for the fetishistic impulse to travel.

Scores on the Eysenck Personality Questionnaire revealed that most of the variant groups tended towards introversion and neuroticism relative to control males (figure 4.2). Analysis of individual items indicated that they were

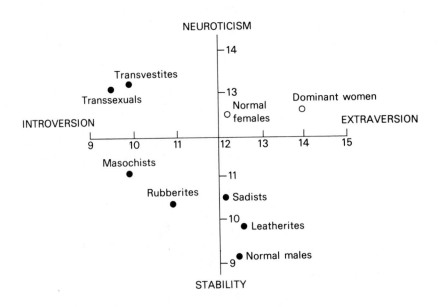

Figure 4.2 Location of variant and normal groups in relation to extraversion and neuroticism
Source: Gosselin and Wilson 1980

inclined to be shy, lonely, sensitive and depressed, and less likely to enjoy telling jokes. All of this suggests some difficulty in social interaction, whether as a cause or effect of the sexual pattern. However, it should be stressed that none of the groups displayed clinically significant levels of neuroticism or psychoticism; their scores were not in the range of hospitalized patients or even outpatients presenting with sex problems. Neuroticism scores, for example, were roughly equivalent to those obtained by normal women. Within this range the term 'emotionality' is probably better used – 'neuroticism' is something of a misnomer when applied to normal samples.

The group of dominant women shown in figure 4.2 was contacted through a magazine called *Superbitch* and consisted of 25 women who specialized in supplying services to sexually submissive men – many of them on a more or less professional basis. Appropriately enough, their personality appeared to complement the variant males, at least with respect to the extraversion – introversion dimension.

As an interesting postscript to these findings on personality, Gosselin and Eysenck (1980) investigated the hypothesis that the personality of gender dysphoric transvestites would change along with the gender of their clothing.

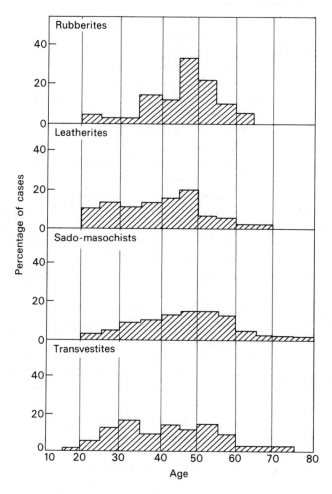

Figure 4.3   Age distribution of subject samples
Source: Gosselin and Wilson 1980

When dressed as women the transvestites reported themselves as more relaxed, confident and extravert, and scores on the EPQ reflected this difference.

The social background of the deviant groups was fairly unremarkable. They were more likely than control males to be without a steady partner, to have perceived their upbringing as restrictive and to have disliked their mother. However, it was not possible to implicate the frequency of corporal punishment in childhood with any of the sexual predilections.

Subjects came from a fairly normal range of socio-economic levels and age groups, though a high proportion of them could be characterized as middle aged (figure 4.3). The rubberites show a marked peak in the age distribution around 45–50 with very few that are either young or much older. This raises the question of whether some particular stressful period could have been responsible for this pattern. In Gosselin (1979) it was found that the majority of rubberites could recall their interest in rubber as originating between the ages of four and ten. Combining this information with the average age of Mackinstosh Society members we can trace the acquisition time to round about the outbreak of the second world war. It is then easy to think of reasons why this might have been a fertile time for such a fetishism to develop. The early war years were anxiety-provoking times with lots of absent fathers, consequently over-protective mothers and family separations due to death or evacuation to the country. Relevant stimuli were also readily available, such as the gas-mask that attracts so many rubberites, raincapes and groundsheets, not to mention the sadistic overtones of Nazi jackboots, rubber raincoats and riding crops. Whether or not the stress of war can be implicated, this was no doubt the peak period in history for the use of rubber materials. The advent of plastic (and hence the PVC fetishist) occurred soon after.

CHALKLEY AND POWELL'S STUDY OF CLINICAL FETISHISTS

While we are not greatly impressed with the value of clinical studies that are based on just one or two individual patients, one clinical study that cannot be overlooked is that of Chalkley and Powell (1983), who surveyed the characteristics of all 48 cases of fetishism seen in the Maudsley Hospital over two decades. All of the information was derived from case notes in the hospital records.

The total number of fetishes found was 122. Seventeen patients had one fetish only, nine had two, twelve had three, six had four, and one each had five, six and seven fetish objects. The most common fetishes related to clothing, especially underwear, stockings, suspenders and other types of lingerie. This type of fetish occurred in 58 per cent of patients. Next most common was rubber and specified rubber articles such as mackintoshes, tubes, babies' dummies and enemas (23 per cent of patients). Footwear fetishisms were found in 15 per cent of patients, particular parts of the body, such as legs, in 15 per cent, leather and leather items in 10 per cent, and clothes made of soft materials and fabrics in 8 per cent.

Patients could also be classified in terms of the kind of behaviour displayed in relation to the fetish object. Wearing the article personally was most popular (44 per cent), followed by stealing it (38 per cent), seeing someone else dressed in it (23 per cent), hoarding it, gazing at it, and inserting it up the rectum (12 per cent each), and fondling, sucking, following, rolling in, burning, and cutting (4 per cent each).

Quite a high proportion of the fetishistic patients had other psychiatric difficulties apart from their fetishism. Three were classified as suffering from paranoid schizophrenia, seven from depression, two from anxiety neurosis, and thirteen from personality disorder. There were nine classifications of sexual dysfunction or deviation other than the labels of fetishism and homosexuality. Five patients were transvestite, and ten stated a homosexual preference. Apart from the formal diagnoses, the case notes revealed many other medical and social difficulties among the fetishists. Over a quarter were judged by the psychiatrist to be socially anxious, 17 had never had sexual intercourse, and 11 suffered from epileptic fits or other stigmatizing conditions such as psoriasis, dermatitis and malformation of the skin of the hands.

While it is tempting to conclude that the fetishism was only one manifestation of a general constitutional weakness, Chalkley and Powell warn against premature acceptance of this conclusion. Fetishisms are found in less than 1 per cent of psychiatric patients and are likely to be at least as common in the general population. Those patients seen in the hospital were frequently referred not because their fetishism was directly disabling but because of some other related problem such as impotence or marital difficulty, because they were referred by the courts after being caught stealing, or because of some completely unrelated psychiatric disorder. The clinical population is thus so biased that it is impossible to assess the normal concomitants of fetishism. This, of course, is why Gosselin and Wilson preferred to study fetishism and related behaviours within non-clinical settings.

AETIOLOGICAL STUDIES

Investigations of the origins of variant male sexuality have implicated several different levels. At the most basic biological level, there is a suggestion that genetic factors may be involved. One or two case studies have been reported in which remarkably similar fetishistic or transvestic behaviour has been observed in identical twins (e.g. Gorman 1964) but these are of course uncontrolled in the sense that the number of discordant twin pairs is not known. The only attempt at a proper twin study in which the concordance of identical twins is compared with that of fraternal twins is that reported by Gosselin and Wilson (1980). Although the samples obtained were rather small (only 14 pairs of each type of twin), there was an indication that transvestic and sadomasochistic tendencies are to some extent influenced by genetic factors. No such genetic factor was detected in this sample for the fetishistic impulse. This study really needs to be repeated with larger samples of twins before definitive conclusions are possible.

Another type of 'cause' for deviant sexuality that has been investigated with clinical subjects is that of minor physiological brain malfunction. Over the last couple of decades there has been growing evidence that some fetishisms, as well as other compulsive sexual behaviours, may be traced to subtle brain damage of the kind that also gives rise to epilepsy (Davies and Morgenstern 1960; Epstein 1961; Kolarsky et al., 1967; Hoenig and Kenna 1979). The damage that is apparently most likely to disrupt sexual behaviour is that located in the temporal lobe and which can be traced to injury incurred either during birth (e.g. forceps delivery) or within the first year or two of life (e.g. infantile meningitis). There are also strong indications that damage to the *dominant* temporal lobe (usually the left side of the brain) is that most likely to be associated with fetishism, transvestism and psychopathic sexual impulses (Flor-Henry 1980). However, it should be noted that deviant sexuality is not the only kind of disruption that may result from such damage; a general loss of libido (hyposexuality) is a more commonly observed outcome (Blumer 1967; Bear and Fedio 1977; Shukla et al., 1979).

The most celebrated ease of linkage between epilepsy and fetishism in the clinical literature is that of the safety-pin fetishist reported by Mitchell, Falconer and Hill (1954). From the age of eight this man had experienced extreme pleasure when he gazed at a safety pin, an activity which he conducted in the privacy of his bathroom. When he was 23 his wife observed the complete sequence, which began with him staring at the safety pin for about a minute. This was followed by a glassy-eyed appearance, vocal humming noises, sucking movements of the lips and total immobility for another minute or two. After the age of 30 there were further elaborations, such as walking backwards and cross-dressing in his wife's clothes while still in a state of confusion. These attacks would only occur when he looked at or imagined whole, shiny safety pins. He was effeminate and partially impotent and enjoyed his seizures more than sexual intercourse. Following a left anterior temporal lobectomy both the epilepsy and fetishism disappeared, and his potency was increased to normal.

Evidence such as this for the involvement of impaired neural circuits in the genesis of fetishistic behaviour is difficult to ignore. On the other hand, we should not assume that just because brain damage *can* be associated with deviant sexuality it is the *only* factor involved. In fact, there are also studies suggesting that conditioning and learning processes may be involved. Rachman and Hodgson (1968) demonstrated that sexual arousal could be conditioned to a picture of a boot in normal men by associating it in the laboratory with pictures of nude women. This conditioned 'fetishism' followed classical principles in that the CS (boot picture) had to precede the UCS (nude woman) in order for conditioning to occur; with the reverse contingency (UCS before CS) no conditioning was observed. McConaghy (1970) has replicated this experiment using coloured geometrical patterns in place of the boot picture, thus showing that possible erotic overtones or 'preparedness' in the CS are not essential ingredients to the acquisition of the conditioned 'fetishism'. However, this laboratory model is not really parallel to a real fetishism, which is highly resistant to extinction and in which there may be little or no response to the UCS (the actual woman).

The possible role of female rejection in devaluation of the human love object, and as a possible contributor to fetishism, has been demonstrated by La Torre (1980). He organized an experimental manipulation of male egos, in which 30 students were given feedback to the effect that they had been turned down by potential girlfriends they had selected from photographs, while another 30 students were informed that the girls had reciprocated interest. The two groups of men were then asked to rate the attractiveness of various pictorial stimuli ranging from an abstract design to lingerie, panties, feet, legs and a complete female. 'Rejected' males showed a decreased interest in the whole woman and an enhanced response to the underwear, feet and legs relative to the ego-boosted males. This would appear to be a more satisfactory analogue of fetishism than the Rachman and Hodgson paradigm in that it accounts for the extinction of interest in women as well as the increased response to impersonal associated articles. If such minor laboratory manipulations of experience with the opposite sex in adulthood can result in measurable changes in the attractiveness of stimuli, how much more effective might critical, early, real-life experiences be?

CONCLUSIONS

Fetishism, sadomasochism and related sexual behaviours remain something of a mystery to the scientist as well as the layman. Since the sex drive has clearly evolved for reproductive purposes, and these behaviours are comparatively non-reproductive, it is reasonable to think in terms of something 'going wrong' in the course of development. Direct genetic effects seem unlikely, since any genes giving rise to these behaviours should be quickly eliminated by natural selection. However, indirect genetic connections are possible; for example, any genes predisposing to difficulty in competing for access to females (attributes such as shyness and submissiveness) might also be associated with the adoption of alternative sexual outlets. It is, of course, impossible for all the males within a social group to be simultaneously dominant and thus equally successful with women. Because of the biological constraints on their fertility, women breed relatively evenly and are thus less competitive in the sexual sphere (Wilson 1981). Viewed within this ethological perspective, sexual variation would appear as a reasonably adaptive solution to the problem of competition difficulty, rather than a pathological symptom in its own right.

Yet this is clearly not the whole story. The surprising specificity and inflexibility of the basis for sexual arousal that is seen in many variant males (e.g. the safety-pin fetish described above), as well as the frequency with which articles prominent in childhood (e.g. babies' dummies) are chosen as fetishes, seems to implicate some process akin to *imprinting*. Presuming that human males have certain broad 'innate releasing mechanisms' for sexual arousal, it would appear that these can be distorted or over-detailed by traumatic events in childhood – either taking the form of minor injury to the brain or accidental, significant experiences with people and articles in the environment, or some combination of these. Again, females have no evolutionary need for a 'targeting' sex drive and are therefore much less prone to such distortions. The fact that only males are susceptible is one of several reasons for thinking that a simple conditioning model would not account for variant sexuality and that brain-wiring must be more fundamentally involved. At this stage it is not possible to say exactly what brain mechanisms are critical. Anterior limbic circuits seen to be important, and the orgasmic response appears to be lateralized to the right (spatial) hemisphere, while the 'ideational trigger' is lateralized to the left (verbal) hemisphere (Flor-Henry 1980). Thus damage to either side can give rise to hyposexuality and impotence, but damage to the left side of the brain is more likely to result in bizarre or unorthodox targets for arousal.

Again, we should not suppose that brain injury is the only cause of variant male sexuality. Damage to certain parts of the brain can give rise to heightened musical appreciation and ability (again more often in males) but this is not the sole basis of musical interest. The choice of fetish objects is far from random; some of the most popular fetishes, such as women's panties, suspenders, high-heeled shoes, leather belts, and whips, have some erotic significance for the majority of normal men. In order to explain this we need to consider attributes that are sensory, associational and symbolic. A black high-heeled shoe, for example, may present a visual configuration that is reminiscent of the pubic triangle (a possible innate releasing mechanism) and at a sight level readily available for imprinting to an infant crawling across the carpet; it may 'fix' fatty acids similar to the copulins produced in a woman's vagina (a pheromonal effect); it may be strongly associated with sophisticated, sexually aware, adult women who are 'dressed to kill'; it may provide overtones of 'threat' in its shape, material and colour, and the clipping noise it makes on hard ground as the authoritarian (mother) figure approaches to administer summary discipline. The excitement experienced by the shoe fetishist could draw on these and other components in any proportion, and in psychoanalytic terms there is likely to be some degree of 'over-determination'. It would be short-sighted not to admit all of these various psychological elements and levels as contributing to the complexity of the fetishist phenomenon.

Likewise, Alex Comfort (1978) has pointed out that sadomasochistic, cross-dressing and other sexual rituals have much in common with dramatic, religious and magical rites, for example in the use of pseudo-aggression, menace, special clothing, compulsion, restraint, chastisement and ordeal to acquire powers, expand self-awareness or alter identity boundaries. Obser-vations of non-dysfunctional couples engaged in behaviours normally classified as sadomasochistic (e.g. commanding, bondage, suspense, mild pain infliction) suggested to Comfort that these people were either engaged in what was ethologically play, or something very like yoga – a ritualized body-image manipulation for the purpose of heightening experience. The relationship of the manipulator to the manipulated, he argues, is not that of master to slave but that of 'facilitator of psychopomp, who uses control to evoke, to push into transcendent experience – almost exactly that of coach to athlete or platoon commander to recruit. . . . The manipulator "compels" the manipulated into states or performances of which the manipulated did not know themselves to be capable.' Comfort argues that psychiatry has too often sought to describe magical and religious behaviours as sadomasochistic guilt expiation when much more understanding would be gained by considering sexual rituals as a kind of magical expansion of consciousness. This viewpoint, if widely accepted, would result in the declassification of a great deal of variant sexual behaviour as psychiatrically abnormal, leading us away from medical concern to a wider anthropological appreciation of the rewards derived from some of the more common 'deviant practices'.

REFERENCES

Aarons, Z. A. (1974). Fetish, fact and fantasy: a clinical study of the problems of fetishism. *International Review of Psychoanalysis*, 2, 199–230.

Abraham, K. (1967). Remarks on the psychoanalysis of a case of foot and corset fetishism. In H. M. Ruitenbech (ed.), *The Psychotherapy of Perversions*, New York: Citadel Press.

Angelini, C., and Maccio, A. M. (1980). The psychosexual self of homosexual subjects. *Rivista Sperimentale di Freniatria e Medicina Legale delle Alenazioni Mentali*, 104, 237–76.

Avery, N. C. (1977). Sadomasochism: a defence against object loss. *Psychoanalytic Review*, 64, 101–9.

Bartholomew, A. A. (1973). Two factors occasionally associated with intravenous drug users: a note. *Australian and New Zealand Journal of Psychiatry*, 7, 206–7.

Bear, D. M., and Fedio, P. (1977). Quantitative analysis of interictal behaviour in temporal lobe epilepsy. *Archives of Neurology*, 34, 454–67.

Bell, A. P. (1974). Homosexualities: Their range and character. In J. K. Cole and R. Dienstbier (eds), *1973 Nebraska Symposium on Motivation*, 21, Lincoln: University of Nebraska.

Bemporad, J. R., Dunton, H. D., and Spady, F. H. (1976). Case report: The treatment of a child fetishist. *American Journal of Psychology*, 30, 303–16.

Benjamin, H. (1966). *The Transsexual Phenomenon*, New York: The Julian Press.

Bethell, M. F. (1974). A rare manifestation of fetishism. *Archives of Sexual Behavior*, 3, 301–2.

Binet, A. (1891). Le fetichisme dans l'amour. *Études de Psychologie Experimentale*, Paris: Octave Doin.

Blumer, D. (1967). The temporal lobes and paroxysmal behaviour disorders. *Szondiana VII*, 51, 273–85.

Buhrich, N., and McConaghy, N. (1977). The clinical syndromes of femmiphilic transvestism, *Archives of Sexual Behavior*, 6, 397–412.

Cath, S., and Cohen, H. (1967). Elbow rubbing and the wish to be beaten: a study of a case and the possible genesis of perversion. *Israel Annals of Psychiatry and Related Disciplines*, 5, 185–97.

Chalkley, A. J., and Powell, G. E. (1983). The clinical description of forty-eight cases of clinical fetishism. *British Journal of Psychiatry*, 142, 292–5.

Comfort, A. (1978). Sexual idiosyncrosies: deviation or magic? *Journal of Psychiatry*, 9, 11–16.

Cooper, E. (1980). Colonialist fetishisms: an answer to the Hong Kong apologists. *Hong Kong Society Bulletin*, 4, 33–43.

Davies, B. M., and Morgenstern, F. S. (1960). A case of cysticeroosis, temporal lobe epilepsy and transvestism. *Journal of Neurological and Neurosurgical Psychiatry*, 23, 247–9.

Ellis, H. (1913). *Studies in the Psychology of Sex*. New York: Random (1936).

Epstein, A. W. (1961). Relationship of fetishism and transvestism to brain and particularly to temporal lobe dysfunction. *Journal of Nervous and Mental Disease*, 130, 107–19.

Epstein, A. W. (1969). Fetishism: a comprehensive view. In J. H. Masserman (ed.), *Dynamics of Deviant Sexuality*, New York: Grune & Stratton.

Flor-Henry, P. (1980). Cerebral aspects of the orgasmic response: normal and deviational. In R. Forbes and W. Pasini, *Third International Congress on Medical*

Sexology, Amsterdam: Elsevier/North Holland Biomedical Press.

Freud, S. (1927). Fetishism, in *Collected Papers*, 5, London: Hogarth.

Gorman, G. F. (1964). Fetishism occurring in identical twins. *British Journal of Psychiatry*, 110, 255–6.

Gosselin, C. C. (1979). Personality attributes of the average rubber fetishist. In M. Cook and G. D. Wilson (eds), *Proceedings of the First International Conference on Love and Attraction*, London: Pergamon Press.

Gosselin, C. C., and Eysenck, S. B. G. (1980). The transvestite double image: a preliminary report. *Personality and Individual Differences*, 1, 172–3.

Gosselin, C. C., and Wilson, G. D. (1980). *Sexual Variations*, London: Faber & Faber.

Greenacre, P. (1969). The fetish and the transitional object. *Psychoanalytic Study of the Child*, 24, 144–64.

Greenacre, P. (1970). The transitional object and the fetish, with particular reference to the role of illusion. *International Journal of Psycho-Analysis*, 51, 447–55.

Hadfield, J. A. (1967). *Introduction to Psychotherapy*, London: Allen & Unwin.

Hirschfeld, M. (1925). *Sexual Anomalies and Perversions*, London: Francis Alder (1946).

Hoenig, J., and Kenna, J. C. (1979). EEG abnormalities and transsexualism. *British Journal of Psychiatry*, 134, 293–300.

Kamel, G. W. L. (1980). Leathersex: Meaningful aspects of gay sadomasochism. *Deviant Behaviour*, 1, 171–91.

Kolarsky, A., Freund, K., Machek, J., and Polak, O. (1967). Male sexual deviation: association with early temporal lobe damage. *Archives of General Psychiatry*, 17, 735–43.

Krafft-Ebing, R. von (1886). *Psychopathia Sexualis*, New York: Stern & Day (1965).

La Torre, R. A. (1980). Devaluation of the human love object: Heterosexual rejection as a possible antecedent to fetishism. *Journal of Abnormal Psychology*, 89, 295–8.

Lenzer, G. (1975). On masochism: a contribution to the history of a fantasy and its theory. *Signs*, 1, 277–324.

Lihn, H. (1970). Fetishism: a case report. *International Journal of Psychiatry*, 51, 351–8.

McConaghy, N. (1970). Penile response conditioning and its relationship to aversion therapy in homosexuals. *Behaviour Therapy*, 1, 213–21.

Mitchell, W., Falconer, M. A., and Hill, D. (1954). Epilepsy with fetishism relieved by temporal lobe lobectomy. *Lancet*, 2, 626–30.

North, M. (1970). *The Outer Fringe of Sex*. London: Odyssey Press.

Panken, S. (1967). On masochism: a re-evaluation. *Psychoanalytic Review*, 54, 135–49.

Prince, V., and Bentler, P. M. (1972). Survey of 504 cases of transvestism. *Psychological Reports*, 31, 903–17.

Rachman, S., and Hodgson, R. J. (1968). Experimentally induced sexual fetishism: replication and development. *Psychological Record*, 18, 25–7.

Sack, R. L., and Miller, W. (1975). Masochism: a clinical and theoretical overview. *Psychiatry*, 38, 244–57.

Shukla, G. D., Srivastava, O. N. and Katiyar, B. C. (1979). Sexual disturbance in temporal lobe epilepsy: A controlled study. *British Journal of Psychiatry*, 134, 288–92.

Smirnoff, V. N. (1969). The masochist contract. *International Journal of Psycho-Analysis*, 50, 665–71.

Socarides, C. W. (1974). The demonified mother: A study of voyeurism and sexual sadism. *International Review of Psychoanalysis*, 1, 187–95.

Spengler, A. (1977). Manifest sadomasochism in males. Results of an empirical study. *Archives of Sexual Behavior*, 6, 441–56.

Stekel, W. (1971). *Sexual Aberrations. The Phenomena of Fetishism in Relation to Sex*, New York: Liveright.

Stolorow, R. D. (1975). The narcissistic function of masochism. *International Journal of Psychoanalysis*, 56, 441–8.

Wilson, G. D. (1981). *Love and Instinct*, London: Temple Smith.

Winnicott, D. W. (1953) Transitional objects and transitional phenomena. *International Journal of Psychiatry*, 34, 89–97.

Yahalom, I. (1967). Sense, affect and image in the development of the symbolic process. *International Journal of Psychoanalysis*, 48, 373–83.

5

Coercive Sexual Behaviour

Kevin Howells

The road to adult sexuality and to patterns of sexual behaviour construed by most in society as 'normal' is subject to many diversions. Money (1981) has used the phrase 'multivariate sequential determinism' to describe the necessary foundation of any attempt to account for the development of both normal and abnormal patterns of sexual expression. The diversities discussed elsewhere in this volume are the product of variation occurring at particular points in the sequence of development. The biological processes determining chromosomal, hormonal and morphological gender, and the social process affecting gender assigment, gender identity, sex-role and sexual preference learning, are potential sources of individual differences. This chapter is concerned with variation in the degree to which sexual behaviour is integrated into dyadic and other relationships. Heterosexual, homosexual, fetishistic and other preferences are often successfully integrated into consensual relationships. It is also possible, however, for humans to engage in sexual behaviour in a coercive manner. 'Coercive sexual behaviour' is the term used in this chapter to describe acts involving the use of force by one person to produce sexual intimacy with another. The word 'force' is itself difficult to define. Here I will follow Russell (1982) in restricting force to the use of physical restraint or harm, or the threat of physical restraint or harm. It is undoubtedly the case that psychological, social and financial pressures can be used to coerce another person into unwanted sexual behaviour, and that such acts have functional similarities to physical coercion. It is nevertheless likely to be more useful to restrict the range of behaviours discussed than to expand it, thereby improving the chances of creating a homogeneous class. The major part of work done in this area will have focused on rape, that is, coerced vaginal–penile intercourse. For this reason I shall use the term rape in the discussion that follows. I will also restrict comments to incidents involving adult female victims. Coerced sexual behaviour with children is different in a number of ways (Cook and

This is an updated and extended version of a paper presented to the Merseyside Annual Conference on Clinical Psychology, September 1982.

Howells 1981) and requires separate discussion, as does male sexual victimization, a phenomenon which appears to be restricted to unusual environments (Lockwood 1980).

PREVALENCE OF RAPE

Massive, and probably insuperable, problems exist in assessing the real prevalence of rape and other forms of coercive sexual behaviour. There are a number of ways of recording prevalence, each beset by difficulties. The fact that rape is illegal in many societies means that such acts will be recorded as crimes, though subtle differences in legal definitions between societies make cross-cultural comparisons difficult.

Approximately 1200 rapes are recorded as known to the police each year in England and Wales. The figure for 'indecent assaults' on females is almost ten times as large (Home Office 1979). It is clear that rape rates vary markedly across cultures and even across subcultures within societies (Schiff 1971; Chappell et al. 1977; Chappell and Singer 1977). The prevalence of rape is typically reported to be substantially greater in the United States than in Europe (Schiff 1971). Without any doubt, rapes recorded as crimes by the police greatly underestimate the actual frequency of such assaults. An alternative approach has been to survey women in the community to establish how many have been victimized. Hindlelang and Davis (1977) report the results of a census survey of 10,000 households in various American cities and estimate that for every 100,000 females aged 12 and over, 315 report being the victim of a rape or an attempted rape during the previous 12 months. Even census methods based on random sampling techniques are likely seriously to underestimate the extent of the problem. It seems intuitively unlikely that many women will admit victimization to a stranger who may him/herself share views of rape that are prejudicial to the victim (Russell 1982). In a recent study of American university students Koss and Oros (1982) report that out of a sample of 2000 females 6 per cent said they had been raped, 18.3 per cent had been subjected to attempts at intercourse where threats of physical force had been used to produce compliance, and 30.2 per cent said a man had used physical force to try to make them engage in kissing or petting when they did not want to. Russell's (1982) survey is one of the most methodologically sophisticated attempts to avoid biases which might suppress the recorded level of sexual assault. The author used 35 female interviewers whose race, age and social class were carefully varied so as to reflect the demographic characteristics of respondents. An intricate and apparently sensitive interview protocol was developed so as to make it easy for victimized women to admit their experiences. The main focus of this study was the rape of women by their husbands or ex-husbands. Fourteen per cent of women who had been married reported such an experience. The results also revealed that 44 per cent of the 930 women interviewed had been subject to at least one rape or attempted rape in the course of their lives.

The large discrepancy between actual and reported assaults requires explanation and a number of causes of failure to report have been suggested. The perceived punishing consequences for victims of proceeding with a rape case, in terms of stigmatizing treatment by the police and courts, may be important. In addition, low reporting may reflect a marked ambivalence in the cultures studied in the social, as opposed to the legal, definition of rape. For an act to be defined as rape by the victim it needs to be attributed to a characteristic of the offender rather than to a characteristic of the victim herself or the circumstances. Popular theories as to the physical impossibility of rape (Schwendinger and Schwendinger 1974) encourage the attribution of responsibility to the victim. The latter may ask herself whether she in some way encouraged the rapist or offered insufficient resistance, and may anticipate that significant others (the police, relatives) will ask similar questions. A study by Klemmack and Klemmack (1976) confirms that many women fail to define some instances of forced intercourse as rape, particularly when the situation involves a sexual assault by a person known to the victim. The internal attribution that 'I wasn't careful enough' or 'I behaved in a stupid way' will undermine incipient plans to report the event.

The failure to report poses major problems for those interested in the psychological study of rapists, problems which are augmented by subsequent equally potent filters in the judicial management of sexual aggressors. The vast majority of (though not all) studies of the characteristics of rapists are based on convicted offenders located in prisons, forensic evaluation clinics or secure psychiatric facilities. Such offenders are the survivors of a series of filters which will have biased the characteristics of the sample in ways which are largely unknown. The features of reported rapes and rapists are likely to differ from those that are not reported, perhaps in the direction of being more violent. When the incident has been reported to the police a series of further filters ensues. The police may or may not decide that a genuine rape has occurred (Wright 1980) and, in the former case, may be successful or not in identifying and finding the suspect. According to McClintock (1980) approximately 75 per cent of sexual crimes are 'cleared up' but those that are cleared up are significantly different from those that are not. Not all, even of this surviving group, will be prosecuted and subsequently convicted, though (at least for England and Wales) the prosecution rate is over 80 per cent (Walmsley 1980). Offenders receiving custodial sentences or psychiatric dispositions will be an even more highly selected group. As I have argued elsewhere with regard to a paedophilic offences (Howells 1981a), misleading conclusions are highly probable if generalizations are made about the aetiology of sexually deviant behaviour on the basis of studies conducted with prison or psychiatric groups.

CROSS-CULTURAL COMPARISONS

I have already alluded briefly to cross-cultural variation in the prevalence of sexual aggression. The striking differences between cultures has led some authors to view rape as a cultural issue rather than as a problem of individual psychology. The relevant task then becomes one of identifying the structural, economic and organizational variables that create and maintain 'rape supportive cultures' (Russell 1982). Margaret Mead (1935) noted with reference to a particular society, 'of rape the Arapesh know nothing beyond the fact that it is the unpleasant custom of the Nugum people to the southeast of them. Nor do the Arapesh have any conception of male nature that might make male rape understandable to them' (p. 104). The absence of rape in this culture had some relationship to the pattern of interaction between the sexes and to the general attitudes to sex and aggression. Levine has provided a detailed anthropological analysis of a culture prone to rape (Levine 1959, 1977). This south-western Kenyan tribe had a high incidence of rape which was also attributable to the pattern of organization of male/female relationships and of sexuality. In this case the tribe construed even legitimate sex as an act in which the man overcomes the resistance of the woman and causes her pain. Relationships between the sexes were generally antagonistic. For Levine, Gusii rape was essentially an extension of a legitimate pattern of behaviour to an illegitimate context, under the pressure of sexual frustration.

Sexual frustration in this instance was a product of societal rules, including the restriction of intra-clan sexual activity and the necessity for a large bridewealth, which had the effect of postponing marriage. An n=1 anthropological study of this sort does not allow the inference that high rape rates and particular cultural configurations are generally significantly correlated. Such an inference would be valid if objective measures of rape frequency and culture were correlated across a range of societies. Sanday has performed an analysis of this sort on a sample of 156 societies, of which 47 per cent were classified as rape-free, 18 per cent as rape-prone and the remainder as not atypical or unknown (Sanday 1981). Rape-prone cultures characteristically promoted male/female antagonism, used rape as a mechanism of social control (e.g. to stop females from observing male sacred ceremonies) and to enhance male dominance. In these societies women were sometimes construed as the economic property of men. Conversely, rape-free societies were characterized by sexual equality, a high value placed on females and female qualities, and generally low levels of interpersonal violence. In a statistical analysis the three societal variables most strongly correlated with rape were the degree of interpersonal violence (r=0.47), ideology of male toughness (r=0.42) and low female decision-making (r=0.33). These observations are consistent with many of the earlier observations of Brownmiller (1975) and the emphasis on the aggressive and dominance components of rape echoes findings at the individual, psychological level of analysis (see below).

DEMOGRAPHIC ASPECTS OF RAPE

Demographic analysis of detected, criminal rapes has cast some light on the nature of the offender himself, the victim and the circumstances in which assaults occur (Toner 1982). Amir's early work is widely regarded as a landmark in this area (Amir 1971), though it has also been severely criticized (see Geis 1977). The study was based mainly on an analysis of police reports in Philadelphia. Amongst important findings were the fact that many rapists and victims knew each other prior to the incident, more than half the rapes occurred in the homes of one of the participants, and two-thirds were planned, rather than spontaneous events. Victims came from all social classes but the rapes were 'ecologically bound', offenders tending to attack women living in the same area as themselves. That subcultural variation may exist in the pattern of offences is demonstrated by studies of other American cities. Chappell and Singer (1977), for example, compared Philadelphia with New York and found marked differences between the two cities. New York rapists were more likely to be older, to be a stranger to the victim, and to be a solitary, rather than group, assaulter.

Intriguing similarities, as well as differences, are revealed by an analysis of an English sample by Wright (1980). This study focused on 'single assaults' and was based on rapes investigated by the police as 'genuine'. Two striking features were the social class and age distributions of the suspects. Seventy-five per cent were unskilled working class and only 2 per cent were classified as professional/ managerial. More than 70 per cent were aged 30 or under. Victims, as in Amir's sample, were predominantly young and came from a range of occupational groups. In 40 per cent of cases victims were well known to the rapist and a similar proportion were strangers. It needs to be reiterated here that all of these surveys are based on reported incidents. Undoubtedly, the characteristics of non-reported incidents will be significantly different.

PSYCHOLOGICAL STUDIES

The last decade has seen significant advances in our understanding of the psychology of coercive sexual behaviour. Investigations are nevertheless at a preliminary stage and many questions remain unanswered. I propose here not to attempt to summarize the entire, fast-burgeoning literature on this topic but to select three central issues which many workers have addressed either directly or indirectly, and which have far-reaching implications, particularly for the clinical management of sexual aggressors. As in other areas, there is a tendency for researchers to focus on their own particular theoretical or clinical concerns, and for lines of enquiry to proceed independently of one another. The three lines of enquiry I shall examine are work on physiological sexual arousal, work on aggressive motivation, and work on the cognitive/attitudinal components of coercive sex.

Physiological sexual arousal

The assessment and modification of patterns of sexual arousal have been major themes in psychological studies of sexual aggression. Such research has flourished partly because of the availability of a technology for assessing sexual response in an objective and apparently reliable way. Of the various physiological changes that accompany sexual arousal in males, changes in penile volume (Freund 1963, 1967) and penile diameter (McConaghy 1974; Crawford 1980) have proven to be the most valid and capable of assessing sexual preference. Penile responses can be measured in response to a wide range of stimuli, including slides, audio-taped verbal descriptions, moving films and internal fantasy, though film and video stimuli produce the highest levels of arousal (Abel et al. 1981; Laws 1984). Whether or not rapists and other sexual aggressors differ in their sexual arousal patterns from normals is an important question. If rapists were abnormal in their responses this would have a number of important implications. Firstly, it might suggest that deviant sexual interests have explanatory power in relation to rape and similar behaviours. For example, if rapists were shown to be aroused by depictions of coercive sexual intercourse and normal males (non-rapists) were not, it could be hypothesized that the behavioural differences between the two groups is caused by their differential arousability. The correlation of two variables is, of course, open to interpretations other than that they are causally related. It is at least possible that engaging in rape behaviour causes the person to be subsequently aroused by depictions of it. Secondly, the finding of a difference between rapists and normals might provide an objective means of predicting the likelihood of a person engaging in rape behaviour in the future. Two sorts of prediction are possible. Deviant patterns of arousal in a person who has not previously raped could suggest that such behaviour is a future possibility, or deviant arousal in a person who has already raped might mean that the behaviour is likely to be repeated. Those attempting such predictions would emphasize, of course, that univariate methods are crude, and that many other factors would need to be taken into account in devising a predictive equation. In clinical contexts the first kind of prediction (new behaviour) is probably less common than the second (repeated behaviour). Laws (1984) has recently argued that:

> although a number of other clinical and actuarial predictors must also be taken into account . . . in my judgement a known violent sex offender who exhibited continuing high levels of deviant sexual arousal should probably not be released to society. The meaning of the measure in this sense is unequivocal: continuing high deviant arousal signals continuing high *risk* for re-offence.

The third reason a difference in arousal is important is that such a difference would suggest that changing arousal patterns should be a central feature of treatment programmes. Early behavioural therapeutic interventions in the field of sexual deviance tended to focus on the modification of deviant arousal, often to the exclusion of other components, though more recent work has been more comprehensive (Crawford 1979, 1981). If rapists are no different from non- rapists in arousal patterns, then a very different treatment strategy would be required. All three of the implications discussed emphasize the need to know how deviant and normal groups compare.

A pioneering study by Abel and his colleagues (Abel et al. 1977) suggested that rapists do differ in their patterns of arousal from controls. The authors reported on rapists' arousal to two-minute audio-taped, verbal descriptions of either mutually consenting sex or rape. The major finding was that rapists were equally aroused by rape and by mutually consenting sex, while non-rapist controls were less aroused by the rape stimuli (see figure 5.1).

The control group in this study were males who were sexually deviant in other ways, but not rapists. A 'rape index' computed by dividing erection to rape stimuli by erection to mutually consenting intercourse proved better able to discriminate rapists from non-rapists than erection to rape stimuli alone. Some of the rapists in this study had raped more than 100 times and are likely to be atypical of rapists as a whole. Indeed it was the high frequency sub-group that had the highest rape-index scores. Barbaree et al. (1979) have replicated this study using a more adequate (though still biased) control group – graduate students. The control subjects responded more to consenting than to rape stimuli, while the rapists showed no significant difference between the two conditions. It was nevertheless the case that the controls did show some arousal to the rape depictions. Barbaree et al.'s interpretation of the results was that the presence of force and violence fail to inhibit arousal in rapists whereas they do in non-rapists. It may well be, of course, that graduate-student volunteers self-select for being free from 'deviant' sexual responses. Barbaree draws attention to another plausible, and perhaps important,

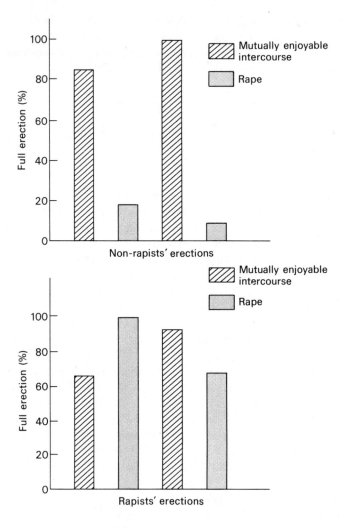

Figure 5.1   Responses of rapists and non-rapists to descriptions of mutually enjoyable intercourse and of rape. (Subjects were assessed on two occasions for each tape, to control for order of presentation.)

Source: Abel et al. 1977. Copyright 1977, American Medical Association; reproduced with permission.

determinant of the failure of rapists to be inhibited by the presence of force. Rapists may have been desensitized to the use of force by their experience of non-sexual violence in prison or in criminal subcultures. The implication of this possibility is that control groups in such studies should be drawn from non-sexual offenders in similar institutions. Such factors were controlled in a recent study by Quinsey et al. (1981), which confirmed the finding of Abel et al. (1977) that the rape index measure distinguished rapists from non-rapists. What was perhaps as striking in this study was that high arousal to rape stimuli was also found in normal community controls when they were given instructions indicating that arousal to deviant material was common in normal males. The evident sensitivity of arousal measures to subtle cognitive influence might lead one to ask whether the arousal responses of both rapists and normals are massively affected by the setting and subjective meaning of the testing session. Rapists are being assessed in forensic, often institutional, settings perceived, perhaps, as part of the 'punishment' for previous offences and as environments in which their dangerousness is being assessed. For normal controls the institution is, perhaps, perceived as the local repository for the criminally deviant, including the sexually deviant. To volunteer to be assessed in such a place is to risk being labelled as also sexually deviant. How such perceptions might affect responses is largely unknown.

A note of caution about assuming that rapists are distinctive in responding sexually to rape depictions is introduced by a series of experiments by Malamuth and colleagues in Canada (Malamuth et al. 1980; Malamuth and Check 1980; Malamuth 1981; Malamuth and Donnerstein 1982). As Malamuth points out, the suggestion that normal males do not respond to representations of coerced sexual behaviour is at variance with observations by other researchers (e.g. Schmidt 1975) and with the high incidence of aggressive themes in widely read popular erotica (Malamuth and Spinner 1980). Erotic magazines with aggressive themes are unlikely to be bought on a large scale unless such themes are reinforcing for substantial numbers of males in the general population. The inconsistency between these observations and those of Abel et al. (1977) may be accounted for by a variety of factors. Malamuth and Donnerstein (1982) suggest two important qualifications to the general statement that normal males do not respond in the same way as rapists to rape depictions. Firstly, males from the general population will show high arousal to rape stimuli when certain conditions are met regarding the description of the victim. In particular, that arousal is high when the victim is portrayed as becoming involuntarily sexually aroused by the rape. In these conditions the response of many 'normal' males is as high as, and sometimes higher than, their response to consenting depictions. When the victim persists in a negative affective response, arousal is less. Secondly, reliable individual differences exist among general population males. Some males are highly aroused by rape stimuli and others are not. Significant differences may exist between responders and non-responders on other measures. In particular sexual responding has some relationship to self-reported 'rape proclivity' (Malamuth 1981; Malamuth and Donnerstein

1982). Rape proclivity is assessed in terms of a high self-rated likelihood of raping 'if you could be assured of not being caught and punished'. About 35 per cent of males report some likelihood on this measure (Malamuth 1981). Malamuth and Donnerstein report that the '(arousal) reactions of the High LR (likelihood of raping) subjects . . . parallel very closely the responses of the rapists studied by Abel et al. (1977).'

The discussion of sexual arousal patterns so far has assumed that the person's sexual responses form a structure that is fixed over time and across situations. It is possible that the pattern of arousal, like other personality traits, is influenced by situational factors. Particular life events and experiences may heighten or diminish deviant arousal. One such situational factor is the ingestion of alcohol. A large number of investigators have suggested a link between alcohol ingestion and aggressive sexual offences. Gebhard and his colleagues (Gebhard et al. 1965), in their massive study of sexual offenders, reported that many had consumed alcohol at the time of the offence. These authors concluded that the commission of sexual crimes requires 'the suspension or distortion of rationality' and that 'in this case alcohol fulfills the requirement'. Rada (1976, 1978) reports a high incidence of drinking in sexual offenders against both children and adults. A number of points need to be made about such studies. Firstly, there are considerable methodological problems in establishing a link between the two variables (Evans 1982). Most studies are based on self-report rather than on direct measurement of blood alcohol levels. It may be that offenders are giving what sociologists have called 'motivational accounts' of the incident, and that situational variables such as alcohol provide a more acceptable 'vocabulary of motives' than do intra-personal factors (McCaghy 1968; Taylor 1972). Secondly, the correlation of alcohol use and sexual aggression is unlikely to be a simple causal one. Deviant sexual propensities may cause a high level of drinking or both forms of behaviour may be the product of some third variable. Finally, even if there were a causal link, it is not clear how the relationship is mediated. A number of forms of mediation are possible. One plausible interpretation is that the social role of being a heavy drinker involves a social deterioration which decreases the capacity to engage in normal non-aggressive sexual relationships (Rada 1976). A second common hypothesis is that alcohol disinhibits the offender and releases behaviours that would normally be restrained. Those who suggest disinhibition effects often fail to make it clear whether it is sexual arousal that is disinhibited or actual behaviour itself. Experimental work has thrown some light on the effects of alcohol on sexual arousal (Lansky and Wilson 1981). Alcohol can often be shown to increase sexual arousal to erotic stimuli; however, this effect is mediated cognitively rather than physiologically – that is, it is the *belief* that you have ingested alcohol that increases arousal rather than the alcohol itself. Briddell et al. (1978) showed that subjects who believed (falsely) that they had consumed alcohol showed greater penile tumescence to erotic stimuli than subjects who believed they had had a non-alcoholic drink. More importantly, arousal to *deviant* sexual stimuli (rape) was more affected than arousal to normal heterosexual stimuli. In this study, subjects who believed they had drunk an alcoholic beverage showed as high arousal to rape as to normal consenting intercourse, whereas those who believed themselves to be sober responded more to normal stimuli. Such cognitive effects are likely to require complex explanations (Lansky and Wilson 1981). In everyday life, of course, actual alcohol ingestion and belief can rarely be disentangled, and both may simultaneously affect sexual behaviour.

The conclusion I would draw from the work on sexual arousal is that, undoubtedly, the advent of sophisticated techniques for assessing sexual responses has produced a significant advance in our knowledge, but that the complexity and ambiguity of the relationship between deviant arousal and deviant behaviour should be appreciated. Rapists may be discriminable from non-rapists in terms of rape indices, but many apparently normal males may show significant arousal to deviant material. It is possible that the deviant response pattern found by Abel et al. (1977) in rapists is neither a necessary nor a sufficient condition for aggressive sexual behaviour to occur. The presence of deviant arousal patterns in the general population has important implications. The exact implications, however, depend on how this fact is interpreted. Are non-convicted males who show deviant arousal simply 'successful' rapists who fail to be apprehended? Or do they fail to act out their deviant interests by controlling their rape proclivity? If the latter is the case, there are clear implications for therapeutic intervention. Attention would need to be directed towards determining how it is that these males inhibit their sexual behaviour, and to using such methods to teach convicted rapists self-control procedures. Fear of aversive consequences, empathic concern for potential victims and cognitions and attitudes which inhibit sexual aggression are all plausible, though largely unresearched, controlling influences. In any event, an exclusive focus in therapy on problems of arousal alone is likely to be inappropriate, as is an over-enthusiastic use of arousal measures to predict future 'dangerousness'.

Aggressive motivation

So far in this discussion I have stressed the sexual aspects of coercive sexual behaviour. An alternative, or (better) complementary, viewpoint is to construe acts such as rape as acts of aggression with significant functional similarities to other non-sexual forms of violent behaviour. The women's movement, in particular, has stressed the aggressive/dominance aspects of rape (Brownmiller 1975; Russell 1975, 1982). There is now research evidence and much informal observation to suggest that too much emphasis has been placed on sexual needs as being the most salient for rapists. Studies have reliably revealed that a substantial subgroup of rapists are generally violence-prone, with histories of non-sexual violent crime. Two British studies (Soothill et al. 1976; Gibbens et al. 1976; Gibbens et al. 1977) identified 'aggressive' rapists of this sort. Gebhard et al. (1965) similarly classified between a quarter and one-third of offenders against adults as 'assaultive'. Less formal accounts by victims often stress the perceived aggressive aim of the assailant (Toner 1982), and a report from the London Rape Counselling Centre suggests: 'our experience has shown us that rape is not "merely" forced intercourse but is an act of violence which uses intercourse as a way of inflicting pain . . . its main aim being to humiliate and degrade the victim' (Roberts 1976). This latter assertion is confirmed by Wright's finding (1980) that 80 per cent of a sample of English rapes involved physical violence and that 30 per cent of victims sustained significant physical injury. The theme of aggression is again dominant in accounts of rape in war. Brownmiller's historical analysis of rape in war suggests that, to the raper and the raped, it has connotations of far more than sex. The context of such incidents suggests that it is the act of a conqueror. As defence of women has been the hallmark of masculine pride, Brownmiller suggests that rape by a conquering soldier is meant to destroy all remaining illusions of power for the defeated side.

Psychological theories of non-sexual aggression often distinguish two classes of aggressive behaviour. Aggression may be 'instrumental' (to obtain some environmental reinforcer) or emotionally mediated ('angry' aggression). A distinction of this sort is made by Bandura (1973) and is implicit in Zillmann's discussion of 'incentive motivated' and 'annoyance motivated' aggression (Zillmann 1979). The question arises whether violence in the context of rape is instrumental or angry. If sexual violence is sometimes anger-motivated, we would expect that it would show three features: the precipitating events would be the aversive kinds of life experiences that induce angry aggression (Berkowitz 1982), the mediating emotion would a negative state of arousal, probably labelled as anger (Bandura 1973), and the reinforcer would be the infliction of pain rather than obtaining sexual release. There is evidence that some rapists (though not all) show these features.

The best source of evidence in relation to such an analysis is the substantial study of Groth (1979), which is based mainly, though not exclusively, on clinical observation rather than on objective psychometric or behavioural analysis. Groth estimated that 40 per cent of his sample of 500 rapists were 'anger' rapists, and it is striking that this group show precisely the characteristics suggested above. The precipitating events were typically arguments, domestic problems, suspicions of infidelity, social rejections and environmental frustrations. Common mediating emotions were a sense of anger and rage, associated with feelings of being wronged, hurt, put down and unjustly treated. The fact that much more violence was present in these rapes than was required to produce compliance also suggested that the reinforcer was the infliction of pain and humiliation. Verbal abuse, swearing and degrading acts were common in the offence situation. Groth's analysis of this group is very similar to a previous description of rape with an 'aggressive aim' by Cohen et al. (1971) and has some correspondence with West et al.'s account (1978) of a group of rapists in therapy.

Groth goes on to describe two other groups of rapists with aggressive components to their motivation. In terms of the angry/instrumental distinction drawn above, both these groups appear to me to be more appropriately described as instrumental. The 'power' rapist intends to 'assert his competency and validate his masculinity. Sexuality is the test and his motive is conquest' (Groth 1979). This might be interpreted as meaning that the reinforcer for the act is, in part, symbolic. The act of intercourse may indeed have multiple meanings in society, and an understanding of some of its non-sexual meanings may be essential to a full analysis of rape. Two examples outside of the area of rape would be the adolescent who engages in sex as much to demonstrate that he or she is 'grown up' as to satisfy a sexual need, and the husband or wife whose sexual involvement with a spouse is maintained by the perception of 'doing one's marital duty'. The symbolic component emphasized by Groth and by many other clinicians and observers (West et al. 1978; Geis 1977) is that of masculinity. Sex roles have also been shown to be important in social psychological studies of attitudes to rape and will be discussed in more detail below. Groth's third type is the 'sadistic' rapist, where aggression itself has become eroticized. This is very much a minority type in Groth's classification and will be discussed in detail here.

While this evidence that aggressive motivation is important is persuasive, some methodological and theoretical difficulties need to be pointed out. The first is that the case for the aggressive view is sometimes overstated. The phrase 'rape is a pseudo-sexual act' occurs frequently in media discussions of rape, sometimes with the implication that the sexual component is negligible. Groth himself goes so far as to say 'Rape is never the result simply of sexual arousal that has no other opportunity for gratification' (Groth 1979, p. 5). Such assertions are hard to sustain. Given that sexual arousal is a necessary condition for rape to occur it is semantically anarchic to label rape as non-sexual or pseudo-sexual behaviour. More accurately, it has 'typically' both sexual and non-sexual components. In particular cases, the aggressive component may sometimes be absent. The second difficulty is that clinical studies such as Groth's are highly dependent on the rapist's self-report, often some time after the offence occurred. It may be that emotional problems and environmental frustration provide a more acceptable vocabulary of motives than sexual proclivities for sexual aggression. Matthews (1980) suggests 'there is good reason . . . to suspect that accounts of illegal deviant sexual behaviour obtained by interview may bear only a tenuous relationship to reality.' The aggressive components of rape are likely to be more difficult to assess objectively in a laboratory setting than the sexual responses described in the previous section. Marques's study (1981) of both aggressive and sexual components of rape in a laboratory is unusual and to be commended for the comprehensiveness of the measures used. Howells and Steadman-Allen (1978) used repertory grid technique to assess rapists' evaluations of the aggressive and sexual aspects of their offences and found evidence that both components were important. The development of objective measures in this area of aggression is an important task for future research.

The conclusion that both sexual and aggressive motivation is involved in coercive sexual behaviour raises the intriguing question of how they might interact. In particular, how is it that anger arousal sometimes induces sexual rather than non-sexual aggression? Why do some of Groth's angry rapists rape rather than simply assault their victims? There are a number of possible explanations. It may be that anger arousal, in some circumstances, facilitates sexual arousal and vice versa. In experimental work both mutual facilitation and mutual inhibition effects have been found for sex and aggression (Malamuth 1977). Zillmann (1971, 1979) has produced some evidence for residual excitation effects from one emotional state to another. Another possibility is that specific developmental experiences may have conditioned sexual arousal to aggressive stimuli for some individuals. Alternatively, rape my be a more effective response than a non-sexual attack, from the rapist's viewpoint. Groth subscribes to the idea that rape is simply the *worst* thing that the person can do and is thereby preferable in a state of intense anger (Groth 1979). It may be that anticipated social evaluations of the act determine its nature. Sexual violence is, perhaps, less incompatible with the perceived masculine role than a non-sexual assault. It is to this topic of social evaluation of sexual aggression that we now turn.

Cognitive/attitudinal aspects

Whereas most of the work reviewed so far has been done within the 'clinical' tradition in psychology, recent years have also witnessed an increasing social psychological contribution. The concern here has been with cognitive evaluations and images of coercive sex. There are many good reasons for investigating these variables. How rape is perceived and evaluated, for example, is likely to affect the reporting of offences, how the police and legal systems process rape cases, jury decision-making, sentencing and a range of extra-legal social reactions to victims and rapists. In addition, it needs to be established whether prevailing cultural attitudes are of the sort that might encourage, or alternatively discourage, sexual aggression. Studies in this field fall into two broad categories: experiments and correlational analyses. (For detailed references see Howells et al. 1984). In the former category subjects are typically presented with an account of a rape and are subsequently asked to make judgements about it. The account may be in the form of a simulated newspaper article, a video-taped interview, a medical file or transcripts of court proceedings. The independent variables may be manipulations of the nature of the offence, the characteristics of the offender or victim, or some attribute of the person doing the experiment. The dependent measures are typically the subjects' ratings of the offender's culpability, of the role of the victim and so on. In correlational surveys, questionnaire measures of attitudes to rape are administered to large groups of subjects, and an attempt is made to assess the degree of association between rape attitudes and sociodemographic or personal characteristics of the subjects. Such studies reveal a number of important facts (Howells et al. 1984). Rape attitudes are complex and multi-dimensional (Feild 1978; Feild and Bienen 1980), and are socially segmented, with differing attitudes in various social groups. In particular, males reliably differ from females in their rape attitudes (Calhoun et al. 1976; Cann et al. 1979; Howells et al. 1984; Feild 1978).

A number of other findings are relevant to the aetiology of rape and to clinical interventions. Firstly, a substantial proportion of people appear to subscribe to beliefs about rape which might serve to justify or disinhibit sexual aggression (Feild 1978; Burt 1980). Burt reports that more than half of an American sample, for example, agree with the statements that 'a woman who goes to the home or appartment of a man on the first date implies she is willing to have sex' and '50% or more of reported rapes are reported as rape only because the woman was trying to get back at a man she was angry with or was trying to cover up an illegitimate pregnancy'. It is the prevalence of such attitudes that leads Russell (1982) to label the United States a 'rape-supportive culture'. Secondly, the tendency of subjects to subscribe to these 'rape myths' does not occur in isolation but forms part of a more general cognitive/attitudinal structure. This finding is consistent with feminist analyses (Brownmiller 1975) and with the anthropological analysis of Sanday (1981). Burt (1980) found that acceptance of rape myths can be predicted from the degree of sex-role stereotyping, the extent to which sexual relationships are seen in adversarial terms, and general acceptance of interpersonal violence. The finding for sex-role stereotyping has been confirmed in a number of other studies (Klemmack and Klemmack 1976; Feild 1978; Krulewitz and Payne 1978; Feild and Bienen 1980; Tieger 1981;

Schwarz and Brand 1983). Given that these studies were all conducted in North America, it is important to know whether these effects are culture-specific. In a recent small British sample (Howells et al. 1984) we found that males who were stereotyped about the female role were less aware of damage to rape victims and were more likely to blame victims for the assault, confirming American findings.

A crucial question is whether rapists themselves occupy an extreme point on the continuum of rape-promoting attitudes that exists amongst males in society. If such attitudes do indeed cause sexual aggression, we would expect rapists to be more sex-role stereotyped, adversarial and violence-accepting than non-rapists. As yet few studies have been addressed to this issue. Tieger (1981) and Malamuth (1981) have presented some evidence that males with a high rape proclivity are more sex-role stereotyped, and Check and Malamuth (1983) report that sex-stereotyped men show more arousal to aggressive pornography. Clearly, comparisons on behavioural rape measures are essential.

IMPLICATIONS FOR ASSESSMENT AND PREVENTION

As the present volume is geared to some extent to the psychologist, psychiatrist or social worker working with sexually deviant people, it is relevant to consider the implications of the above research for the understanding and assessment of the individual. It should now be clear that any particular sexually coercive act requires a comprehensive and multi-faceted analysis. The details of such an analysis follow logically from what has been established by the studies. Such an analysis would need to include the individual's pattern of sexual arousal and factors tending to disinhibit restraint of deviant arousal (low self-control, alcohol use, poor anticipation of consequences). In addition, the relationship between the coercive behaviour and internal state of anger and external frustrations and stresses would need to be determined.

Finally, cognitive beliefs and judgements about women, sexual relation-ships and sex-appropriate behaviour would require exploration. Even such an apparently broad analysis is not exhaustive. The subgroup of sexual aggressors who have instrumental problems (poor social skills, deficient sexual information) has not been discussed in the present chapter, though they may be frequent in psychiatric settings (Howells 1976; Howells and Wright 1978; Crawford and Allen 1979; Crawford and Howells 1982). It is clear that, given the multiplicity of contributing factors, two individual sexual aggressors could engage in behaviour that was topographically similar (e.g. rape) but functionally very different. The likely heterogeneity of populations of rapists is evident from the above discussion.

Which preventative interventions are most appropriate will depend on the level at which the problem of coercive sexual behaviour is analysed, and which factors are given causal status. The culture, the aggressor himself, the situational aspects of the encounter or the victim's behaviour could all be identified as causes and become the focus for attention (Brodsky 1976a). Changing cultures and societies has a sociological, historical, economic and political dimension which puts it outside the scope of this chapter and beyond the competence of its author. Situational changes (e.g. improved street-lighting) may well reduce the opportunity for sexual assaults. Prevention possibilities at the level of the victims's behaviour are largely unexplored. Women's differential success in resisting rape attempts has led some psychologists to attempt to discover what kinds of victim's behaviour might be successful in preventing a rape (Brodsky 1976b; Marques 1981) with a view to teaching other women effective resistance strategies. Finally, attempts to reduce the level of assaults by 'treating' the aggressor are perhaps the least likely to make a major impact on the numbers of incidents occurring, but it is in this area that we find the main application of psychological theories and effort.

The psychological or psychiatric treatment of individual sexual aggressors is sometimes neither necessary nor possible. Formal treatment may be unnecessary in the sense that the deviant behaviour is unlikely to be repeated. The majority, for example, of sexual offenders appearing in court for the first time are not subsequently reconvicted for sexual crimes. The consequences of first conviction may be so aversive that the behaviour is not repeated, without any formal psychological intervention. It is possible, of course, that recorded convictions are a poor measure of the occurrence of offending behaviour. In any event, therapeutic attention is more appropriately directed at the subgroup of repeated offenders.

Formal treatment may be impossible in the sense that the aggressor may have no wish to receive treatment. The absence of motivation for change in offender groups is a major obstacle to therapeutic progress. Most of the treatments devised (see below) require a collaborative relationship between offender and therapist and the presence of common treatment goals. Where these are absent the essential basis for treatment does not exist. Formal 'consent' to treatment may sometimes mask resistance or lack of desire to change, and be the product of situational pressures in the psychiatric or penal setting. The work of Perkins (1982, 1983a, 1983b) illustrates the difficulties caused by lack of motivation. This author found that a large proportion of sex offenders in a British prison were 'unsuitable for treatment' for reasons of this sort, and that, even when they did agree to enter treatment, a substantial proportion failed to complete it (Perkins 1983b).

Where the motivational basis for therapy is present, the nature of the therapeutic programme is determined by a full analysis of the individual case.

The general discussion of aetiology presented above suggests that any programme would need to be comprehensive. Broad-based interventions of this sort, including sexual, aggressive and attitudinal components, are increasingly advocated for sexual aggressives and related forms of sexual deviance (Barlow 1974; Abel et al. 1978, Crawford 1979, 1981; Perkins 1982, 1983a, 1983b).

Given the complex aetiology of behaviours such as rape, an exclusive focus on changing patterns of sexual arousal in therapy is inappropriate. In the past, sexual arousal has been the major target for many workers. Castration, for example, has been used in some European countries to reduce sexual recidivism (for a discussion see Crawford 1981). Ethical objections aside, such a treatment approach takes an entirely sexual view of sexual offending and ignores the evidence that aggressive forms of motivation are important for some. Chemical treatments developed to reduce sexual drive (oestrogen, benperidol, cyproterone acetate, etc.) share this oversimplified view. If used in isolation, or without reference to a proper analysis of the problem, they are equally inappropriate as standard treatments.

The modification of sexual arousal patterns still has some part to play in comprehensive treatment programmes. The emphasis in contemporary therapies, however, is increasingly on enhancing non-deviant arousal rather than on eliminating deviant arousal (Abel et al., 1978; Crawford 1981; Perkins 1982). Stimulus-fading, masturbatory reconditioning, biofeedback and exposure to non-deviant sexual material have all been used to this end (Crawford 1981; Perkins 1983a). Covert sensitization (Cautela and Wisocki 1971), satiation (Marshall 1979) and other procedures have also been used to reduce deviant arousal where it is appropriate. The work discussed earlier in this chapter would suggest that programmes should, perhaps, place greater emphasis on the control (particularly self-control) of deviant arousal rather than on its elimination. A relevant strategy would be to attempt to remove influences that diminish control. Cognitive/attitudinal processes are likely to be influences of this sort. Beliefs about women, sex roles and sex-appropriate behaviour may diminish control and need to be targets for change. Structured feedback from women themselves, perhaps in a group setting, might serve to modify inaccurate perceptions of the opposite sex. The major obstacle to cognitive restructuring of this sort is the fact that therapeutic sessions may be embedded in a wider and more powerful social environment which actively promotes rape-engendering attitudes and beliefs.

Where alcohol ingestion can be shown to be a likely cause of impairment of control it may be relevant to try to change the pattern of alcohol use. In some cases, of course, poor control of sexual impulses is part of a broader impulsivity, which shows itself in the 'acting out' of a range of impulses apart from the sexual. It follows that self-control training of a wider sort may be of use for some offenders.

The fact that some sexual assaults are aggressively motivated suggests that treatments developed for non-sexual aggression should also be used for sexual aggressors. Reconceptualizing rape as aggressive can expand the range of therapeutic methods available. The environmental, cognitive and affective components of angry aggression, and corresponding therapies, have been delineated elsewhere (Novaco 1978; Howells 1981b). As angry aggression is often a response to aversive/frustrating life experiences, interventions which reduced the aversiveness of the external environment would be expected to reduce the probability of both sexual and non-sexual aggression. A sexual offender, for example, who was induced to behave in a aggressive way by the experience of failure in relationships and by work difficulties would be less prone to aggression if he could be helped to be more successful in relationships and at work. Self-control strategies for the management of anger (Novaco 1978) are similarly relevant to the problems of sexual aggressors.

Comprehensive intervention programmes would also need to make provision for the sexual offender who has such poor instrumental skills in sexual relationships that aggression is used to obtain sexual contact. Social skills training to remedy such deficits will be appropriate for some (Crawford and Allen 1979). A sense of incompetence in relationships with potential sexual partners may be increased by poor knowledge and information about sexuality in general. Crawford and Howells (1982) devised a sex-education programme to improve such knowledge, and found that a number of therapeutically useful changes were brought about.

There are major difficulties in implementing treatment programmes for sexual aggressors, particularly in penal settings, some of which have been discussed above and by authors elsewhere (West 1980). Even where therapy can be provided within institutions, massive problems of generalization of treatment effects to real-life environments exist. Such difficulties suggest, once again, the necessity for psychologists, psychiatrists, social workers and other professionals to look beyond the individual therapeutic approach in their attempts to reduce the level of sexual violence in society.

SUMMARY

The research reviewed in this chapter indicates that coercive sexual behaviour in humans is far more common in many societies than the frequency of reported crimes would suggest. The variation in prevalence between cultures and subcultures, and the association of such behaviour with particular configurations of attitudes, suggest that sexual aggression is as much a cultural problem as a problem of individual psychology. However, a 'culture *versus* individual' dichotomy is not useful in that, within societies, individual differences exist in the propensity of males for coercive sexual behaviour. Psychological studies demonstrate that acts such as rape have some relationship to deviant patterns of physiological arousal but that arousal itself does not clearly differentiate rapists from non-rapists. The limitations of a purely sexual view are revealed by studies of the aggressive/dominance and cognitive/attitudinal determinants of this behaviour. Consequently, individual assessments and therapeutic interventions will need to be multi-faceted and broad-based.

REFERENCES

Abel, G. G., Barlow, D. H., Blanchard, E. B., and Guild, D. (1977). The components of rapists' sexual arousal. *Archives of General Psychiatry*, 34, 395–403.

Abel, G. G., Blanchard, E. B., and Barlow, D. H. (1981). Measurement of sexual arousal in several paraphilias: the effect of stimulus modality, instructional set and stimulus content. *Behaviour Research and Therapy*, 19, 25–33.

Abel, G. G., Blanchard, E. B., and Becker, J. V. (1978). An integrated treatment program for rapists. In R. T. Rada (ed.), *Clinical Aspects of the Rapist*, New York: Grune & Stratton.

Amir, M. (1971). *Patterns in Forcible Rape*, Chicago: University of Chicago Press.

Bandura, A. (1973). *Aggression: a Social Learning Analysis*, Englewood Cliffs, NJ: Prentice-Hall.

Barbaree, H. E., Marshall, W. L., Lanthier, R. D. (1979). Deviant sexual arousal in rapists. *Behaviour Research and Therapy*, 17, 215–22.

Barlow, D. H. (1974). The treatment of sexual deviation: toward a comprehensive behavioral approach. In K. S. Calhoun, H. E. Adams and K. M. Mitchell (eds), *Innovative Treatment Methods in Psychopathology*, New York: Wiley.

Berkowitz, L. (1982). Aversive conditions as stimuli to aggression. In L. Berkowitz (ed.), *Advances in Experimental Social Psychology*, 15, New York: Academic Press.

Briddell, D., Rimm, D., Caddy, G., Krawitz, G., Scholis, S., and Wunderlin, R. (1978). Effects of alcohol and cognitive set on sexual arousal to deviant stimuli. *Journal of Abnormal Psychology*, 87, 418–30.

Brodsky, S. L. (1976a). Sexual assault: perspectives on prevention and assailants. In M. J. Walker and S. L. Brodsky (eds), *Sexual Assault*, Lexington, Mass.: Lexington Books.

Brodsky, S. L. (1976b). Prevention of rape: deterrence by the potential victim. In M. J. Walker and S. L. Brodsky (eds), *Sexual Assault*, Lexington, Mass.: Lexington Books.

Brownmiller, S. (1975). *Against Our Will: Rape, Women and Men*, London: Secker & Warburg.

Burt, M. R. (1980). Cultural myths and supports for rape. *Journal of Personality and Social Psychology*, 38, 217–30.

Calhoun, L. G., Selby, J. W., and Warring, L. J. (1976). Social perceptions of the victim's causal role in rape: an exploratory examination of four factors. *Human Relations*, 29, 517–26.

Cann, A., Calhoun, L. G., and Selby, J. W. (1979). Attributing responsibility to the victim of rape: influence of information regarding past sexual experience. *Human Relations*, 32, 59–67.

Cautela, J. R., and Wisocki, P. A. (1971). Covert sensitisation for the treatment of sexual deviations. *Psychological Record*, 21, 37–48.

Chappell, D., Geis, G., Schafer, S., and Siegel, L. (1977). A comparative study of forcible rape offences known to the police in Boston and Los Angeles. In D. Chappell, R. Geis and G. Geis (eds), *Forcible Rape: the Crime, the Victim and the Offender*. New York: Columbia University Press.

Chappell, D., and Singer, S. (1977). Rape in New York city: a study of material in the police files and its meaning. In D. Chappell, R. Geis, and G. Geis (eds), *Forcible Rape: the Crime, the Victim and the Offender*, New York: Columbia University Press.

Check, J. V. P., and Malamuth, N. M. (1983). Sex role stereotyping and reactions to depiction of stranger versus acquaintance rape. *Journal of Personality and Social Psychology*, 45, 344–56.

Cohen, M. L., Garofalo, R., Boucher, R., and Seghorn, T. (1971). The psychology of rapists. *Seminars in Psychiatry*, 3.

Cook, M., and Howells, K. (eds) (1981). *Adult Sexual Interest in Children*, London: Academic Press.

Crawford, D. A. (1979). Modification of deviant sexual behaviour: the need for a comprehensive approach. *British Journal of Medical Psychology*, 52, 151–6.

Crawford, D. A. (1980). Applications of penile response monitoring to the assessment of sexual offenders. In D. J. West (ed.), *Sex Offenders in the Criminal Justice System*, Cambridge: University of Cambridge Institute of Criminology.

Crawford, D. A. (1981). Treatment approaches with pedophiles. In M. Cook and K. Howells (eds), *Adult Sexual Interest in Children*, London: Academic Press.

Crawford, D. A., and Allen, J. V. (1979). A social skills training programme with sex offenders. In M. Cook and G. Wilson (eds), *Love and Attraction*, Oxford: Pergamon.

Crawford, D. A., and Howells, K. (1982). The effect of sex education with disturbed adolescents. *Behavioural Psychotherapy*, 10, 339–45.

Evans, C. H. (1982). Alcohol and sexual assault. *British Journal of Sexual Medicine*, 9, 40–2.

Feild, H. S. (1978). Attitudes toward rape: a comparative analysis of police, rapists, crisis counselors and citizens. *Journal of Personality and Social Psychology*, 36, 156–79.

Feild, H. S., and Bienen, L. B. (1980). *Jurors and Rape*, Lexington, Mass.: Lexington Books.

Freund, K. (1963). A laboratory method for diagnosing predominance of homo- or hetero-erotic interest in the male. *Behaviour Research and Therapy*, 1, 85–93.

Freund, K. (1967). Diagnosing homo- or heterosexuality and erotic age preference by means of a psychophysiological test. *Behaviour Research and Therapy*, 5, 209–28.

Gebhard, P. H., Gagnon, J. H., Pomeroy, W. B., and Christenson, C. W. (1965). *Sex Offenders*, New York: Harper & Row.

Geis, G. (1977). Forcible rape: an introduction. In D. Chappell, R. Geis and G. Geis (eds), *Forcible Rape: the Crime, the Victim and the Offender*, New York: Columbia University Press.

Gibbens, T. C. N., Way, C., and Soothill, K. E. (1977). Behavioural types of rape. *British Journal of Psychiatry*, 130, 32–42.

Groth, A. N. (1979). *Men Who Rape*, New York: Plenum.

Hindelang, M. J., and Davis, B. J. (1977). Forcible rape in the United States: a statistical profile. In D. Chappell, R. Geis and G. Geis (eds), *Forcible Rape: the Crime, the Victim and the Offender*, New York: Columbia University Press.

Home Office (1979). Sexual offences, consent and sentencing. Home Office Research Study No. 54. London: HMSO.

Howells, K. (1976). Interpersonal aggression. *International Journal of Criminology and Penology*, 4, 319–30.

Howells, K. (1981a). Adult sexual interest in children: considerations relevant to theories of aetiology. In M. Cook and K. Howells (eds), *Adult Sexual Interest in Children*, London: Academic Press.

Howells, K. (1981b). Social relationships in violent offenders. In S. Duck and R. Gilmour (eds), *Personal Relationships, 3: Personal Relationships in Disorder*, London: Academic Press.

Howells, K., Shaw, F., Greasley, M., Robertson, J., and Gloster, D. (1984). Perceptions of rape in a British sample: effects of relationship, victim status, sex, and attitudes to women. *British Journal of Social Psychology*, 23, 35–40.

Howells, K., and Steadman-Allen, R. (1978). Emotional antecedents of rape, unpublished manuscript.

Howells, K., and Wright, E. (1978). The sexual attitudes of aggressive sexual offenders. *British Journal of Criminology*, 18, 170–4.

Klemmack, S. H., and Klemmack, D. L. (1976). The social definition of rape. In M. J. Walker and S. L. Brodsky (eds) *Sexual Assault: the Victim and the Rapist*, London: Lexington Books.

Koss, M. P., and Oros, C. J. (1982). Sexual experiences survey: a research instrument investigating sexual aggression and victimization. *Journal of Consulting and Clinical Psychology*, 50, 455–7.

Krulewitz, J. E., and Payne, E. J. (1978). Attributions about rape: effects of rapist force, observer sex and sex role attitudes. *Journal of Applied Social Psychology*, 8, 291–305.

Lansky, D., and Wilson, G. T. (1981). Alcohol, expectations, and sexual arousal in males: an information-processing analysis. *Journal of Abnormal Psychology*, 90, 35–45.

Laws, D. R. (1984). The assessment of dangerous sexual behaviour in males. *Medicine and Law: an International Journal*, 3, 127–140.

Levine, R. A. (1959). Gusii sex offences: a study in social control. *American Anthropologist*, 61, 965–90. (also in D. Chappell, R. Geis and G. Geis (eds), *Forcible Rape: the Crime, the Victim and the Offender*, New York: Columbia University Press.

Lockwood, D. (1980). *Prison Sexual Violence*, New York: Elsevier North Holland.

McCaghy, C. H. (1968). Drinking and deviance disavowal: the case of child molesters. *Social Problems*, 16, 43–9.

McClintock, F. H. (1980). Criminal careers of sexual offenders: sexual recidivism, criminal justice and politics. In D. J. West (ed.), *Sex Offenders in the Criminal Justice System*, Cambridge: University of Cambridge Institute of Criminology.

McConaghy, N. (1974). Measurements of change in penile dimensions. *Archives of Sexual Behavior*, 3, 381–8.

Malamuth, N. M. (1977). Sexual arousal and aggression. *Journal of Social Issues*, 33, 110–33.

Malamuth, N. M. (1981). Rape proclivity among males. *Journal of Social Issues*, 37, 138–57.

Malamuth, N. M., and Check, J. V. P. (1980). Sexual arousal to rape and consenting depictions: the importance of the woman's arousal. *Journal of Abnormal Psychology*, 89, 763–6.

Malamuth, N. M., and Donnerstein, E. (1982). The effects of aggressive–pornographic mass media stimuli. In L. Berkowitz (ed.), *Advances in Experimental Social Psychology*, 15, New York: Academic Press.

Malamuth, N. M., Heim, M., and Feshbach, S. (1980). The sexual responsiveness of college students to rape depictions: inhibitory and disinhibitory effects. *Journal of Personality and Social Psychology*, 38, 399–408.

Malamuth, N. M., and Spinner, B. (1980). A longitudinal content analysis of sexual violence in best-selling erotic magazines. *Journal of Sex Research*, 16, 226–37.

Marques, J. K. (1981). Effects of victim resistance strategies on the sexual arousal and attitudes of violent rapists. In R. B. Stuart (ed.), *Violent Behavior: Social Learning Approaches to Prediction, Management and Treatment*, New York: Brunner/Mazel.

Marshall, W. L. (1979). Satiation therapy: a procedure for reducing deviant sexual arousal. *Journal of Applied Behavioral Analysis*, 12, 377–89.

Matthews, R. (1980). Assessment of sexual offenders at Wormwood Scrubs. In D. J. West (ed.), *Sex Offenders in the Criminal Justice System*, Cambridge: University of Cambridge Institute of Criminology.

Mead, M. (1935). *Sex and Temperament in Three Primitive Societies*, New York: William Morrow.

Money, J. (1981). The development of sexuality and eroticism in humankind. *Quarterly Review of Biology*, 56, 379–404.

Novaco, R. W. (1978). Anger and coping with stress. In J. P. Foreyt and D. P. Rathjen (eds), *Cognitive Behavior Therapy*, New York: Plenum.

Perkins, D. (1982). The treatment of sex offenders. In P. Feldman (ed.), *Developments in the Study of Criminal Behaviour*, 1: *The Prevention and Control of Offending*, Chichester: Wiley.

Perkins, D. (1983a). Assessment and treatment of dangerous sex offenders. In J. Hinton (ed.), *Dangerousness: Problems of Assessment and Prediction*, London: Allen & Unwin.

Perkins, D. (1983b). The psychological treatment of sex offenders in the prison and the community. Paper presented to a meeting of the British Psychological Society, Division of Criminological and Legal Psychology, Oxford.

Quinsey, V. L., Chaplin, T. C., and Varney, G. A. (1981). A comparison of rapists' and non-sex offenders' sexual preference for mutually consenting sex, rape and physical abuse of women. *Behavioral Assessment*, 3, 127–35.

Rada, R. T. (1976). Alcoholism and the child molester. *Annals of the New York Academy of Sciences*, 273, 492–6.

Rada, R. T. (1978). *Clinical Aspects of the Rapist*, New York: Grune & Stratton.

Roberts, C. (1976). *Report of the Rape Counselling and Research Project*, London: Rape Crisis Counselling Centre.

Russell, D. E. H. (1975). *The Politics of Rape*, New York: Stein & Day.

Russell, D. E. H. (1982). *Rape in Marriage*, New York: MacMillan.

Sanday, P. R. (1981). The socio-cultural context of rape: a cross-cultural study. *Journal of Social Issues*, 37, 5–27.

Schiff, A. F. (1971). Rape in other countries. *Medicine Science and the Law*, 11, 25–30.

Schmidt, G. (1975). Male–female differences in sexual arousal and behaviour. *Archives of Sexual Behavior*, 4, 353–64.

Schwarz, N., and Brand, J. F. (1983). Effects of salience of rape on sex role attitude, trust and self-esteem in non-raped women. *European Journal of Social Psychology*, 13, 71–6.

Schwendinger, J., and Schwendinger, H. (1974). Rape myths: in legal, theoretical and everyday practice. *Crime and Social Justice*, 13, 18–26.

Soothill, K. L., Jack, A., and Gibbens, T. C. N. (1976). Rape: a 22-year cohort study. *Medicine, Science and the Law*, 16, 62–9.

Taylor, L. (1972). The significance and interpretation of replies to motivational questions: the case of sex offenders. *Sociology*, 6, 23–39.

Tieger, T. (1981). Self-rated likelihood of raping and the social perception of rape. *Journal of Research in Personality*, 15, 147–58.

Toner, B. (1982). *The Facts of Rape* (2nd edn), London: Arrow Books.

Walmsley, R. (1980). Prosecution rates, sentencing practice and maximum penalties for sexual offences. In D. J. West (ed.), *Sex Offenders in the Criminal Justice System*, Cambridge: Cambridge University Institute of Criminology.

West, D. J. (1980). Treatment in theory and practice. In D. J. West (ed.), *Sex Offenders in the Criminal Justice System*, Cambridge: University of Cambridge Institute of Criminology.

West, D. J., Roy, C., and Nichols, F. L. (1978). *Understanding Sexual Attacks*, London: Heinemann.

Wright, R. (1980). Rape and physical violence. In D. J. West (ed.), *Sex Offenders in the Criminal Justice System*, Cambridge: Cambridge University Institute of Criminology.

Zillmann, D. (1971). Excitation transfer in communication-mediated aggressive behaviour. *Journal of Experimental Social Psychology*, 7, 419–34.

Zillmann, D. (1979). *Hostility and Aggression*, Hillsdale, NJ: Erlbaum.

6

Sexual Inadequacy

Derek Jehu

Human sexual functioning may be considered inadequate because it is accompanied by pain, vaginal spasm or anxiety, or because of some impairment of sexual motivation, arousal, climax or satisfaction (Jehu 1979; Kaplan 1979; Schover et al. 1982). Coital pain or dyspareunia is experienced during intromission or thrusting by some women, and in men it may occur during erection, insertion, thrusting or ejaculation.

The condition of vaginismus can be defined as a spastic contraction of the muscles at the outer third of the vagina and the perineum, which occurs as an involuntary reflex response to the threat of vaginal penetration. Consequently, intromission is either completely prevented or only possible with great difficulty and pain. The muscular spasm is often accompanied by considerable fear of penetration. This is one instance of a sexual phobia in which certain specific features of sexual activities elicit intense, irrational anxiety. This reaction often involves physiological components such as profuse sweating, nausea, vomiting, diarrhoea or palpitations. It is understandable that phobias also include the avoidance of eliciting events. Consequently, sexual motivation is liable to become impaired, the range of foreplay is restricted, and the frequency of intercourse is reduced. Even purely affectionate acts, such as a hug or a kiss, may evoke anticipatory anxiety unless the circumstances are such that a possible progression to sex is ruled out.

Members of both sexes sometimes report that they do not experience any urge or desire for sex, they could go on indefinitely without it and abstinence is often a relief for them. This lack of motivation may extend to all sexual activities and partners. In other cases, it is more restricted, so that interest may be retained, for example, in masturbation or towards extra-marital partners.

Complaints of inadequate sexual arousal can involve its psychological and/or physiological components. Psychologically, there may be a deficiency of erotic sensations and feelings in response to sexual stimulation. Physiologically, men may experience persistent difficulty in obtaining or maintaining full erections, and women may lack the analogous responses of vaginal lubrication and swelling.

Similarly, either or both of the psychological and physiological components of climax may be impaired. Men or women may report that the subjective feelings of pleasure that usually accompany orgasm are attenuated or absent. Other impairments of climax in males are premature, retarded or retrograde ejaculation. Premature ejaculation means that the individual reaches climax involuntarily, when he would prefer to maintain his control for a longer period of time. In contrast, retarded ejaculation comprises a persistent delay or failure in reaching climax, despite a full erection and intense stimulation for unusually lengthy periods. It is important to note that both orgasm and ejaculation are retarded or absent in this dysfunction, for it needs to be distinguished from retrograde ejaculation which consists of the involuntary discharge of semen backwards into the bladder rather than forwards through the urethra, so that the man still has erections and orgasms but there is no visible ejaculate. Another impairment of climax in women is orgastic dysfunction in which difficulty is experienced in releasing the reflex contractions of the vaginal and pelvic musculature that are the physiological components of orgasm, making this problem analogous to retarded ejaculation in the male.

Lastly, it is important to appreciate that some men and women complain of sexual dissatisfaction despite the fact that motivation, arousal and climax are relatively unimpaired, at least in the earlier stages of the dissatisfaction. This may arise from the frequency, timing, location or nature of sexual activities. It may also occur if sex is perceived as dirty, disgusting, monotonous or boring. Finally, sex may be unsatisfying if the partners are not attracted to each other, if they are insensitive to the other's sexual needs and preferences, if one feels that the other is only interested in him or her for sex, or if there is a role strain or serious conflict in their relationship (Frank et al. 1979; Hudson et al. 1981; Perlman and Abramson 1982).

There are two general points to note about the above outline of various types of sexual inadequacy. First, it categorizes problems not people, so that more than one problem may co-exist in the same individual. Second, it will be apparent that the definitions of the various dysfunctions involve subjective judgements of inadequacy by the individuals concerned. Thus, the avoidance of sexual activity because of dyspareunia, vaginismus or a sexual phobia may not be at all distressing to some individuals, and there are no absolute or prescribed standards of sexual motivation, arousal, climax or dissatisfaction against which an individual could be judged objectively to be inadequate.

INCIDENCE OF INADEQUACY

This variability and subjectivity in the judgement of sexual inadequacy influences the few estimates available of its incidence in general populations. One such estimate is based on 100 predominantly white, well-educated, middle-class and happily married couples in the USA (Frank, Anderson and Rubenstein 1978). Current erectile or ejaculatory dysfunctions were reported by 40 per cent of the men, and 63 per cent of the women were currently experiencing an impairment of their arousal or ability to reach orgasm. Despite these problems however, 80 per cent of the couples considered their sexual relations to be satisfying. Thus impairments of sexual performance appeared to be widespread even in this well-favoured and happily married group, but the couples concerned did not necessarily judge these impairments to be detrimental to their sexual relationship.

Among a representative sample of 58 married Swedish men, 39 per cent had experienced premature ejaculation, 10 per cent retarded ejaculation, and 7 per cent impotence. As in the Frank et al. study above, these sexual dysfunctions were not significantly related to the sexual satisfaction of the couple (Nettelbladt and Uddenberg 1979).

In a study of diabetic patients in Denmark a control group was used comprising 40 men and 40 women, aged 26 to 45 years, who were attending their general practitioners but who were not suffering from any kind of chronic somatic disease and had not been referred previously for psychiatric treatment. Among the men in this control group, 2.5 per cent reported reduced libido and 10 per cent reported premature ejaculation, while none complained of erectile dysfunction or retarded ejaculation. Among the women, 23 per cent reported reduced libido and 7.5 per cent orgastic dysfunction, while none experienced general sexual dysfunction or vaginismus (Jensen 1981).

Among the very few studies that have been conducted the three that are reviewed here are perhaps the most representative, but it is clearly impossible to draw any reasonably precise estimates of the incidence of sexual inadequacy in general populations. Two of the studies do indicate that difficulties in sexual performance are not necessarily associated with sexual dissatisfaction.

CAUSES OF SEXUAL INADEQUACY

The causes of sexual inadequacy can be conceptualized in the general categories of organic factors, previous learning experiences and current conditions, operating singly or in combination in particular cases. These causal factors are illustrated only very selectively in this chapter and comprehensive reviews are available in several texts (e.g. Jehu 1979; Kaplan 1974, 1979; Kolodny et al. 1979; Leiblum and Pervin 1980; Lo Piccolo and Lo Piccolo 1978; Masters and Johnson 1970). .

Organic factors

The relevant organic factors include certain disease conditions, together with the side-effects of some types of medication or surgery. Sexual inadequacy is sometimes a direct result of physiological impairments involved in these diseases or treatments, or it may arise from the patient's psychological reactions to these experiences. Even when there is a physiological impairment, its effects may be influenced by psychological factors; for instance, a temporary or moderate physiological impairment of sexual capacity may persist or worsen if the patient becomes unduly anxious or depressed about this. Some selected examples of medical conditions that may have an adverse influence on sexual functioning are outlined below.

Spinal-cord lesions.   A wide range of sexual difficulties in both men and women are associated with spinal-cord lesions arising from injuries, tumours, inflammations, multiple sclerosis or spina bifida. To some extent at least, the difficulties are likely to be due to the physiological impairment of the central nervous system mechanisms that subserve sexual responses, although psychological reactions may also be involved in some cases.

Varying proportions of spinal-cord-injured men, ranging up to about 50 per cent, suffer some impairment of arousal or climax (Higgins 1979). The major reason for the wide range in residual capacity is variation between clients in the level and completeness of the lesion. Generally speaking, lower-level lesions are more destructive of sexual response than those at higher levels, and the same is true of complete compared to incomplete lesions.

About 85 per cent of spinal-cord-injured people are male, while only 15 per cent are female. This may be one reason why the sexual responses of spinal-cord-injured women have been even less well investigated than those of their male counterparts. In the best study to date (Bregman 1975, 1978) the results are not altogether clear but they seem to indicate that about 90 per cent of the 31 spinal-cord-injured women experienced vaginal lubrication and about 73 per cent could reach orgasm.

Apart from the impairment of specific sexual responses, there are other common physical sequelae of spinal injuries that may have an adverse effect on sexual functioning. For instance, involuntary defaecation or urination may occur during intercourse. Intercourse may also be precluded or disrupted by an abnormality of the trunk and lower limbs, such as an occurrence of muscular spasms that are strong and unpredictable, or by weakening of the bones through atrophic changes so that they are easily fractured in some coital positions. While spinal-cord lesions are often accompanied by losses of sensation in certain areas of the body, it is also true that heightened sensitivity to erotic stimulation may occur in other areas. For instance, sensation may become more acute at the body level just above the sensory loss, and this area may become a new or enhanced erogenous zone.

Diabetes mellitus.   One of the commonest organic causes of erectile dysfunction is diabetes mellitus. In a typical study (Barnett 1973) of sexual difficulties among 175 diabetic men it was found that 49 per cent suffered from erectile dysfunction. The incidence of erectile dysfunction was not related to the control, duration or severity of the disease. In another study (Rubin and Babbott, 1958) erectile dysfunction was found to be related to age; among diabetic men aged between 30 and 34, the incidence was 25 per cent, while in those between 60 and 64 it rose to 74 per cent.

There has been considerable controversy over the nature of the physiological impairment contributing to erectile dysfunction in diabetic men; neurogenic, endocrine and vascular factors have all been implicated but there now seems little doubt that damage to the autonomic nervous system is at least partly responsible in many cases (*British Medical Journal* 1974). To the extent that neural damage is responsible, the erectile dysfunction is irreversible. This does not necessarily imply a similarly poor prognosis for the erectile problem when this arises either from physical causes, such as transient periods of hypoglycaemia or general ill health, or from the patient's psychological reactions to diabetes. For instance, he may become anxious about his sexual performance after learning that it can be adversely affected by diabetes or following a temporary loss of erectile capacity due to the kind of transient physical causes mentioned above.

The effect of diabetes on the sexual functioning of women is at present undetermined. There is a direct conflict of evidence over whether diabetic women have more difficulty in reaching orgasm compared to non-diabetic women (Ellenberg 1977; Jensen 1981; Kolodny 1971). Furthermore, in one major study (Ellenberg 1977) it was found that diabetic women who showed clear evidence of neurological abnormality were not more sexually dysfunctional than other diabetic women who did not show signs of neural damage. The results of this study concerning the incidence of sexual dysfunction in diabetic women and the role of neuropathy as a cause of these difficulties are markedly discrepant from the equivalent findings in respect of male diabetics, and at present there are no adequate explanations for these discrepancies.

Arthritic disorders.   Some degree of sexual difficulty is reported by a high proportion of arthritic patients (Richards 1980), and this is readily understandable in the light of the impediments to sexual activity presented by the inflammation, pain, stiffness, immobility and deformity of the affected joints and connective tissues. For instance, the involvement of a woman's hip joints may prevent her from abducting and externally rotating them so that it is impossible for her to have intercourse in the male-superior position with her partner lying between her open legs. Similarly, a man whose lower spine is painful or rigid will be unable to engage in thrusting movements during intercourse. In a recent survey (Ferguson and Figley 1979) of 70 women and 30 men suffering from arthritic disorders it was found that 54 per cent of the women and 56 per cent of the men reported sexual difficulties, with pain being the major problem in both sexes.

Without underestimating the contribution of pain and the other impediments mentioned above to the sexual difficulties of arthritic people, it is likely that other physical and psychological factors may also play a part. Relevant physical factors include fatigue and the side-effects on sexual functioning of the medication used to treat arthritis, such as corticosteroids and narcotics. The stresses and limitations entailed by the disability may also evoke psychological reactions such as lowered self-esteem and depression, which may in turn have adverse effects on an arthritic person's confidence in heterosocial relationships, interest in sex, and sexual performance. His or her partner may also be inhibited by fear of inflicting pain on the arthritic person during sexual activity. Some support for the importance of such psychological reactions arises from the fact that relief from pain, for example by hip replacement, is not regularly followed by an alleviation of sexual difficulties (Richards 1980). Patients may wholly attribute these difficulties to their pain when other causal factors are also operating.

Cancer.   Many cancer patients will experience sexual difficulties as a result of physiological impairments arising either from certain side-effects of malignancy, such as anaemia, anorexia, muscle atrophy and neurological deficits; or from the methods used to treat the malignancy, such as chemotherapy, surgery and radiation. The psychological reactions of clients and their partners to the malignancy are also likely sources of sexual difficulty. For instance, this may result from feelings of anxiety, anger and depression evoked by the life-threatening nature of cancer, as well as the pain and mutilation often associated with its treatment. These physiological and psychological causal factors are illustrated in the following discussion of the sexual implications of two particular forms of cancer.

The commonest form of cancer among women is cancer of the breast, and it is most usually treated by a radical or simple mastectomy. At present, only very limited evidence is available on the sexual implications of this disability and its surgical treatment, although there are some preliminary indications of difficulties being experienced. For instance, Maquire (1978) found that mastectomy patients reported many more sexual problems than did a control group of benign-breast-tumour biopsy patients. At a four-month post-operative follow-up, 40 per cent of mastectomy patients reported difficulties, compared to 11 per cent of control group patients. At one-year follow-up, the equivalent figures were 33 per cent of the mastectomy patients, and 8 per cent of the controls. Similarly, in a retrospective pilot study of women who had undergone mastectomies an average of eight years previously, it was found that a third of them had not resumed intercourse within six months of their surgery, and that there were pre-postoperative decreases in the frequencies of the woman initiating sex, of breast stimulation, of intercourse and of female orgasm (Frank, Dornbush, Webster and Kolodny 1978).

There are some physical side-effects of breast cancer and its treatment that may adversely affect sexual functioning (Kolodny et al. 1979), but the psychological reactions of the woman and her partner are likely to be especially important sources of sexual difficulty. While these reactions are varied in their nature, intensity and duration, some of them do appear to be very prevalent (Meyerowitz 1980). For example, depression, anxiety and anger are commonly reported responses to concerns about relapse and death, mutilation by surgery and rejection by a partner. The woman's body image and self-concept are often damaged, a reaction which is readily understand-able in the light of the importance of the breast as a symbol of femininity and attractiveness in our society (Polivy 1977). There is evidence also that while most men adjust well to their partner's mastectomy, there are others who have marked difficulty in this regard (Wellisch et al. 1978).

Malignancies of the colon or rectum are among the commonest forms of cancer in men. These disabilities are often treated by the surgical excision of some part of the colon, together with the rectum. Additionally, a colostomy is constructed by bringing a remaining portion of the colon to a stoma, or opening, in the abdominal wall through which faeces are discharged, usually into a bag. Substantial proportions of men who have undergone this surgical intervention appear to suffer both erectile and ejaculatory difficulties, although more systematic evidence is lacking (Kolodny et al. 1979). In particular, retrograde ejaculation occurs in perhaps half such cases.

This problem of retrograde ejaculation is due to neural damage incurred as an inevitable side-effect of the surgical excision of the rectum. Such damage may also contribute to some of the other sexual difficulties exhibited by colostomy patients. In addition to this physiological impairment, however, there are many psychological factors that may contribute to such difficulties. These factors include the common concerns and reactions arising from the diagnosis of cancer that are discussed above, but some issues are of particular relevance to colostomy patients. They often fear that the stoma will be damaged during sexual activity. Another potential source of distress is the possibility of any leakage, noise or odour from the stoma itself. Finally, they may regard themselves as much less attractive, if not repulsive, to a partner, who it is feared may therefore reject or desert them.

Myocardial infarction.   Sexual difficulties are common among men who have experienced myocardial infarction. These difficulties include lack of sexual desire, erectile dysfunction, ejaculatory problems, lowered frequency of intercourse, and failure to resume intercourse after the heart attack (Friedman 1978; Kolodny et al. 1979; Mehta and Krop 1979; Papadopoulus 1978; Wabrek and Burchell 1980). At present, no satisfactory data are available on the sexual functioning of women who have experienced myocardinal infarction, so this discussion is focused upon male patients.

An occasional coronary patient may experience sexual difficulties as a side-effect of organic factors such as antihypertensive medication or chest pain, but in the vast majority of such patients these difficulties are psychogenic in origin. Thus a man may react with anxiety, depression, avoidance and impaired self-concept to the threats to his survival, life-style and sexual and marital relationships which he perceives as necessary consequences of his heart attack (Krop et al. 1979). In particular, coronary patients and their partners are very prone to fear a repeat infarct or sudden death during intercourse, therefore they often avoid it. Apart from the deprivation this entails, there is some evidence to suggest that rather than decreasing the risk of another infarct, such avoidance might actually increase this risk because of the stress associated with abstinence (Wabrek and Burchell 1980). There is good evidence that the typical middle-aged male patient can fulfil the physiological demands of resuming intercourse within an established marital relationship, without incurring significant risk of a repeat infarct (Hellerstein and Friedman 1970; Masur 1979; Stein 1977). Similarly, the risk of death during intercourse in such relationships is extremely low, although it appears to become appreciably higher if the man is with an extramarital partner in an unfamiliar setting, especially if he has recently eaten a heavy meal and/or consumed alcohol (Massie et al. 1969; Ueno 1963). Naturally, these general statements must be tailored to particular patients in the light of individual characteristics such as general health, exercise tolerance, severity of damage to the heart, frequency of pain or arrythmias, age and preinfarct sexual activity.

Previous learning experiences

Many early experiences are alleged to contribute to later sexual dysfunction, but the evidence for this is often extremely inadequate. Commonly, it is based upon a small and unrepresentative sample of clinical cases, without any comparable enquiry among suitably selected control subjects. Furthermore, when certain early experiences are identified in the histories of dysfunctional patients, these factors are often assumed to have contributed to the dysfunction without eliminating other possible explanations. Among the early experiences that may contribute to sexual dysfunction are an excessively restrictive upbringing and sexual victimization (Jehu 1979).

Restrictive upbringing.   Many factors indicating an excessively strict moral or religious upbringing are commonly reported in the histories of dysfunctional patients, and their sexual impairments are often alleged to have originated in these early experiences. Thus, on the basis of their extensive clinical experience, Masters and Johnson (1970) repeatedly indicted severe religious orthodoxy as an important cause of sexual dysfunction in a significant proportion of their patients.

In restrictive homes either there tends to be no discussion of sexual matters, together with censorship of television, radio and reading material, or else the children are constantly admonished about the sinfulness, immorality and dirtiness of sex. It is often described as having the sole purpose of reproduction rather than being a legitimate source of pleasure. Boys are warned that impure thoughts, masturbation, nocturnal emissions and petting or intercourse before marriage are all unacceptable as well as carrying the risks of mental or physical illness. Fear of an unmarried pregnancy is instilled into girls, who are vehemently cautioned about the dangers of sexual advances from men and the importance of preserving virginity until marriage. Even then, intercourse is to be regarded as a painful and nasty wifely duty and not something to be enjoyed. In childhood, any manifestation of sexual interest or exploration is viewed as disgusting or immoral, and discovery entails humiliation, disapproval and punishment. Later, a young person's social activities have to be approved and scrutinized to prevent any sexual involvement arising and even engaged couples may have virtually no physical contact with each other before marriage.

The alleged outcome of such a restrictive upbringing is a young adult who is grossly lacking accurate sexual knowledge and deeply imbued with negative sexual attitudes. The long association of fear, guilt and disgust with sexuality may not be easily reversible on marriage; instead it may persist and overgeneralize so that what should be an enjoyable and socially valued sexual relationship is impaired by some form of dysfunction. However, while the clinical literature is persuasive about the occurrence of such adverse effects in some individuals, these are not inevitable consequences of an excessively restrictive upbringing.

Sexual victimization.   The term 'sexual victimization' is used to refer to sexual experiences between juveniles and older persons that are exploitive because of the juvenile's age, lack of sexual sophistication, or relationship to the older person (Finkelhor 1979). The experiences covered range from exhibitionistic display of the offender's genitals through to sexual intercourse. They may or may not involve the use of force, and it is assumed that a juvenile is not competent to give an informed consent to the sexual activity. On the basis of a review of the major surveys Herman concludes that their results are remarkably consistent in showing that 'one fifth to one third of all women reported that they had had some sort of childhood sexual encounter with an adult male. Beween four and twelve per cent of all women reported a sexual experience with a relative, and one woman in a hundred reported a sexual experience with her father or stepfather' (1981, p. 12). All the surveys on which this conclusion is based were conducted in the United States, and there is no comparable information available in respect of other countries.

Sexual dysfunction appears to be common among women who were sexually victimized in childhood or adolescence. In a questionnaire study of volunteers from the general population in the United States, Glasner (1980) found that sexual dysfunction in adulthood was experienced by 65 per cent of 28 women who were sexually molested in childhood, while the comparable proportion for 15 unmolested women was 28 per cent. This difference is significant at the 1 per cent level. Conversely, in a study of 240 women who were seeking counselling for sexual dysfunctions (Baisden and Baisden 1979) it was found that 90 per cent reported sexual encounters before they were 18 years old with males who were at least four years older.

In a small group of 12 incest victims who volunteered for a research study, a sexual phobia was reported by 75 per cent of the victims (Becker et al. 1982). Among the features of lovemaking that may evoke such phobic reactions is the occurrence of 'flashbacks' to the victimization experience. If something happens during the current encounter that reminds the woman of the traumatic incidents, then she may have a vivid memory or image of them which is very disturbing to her. Consequently, her response is more appropriate to the past incidents than to the present activity with a partner whom she may love very much. Another common disturbing feature is any element of being coerced, used or controlled by the current partner. This is also liable to recapitulate the earlier victimization experience and to evoke aversive reactions. For some victims, arousal is possible providing that they initiate and remain fully in control of the lovemaking. Finally, some victims experience phobic reactions to the slightest hint of pleasure arising in a sexual encounter. Possibly, any such pleasure during the earlier victimization was associated with considerable guilt and distress, so that it has become threatening to the victim.

In the same study (Becker et al. 1982), 33 per cent of the victims were reported to be exhibiting a lack of sexual motivation. There are a number of possible causes for such impaired motivation in victims, including poor physical health, depression, conflict between the partners, fear of intimacy or romantic success, and the avoidance of sex because it is a painful, distressing or unsatisfying experience for the woman (Jehu 1979; Kaplan 1979). Some of these possible causes have been covered already, and the factors of depression and relationship difficulties are discussed next.

Loss of interest in sex is a well-recognized symptom of depression, and this disorder is very commonly reported among victims. For example, in a study of 40 father–daughter incest victims in psychotherapy, 60 per cent exhibited major depressive symptoms (Herman 1981). This incidence is not surprising in view of the prevalence of guilt and low self-esteem among victims. Their guilt may be attributed to three factors. First, the child victim was often pressured to keep the molestation secret, and this may have conveyed the idea that what happened was something that she should be ashamed of and not reveal to others. Second, guilt may arise from the experience of physical pleasure during the molestation, despite its repugnance to the victim. Third, she may blame herself for allowing the molestation to continue over an extended period of time. Help to end it may not have been sought because of the pressure for secrecy, fear of not being believed, or reluctance to cause discord or disintegration in the family. The victim may feel, however, that she must have contributed in some way to the continuance of the molestation, perhaps by being seductive, and that there must have been something more she could have done to stop it. Closely related to feelings of guilt is the low self-esteem of many victims; they often regard themselves as inferior or worthless compared to other people. For instance, among Herman's father–daughter incest victims, 60 per cent had a predominantly negative self-image. She comments that 'Many women felt that what set them apart from others was their own evilness. With depressing regularity, these women referred to themselves as bitches, witches, and whores. The incest secret formed the core of their identity' (Herman 1981, p. 97).

Difficulties in relationships with partners are another common cause of lack of sexual motivation, and a variety of such difficulties are reported among victims. They tend to have numerous sexual relationships of a transient and casual nature. For instance, Tsai et al. (1979) studied three groups, each consisting of 30 women: (1) a clinical group comprising women currently seeking therapy for problems associated with childhood molestation. In this group 43 per cent of the women reported having 15 or more consensual sexual partners. The equivalent proportions were (2) 17 per cent in a non-clinical group consisting of women who had been molested as children but who had never sought therapy, and (3) 9 per cent in a control group of women who had never been molested and who were matched to the non-clinical group. Some victims are also described as having a tendency to sexualize all their relationships. There are several possible reasons for this tendency. The victims may not be able to distinguish sex and affection because of the confusion of parental love and sexuality in childhood. They may have learned to use sex as an effective means of getting favours, and some may have a compulsive need for sex as proof of being loved and of being an adequate woman. Whatever the reason, the result is often a constant series of brief, unsatisfying, hurtful and damaging relationships, which only serve to increase the victim's distrust of other people.

A related issue is the tendency of victims to engage repeatedly in relationships with apparently unsuitable partners who often misuse the women. Thus, among Meiselman's (1978) psychotherapy patients, 42 per cent of 26 father–daughter incest victims were said by their therapists to be 'masochistic', meaning that the women sought out and passively tolerated relationships in which they were mistreated. Terms such as 'doormat', 'punching bag', and 'dish rag', were often used to describe these women. On the basis of their experience in running therapy groups for women who were sexually molested as children, Tsai and Wagner (1978) also note the seeming compulsion of some of these victims to get involved with unworthy men, who not infrequently resemble the molester. Several speculations have been advanced to account for this tendency towards ill-matched and punishing relationships. The victim's self-esteem is often so low that she always selects partners beneath her and who do not embody high standards which she feels she cannot live up to. She may never have learned the skills required to protect herself and assert her rights in a relationship, and she may have acquired only very limited expectations of what she might reasonably demand from a partner. Any such deficiencies in skills and expectations could stem from the victim's modelling of her mother's passive role in relation to a dominant father, a situation that is typical of many incestuous families (Herman 1981; Meiselman 1978).

Finally, some victims have difficulty in maintaining a longer-term relationship with a man, because of the increasing closeness and intimacy that this involves. Therefore they tend to have a series of shorter-term, more superficial relationships. One reason for such difficulties in victims is that the more intimate a relationship becomes the greater the likelihood that it will recapitulate the earlier traumatic experiences with an offender who was emotionally close to the victim. Another possible reason is a profound distrust of intimate relationships arising from having being exploited by the offender and inadequately protected by the mother.

In addition to sexual phobias and lack of motivation, some victims suffer from impairments of arousal. In the Becker et al. (1982) study, 42 per cent of the 12 incest victims were reported to have such impairments. One reason for them is the evocation during lovemaking of the phobic reactions discussed above. It is well known that excessive anxiety can disrupt arousal, and this is also likely to be terminated by the occurrence of physiological symptoms such as nausea, retching and vomiting. Additionally, those aspects of lovemaking that are disturbing will be physically avoided; consequently effective sexual stimulation may not be received.

Whether as a result of impaired arousal or for other reasons, some victims experience difficulty in reaching climax during their current sexual encounters. Thus 42 per cent of the 12 incest victims studied by Becker et al. (1982) exhibited primary or secondary nonorgasmia. In contrast, there are some victims who can reach climax quite easily, even though they may not be sexually motivated or aroused. The orgasm seems to come 'out of the blue'. Often these victims can only climax during intercourse and not in response to other stimulation by a partner. In some cases, the orgasm is not an enjoyable or satisfying experience. It is almost as if the victim has acquired the response at an early age, but in traumatic circumstances so that it has never been associated with pleasure.

In the case of some victimized women there is evidence to suggest that their sexual relationships tend to be characterized by dissatisfaction as well as other dysfunctions. Thus, in the study by Tsai et al. (1979), (1) the clinical group of women currently seeking therapy for problems associated with childhood molestation reported significantly less satisfaction than either (2) the non-clinical group of women who had been molested but had never sought therapy, or (3) the control group of women who had never been molested. The additional findings that the non-clinical molested group and the control unmolested group did not differ in sexual satisfaction highlights the fact that dissatisfaction is not universal among molested women. When it is present, it may be a consequence of other sexual dysfunctions or of the depressive reactions or relationship difficulties outlined above.

Current conditions

Although sexually dysfunctional responses may have been acquired during previous learning experiences, these responses are initiated and maintained by certain current conditions (Jehu 1979). For example, a sexual assault in the past may have led to the irrational belief that intercourse is certain to be a painful or unpleasant experience; consequently the current prospect of sex initiates anxiety and avoidance reactions. Likewise, if an incident of sexual dysfunction is followed by a humiliating, critical or angry reaction from the partner, then this is likely to increase performance anxiety and to maintain the dysfunction in future encounters. Among the contemporary conditions that may initiate and maintain inadequate sexual responses in this way are psychological stress, and discord between the partners.

Psychological stress.   Many forms of psychological stress may contribute to sexual dysfunction. Certain aspects of sexual anatomy or activity may be stressful for some individuals, for example, the threat of penile penetration for a woman suffering from vaginismus. Some patients anticipate that sex will harm them in some way, such as the post-coronary patient and his partner who fear that a relapse or death may occur during intercourse. Others anticipate failure in sexual encounters, including the possibility of ejaculating prematurely or of not reaching orgasm. There are also stressful situations arising from contraventions of an individual's moral or religious standards. Thus people whose standards include a complete prohibition on intercourse before marriage may be sexually unresponsive if they attempt to engage in this. Moreover, it is important to recognize that stresses of a non-sexual nature can also impair sexual functioning. A person who is worried about loss of a job or a sick relative may experience some repercussions in the area of sexual relationships.

Any of these stresses may evoke reactions that impair sexual responses. Among these reactions are negative emotions such as anxiety, depression and anger. For instance, it is commonly held that sexual arousal is especially vulnerable to disruption by anxiety concerning sexual performance. The physical avoidance of stressful sexual events is another common reaction, so that sexual encounters tend to be progressively reduced by couples for whom they have become distressing. Cognitive avoidance may also occur, so that erotic thoughts and feelings that are disturbing are excluded from the person's awareness. Another cognitive reaction to stress is the monitoring or 'spectatoring' of sexual performance. For instance, a man who anticipates erectile failure is prone to observe himself to see if he is getting an erection, how full it is becoming, and whether or not he is losing it. This puts him in the role of a spectator rather than a participant in his sexual encounters, and this detachment, together with the distraction of the cognitive monitoring process, results in his being cut off from effective sexual stimulation.

Partner discord.   Discord between the partners is another current condition that often contributes to sexual inadequacy. There are certain patterns of discord that seem to be quite commonly implicated. One of these is the rejection of a partner who is perceived as unattractive or disliked, and whose sexual approaches therefore tend to be insufficiently stimulating, and annoying rather than arousing. Another pattern is competition between the partners to dominate the relationship, so that power struggles occur which sometimes impair sexual functioning in specific ways. For example, a wife may not respond or reach orgasm because this would represent submission to her husband, or a man may ejaculate before intromission to avoid compliance with his wife's demand for intercourse. Any insecurity arising from a threat of criticism or desertion by the partner can also impair sexual functioning. Performance anxiety is likely to be compounded if failure is expected to be met with criticism or desertion rather than understanding, and individuals who fear such consequences may be so concerned to ensure their partner's sexual pleasure that they completely subordinate their own satisfaction. Similarly, any friction or hostility between partners, from whatever cause, may well disrupt their sexual relationship. It is difficult for individuals to respond sexually with a partner towards whom they are experiencing considerable feelings of anger, and hostility may be expressed not only by verbal abuse and physical assault, but also in quite subtle ways that damage the sexual relationship. When lovemaking is anticipated, it may be prevented or spoiled by one of the partners provoking a quarrel. Sexual approaches may be made only at times when intercourse is impracticable or not desired by the other partner; alternatively a hostile recipient may respond consistently with apathy, complaints of fatigue or illness, or outright refusal. Some individuals persist in presenting themselves in a physically unattractive manner, or in behaving in annoying ways, so that it is difficult for their partner to respond sexually to them. For instance, a wife may not become aroused if her husband is unwashed, smells of alcohol, or uses foul language. Finally, during sexual encounters, one partner may withhold pleasurable and effective stimulation from the other, and dysfunctions such as premature ejaculation can serve to frustrate a spouse's satisfaction.

Little empirical work has been done on the relationship between partner discord and sexual dysfunction but one exception is a study by Frank et al. (1979). They demonstrated an association between marital role strain and sexual dissatisfaction. Eighty non-patient couples, 50 marital-therapy couples and 50 sex-therapy couples completed an extensive self-report questionnaire concerning their marital relationships. Questions were included on the actual and ideal roles of each spouse in (1) caring for the home, cooking and shopping, (2) making major family decisions, (3) having a career, (4) being sexually faithful, (5) having responsibility for the care of the children, (6) being sexually aggressive, (7) having interests and activities that do not include one's spouse, and (8) determining how money is spent. The degree of discrepancy between the actual and ideal roles was taken as an index of marital role strain, and this was found to correlate positively with responses indicating sexual dissatisfaction in all three groups. The investigators comment that positive feelings about oneself are a necessary precondition for an intimate relationship with another person. Since one aspect of how one evaluates oneself is the degree to which one is fulfilling the roles one wants to fulfil, it is understandable that individuals who are dissatisfied with the role assignments in their marriages may also experience sexual dissatisfaction.

In the previous section on the incidence of sexual inadequacy, it was noted that many couples do not judge an impairment of sexual performance to be detrimental to their sexual relationship. One factor that influences such judgements is the quality of the overall interaction between the partners. Thus, in the study by Frank, Anderson and Rubenstein (1978), the researchers concluded that it was not the absolute level of sexual functioning but the 'affective tone' of the marriage which determined a couple's degree of sexual satisfaction. In another study (Chesney et al. 1981) a group of couples who had attended a sex therapy clinic was compared with a demographically similar group of couples who had not sought therapy. While these couples had experienced some of the same sexual problems as those who had attended for treatment, the comparison couples were able to communicate effectively and to solve these problems constructively, whereas the treatment couples could not handle their sexual problems on their own. Thus the most important factor in determining sexual satisfaction appeared to be not the occurrence of sexual problems but how a couple perceived and reacted to these problems.

TREATMENT OF SEXUAL INADEQUACY

Many of the interventions used in the treatment of sexual inadequacy are listed below under subheadings indicating the major, though not the exclusive, purpose of each procedure. These are described fully elsewhere (Jehu 1979), and their use is illustrated below in the context of two intervention packages: (1) for non-partnered men who are experiencing erectile dysfunction, and (2) for women who were sexually victimized in childhood or adolescence.

General therapeutic conditions

Therapeutic relationship
Causal explanation
Prognostic expectancy

Sexual assignments

General pleasuring
Genital stimulation
Sexual intercourse

Specific procedures

Provision of information
Verbal
Bibliographical
Audio-visual

Modification of attitudes and beliefs
Sanctioning
Self disclosure

Role-playing
Cognitive restructuring

Reduction of stress
Relaxation training
Desensitization
Flooding
Guided imagery
Thought stopping
Modelling
Vaginal dilatation
Sexual enhancement
Classical conditioning
Biofeedback
Hypnosis
Exposure to erotic material
Pelvic muscle exercises — *Kegel exercises*
Drugs/hormones
Prosthetic/mechanical aids — *Toys*
Relationship enhancement
Increasing positive exchanges
Communication training
Problem-solving training
Assertiveness training
Heterosocial skills training

Treatment of non-partnered men experiencing erectile dysfunction

Masters and Johnson (1970) insist that the treatment of sexual dysfunction must be conjoint, and their emphasis on the necessary involvement of two willing and co-operative partners has been followed by many other therapists who will only accept couples as clients. This denies treatment to a significant number of dysfunctional individuals at least until they are able to establish a relationship with a partner who is willing to participate and co-operate in a treatment programme. Unfortunately, the establishment of such a relationship is in itself a problem for many individual clients, for they have often experienced difficulty and distress in earlier sexual encounters which has caused them to avoid even social contacts with members of the opposite sex in case these should lead on to sexual situations where their inadequacy will be exposed. Thus a vicious circle develops in which these individuals cannot obtain treatment for sexual dysfunction because they do not have a regular partner, and they cannot obtain such a partner because of their sexual dysfunction. Therefore, despite the very real difficulties involved, it does seem important to try to find ways of helping dysfunctional clients who do not have a regular partner. One such way is the 'psychoeducational' approach (Lobitz and Baker 1979; Price et al. 1981; Reynolds et al. 1981; Zilbergeld 1975, 1978, 1980) which in our own clinic comprises the following components.

Information is provided on topics such as male and female sexual anatomy and responses, and changes in sexual response during the ageing process.

There is a strong emphasis on the modification of attitudes and beliefs that might be contributing to the erectile dysfunction. These include views that (1) it is performance rather than enjoyment that counts in sex, (2) women value performance more than the gentle expression of physical affection and caring, (3) a man must take charge of and orchestrate sex, (4) all physical contact must lead to sex, (5) sex equals intercourse, (6) sex requires an erection, and (7) that a man always wants and is always ready to have sex (Zilbergeld 1978). In fact, men are not sex machines; on the contrary they can only respond when the conditions are appropriate for them.

It follows that another component in the programme is the identification of the conditions that the patient requires for good sex. These are likely to include (1) feelings of sexual attraction and excitement towards the partner, (2) an absence of emotional or physical blocks to sexual response, such as guilt, anger, anxiety, fatigue or alcohol, (3) effective sexual stimulation, and (4) an appropriate setting, providing privacy, warmth and comfort.

The next component in the programme is social skills training to help the patient to establish a relationship with a partner and to obtain the conditions he needs for good sex. This training includes (1) initiating contact with women, (2) coping with rejection, (3) receiving and sending messages, (4) starting conversations, (5) assertiveness and setting limits, (6) initiating dates, (7) initiating touching with a partner, (8) disclosing erectile difficulties to a partner, and (9) obtaining a partner's collaboration in therapeutic sexual assignments.

These assignments are another component; they are undertaken by the patient at home between therapeutic sessions. They include (1) a ban on intercourse throughout the programme, (2) self-exploration and pleasuring of the patient's own body, (3) masturbation with focus on sensations, (4) deliberately losing and regaining erections during masturbation, (5) masturbating to fantasies of sex with a partner, including losing and regaining erections or having no erection, (6) techniques to improve ejaculatory control, and (7) sensate focus and non-demand intercourse with a partner (see below).

As a final component in the programme, patients are asked to design a plan for maintaining any gains they have made during treatment. These plans include (1) the thoughts and/or actions that have contributed to the patient's problems, (2) what he has learned in the programme, (3) what difficulties he anticipates following treatment, and (4) some solutions to these difficulties.

All these components are covered in various ways in the programme, including (1) didactic presentations by the therapist, (2) films, (3) prescribed readings, (4) role-playing, (5) group discussion, if therapy is in a group format, and (6) homework assignments of a sexual or social skill nature.

Treatment of women who were sexually victimized in childhood or adolescence

In our clinic we are developing a treatment package that is individually tailored to suit particular women victims and their partners. Within the broad context of a good therapeutic relationship and an expectation of receiving effective help, the package comprises several more specific modules.

Relaxation training. The first of these is often relaxation training, which is given to help the patient to cope with the anxiety that is frequently evoked by having to explore and confront the victimization experience.

Cognitive restructuring. It does seem necessary for patients to deal with the victimization experience before the specific treatment of sexual dysfunction can be implemented successfully. For this reason, a second module in the package is often the cognitive restructuring of the false beliefs that contribute to a patient's guilt, low self-esteem and depression. The following procedures are among those used in this task.

Factual data are provided to correct any inaccurate information that may be contributing to a patient's false beliefs. For example, feelings of difference and alienation from other people may be based upon the belief that sexual victimization is extremely rare in childhood, and accurate information about its prevalence may serve to modify the false belief and to alleviate the associated negative feelings.

The patient's logic is reviewed to determine whether the evidence supports the conclusion she has drawn. For instance, 'No man can be trusted' is an over-generalization, and an arbitrary inference is being drawn by a patient who concludes that 'I must have been to blame because I was removed from home.'

When predicting the direst consequences for herself a patient may not utilize all the information available. Thus 'I will never be able to lead a normal life, the damage is permanent' ignores the fact that some victims do succeed in making a satisfactory adjustment or recover. The therapist can widen the patient's perspective in this respect and thus 'decatastrophize' her thinking.

'Distancing', or vicarious exposure to the victimization of other women, may enable the patient to take a more objective view of her own experience. For example, if she does not blame another woman for being victimized, she may be less inclined to blame herself.

'Decentring' refers to the process of having a patient challenge the basic belief that she was the focal point of the victimization. For instance, 'I must have been seductive' might be challenged by the patient looking at the experience from the offender's perspective and recognizing that his insistence on secrecy is a clear indication of his awareness that his behaviour is unacceptable and of his own responsibility for the transgression.

The procedure of 'reattribution' follows logically from distancing and decentring and it is designed to correct a patient's tendency to assume total responsibility for the victimization and not to take into account factors that were beyond her control. These might include her immaturity and lack of power compared to the offender.

Interpersonal skills training. The relationship difficulties exhibited by many victims are noted in the earlier section on previous learning experiences. Some of these patients will need treatment aimed specifically at improving their capacity to establish and/or maintain satisfying personal relationships. This is particularly important when the cognitive structuring component is accompanied by an exacerbation of conflict between a victim and her partner. Such deterioration is quite understandable in the light of the changes that may have occurred in the victim, so that she is no longer prepared to tolerate an ill-matched or oppressive relationship. Consequently, the respective roles of the partners and the implicit or explicit rules governing their relationship need to be renegotiated between them. In such circumstances, an interpersonal skills module is implemented to enhance the couple's abilities to communicate with each other and to collaborate in the resolution of conflicts.

Basic communication skills are required to be an effective speaker and listener. Training in effective speaking emphasized three features: (1) being direct, speaking for oneself, (2) being emotionally expressive about one's feelings, and (3) being specific about the particular events that evoke these feelings. Effective listening requires the skills of summarizing, reflecting and validating, in order to demonstrate to a speaker that one has heard and understood what has been said.

Training in conflict resolution teaches a couple (1) to define their conflicts, (2) to generate possible solutions, (3) to evaluate these solutions, and (4) to negotiate agreements embodying particular solutions.

When a patient's false beliefs concerning the victimization have been cognitively restructured and any partner discord alleviated, then it is feasible to implement a module for the specific treatment of sexual inadequacy.

Specific procedures for sexual inadequacy. This module may include any of the procedures listed on pp. 150-1 and they are exemplified here by a programme of sexual assignments (Heiman et al. 1976) that is often useful in the treatment of a range of dysfunctions including sexual phobias, lack of motivation, difficulties in arousal, and problems in reaching orgasm.

The general aim in using this programme with victimized women is to reduce the disturbing nature of those features of sexual activity that are stressful for them. This is done by gradually exposing the client to these stressful features while she remains in a non-anxious state:

1. Many victimized women regard their genitals particularly as an unfamiliar, isolated, bad or dirty part of their body. The first step in the programme may be especially useful in helping such clients to become more aware, comfortable and positive towards their bodies as a whole and their genitals specifically. The client is asked to examine her nude body and to appreciate its attractive features. Additionally, it is recommended that she use a handmirror to explore her genitals and to identify the various parts with the aid of a diagram.

2. The slightest sign of sexual pleasure may evoke phobic reactions in some victimized women and the next step in the programme is useful in beginning the process of helping these clients to tolerate and enjoy such pleasurable feelings. The client is asked to explore her genitals tactually, with the aim of locating sensitive areas that are pleasurable to touch. She is not given any expectation of sexual arousal at this stage.

3. The process of accepting and enjoying sexual pleasure is continued in this and the following steps. In step 3 it is suggested that the client stimulate manually those sensitive areas that she located in the previous step.

4. In step 4 the client is asked to increase the intensity and duration of the manual stimulation. She may also be encouraged to explore the use of erotic materials and fantasies to extend and enhance her capacity for arousal. In the cases of clients who fear loss of control during orgasm, it may be helpful if they role-play their conception of the orgastic response in an exaggerated manner. The simulation of anticipated reactions such as involuntary screaming or gross muscular movements may alleviate their stressfulness and sometimes results in the occurrence of a real orgasm during the role-play.

5. Again, particularly in the cases of those women who have difficulty in climaxing, the next step may be to repeat the previous step using a vibrator instead of manual stimulation, or some combination of the two.

6. From here on, the subsequent steps in the programme involve both partners. Accordingly, it is important to emphasize some general points concerning partner-related activities for victimized women. First, because of their vulnerability to adverse reactions to any feelings of coercion or exploitation, they should be given control of partner-related activities,

includig their initiation and duration. Second, if the woman experiences flashbacks to the victimization that adversely affect her current responses with her partner, then she should let him know that she is flashing, so that he can understand what is happening and not blame her or himself. Third, the woman may experience strong feelings of anger during current activities with her partner that he has done nothing to evoke. Again, these feelings should be recognized as arising from the past rather than the present circumstances.

Often the first partner-related activity to be prescribed in the programme is general pleasuring or sensate focus. Briefly, this means that the partners take it in turns to explore the sensual pleasures of touching and caressing each other's bodies with tenderness and affection. At this stage the breast and genital areas are excluded, but otherwise the couple are left to discover for themselves where and how they like to be touched and to communicate these preferences to each other. One reason for this assignment is the reduction of avoidance reactions. Quite often victimized women and their partners have been avoiding any physical expression of affection as well as sexual foreplay in case these should involve or lead on to activities that are very stressful for the woman. This threat is removed by the therapeutically negotiated limits to general pleasuring, and the associated avoidance reactions are correspondingly alleviated.

7. Once couples are able to respond positively to general pleasuring, then they can move on to the next step of including the breast and genital areas. It is very important to stress that this genital pleasuring is a gradual extension of general pleasuring, which is not superseded by the incorporation of the genitals. At this stage, the woman will communicate to her husband what she has learned earlier about the most effective means of stimulation for her, and it is important that he follows her guidance concerning her preferences.

8. When the woman is anxiety-free and aroused during general and genital pleasuring the couple might move on to the next step of 'non-demand coitus'. She adopts the female superior position and inserts her partner's penis into her vagina. Initially, she simply contains the penis while experiencing the sensations and feelings this evokes. These may be enhanced by the woman contracting her vaginal muscles on the penis, and subsequently, as her arousal mounts, by moving slowly up and down and experimenting with other different movements. She is told to concentrate on her own sensations and pleasure without worrying about her partner's gratification at this stage. If he becomes too aroused, then movement can be stopped for a while, and he can either remain inside his partner or withdraw until the excitement subsides. Such withdrawal and reinsertion is often a teasing and arousing experience for the woman, and her arousal may also be maintained by clitoral stimulation while penile movement is suspended. This assignment continues for as long

as the woman wishes, at which point her partner might reach climax either intravaginally or by manual or oral stimulation as long as this is not stressful for the woman. An important feature of this assignment for the victimized woman is that it provides an opportunity for her to explore and appreciate the vaginal sensations and erotic feelings evoked by the man's penis, without having to subordinate her own preferences and pleasure to those of her partner.

9. The final step is for the couple to proceed to full intercourse, while either the woman or her partner concurrently stimulates the woman's genitals either manually or with a vibrator. If the couple so desire, this concurrent stimulation can gradually be faded out by stopping when the woman is near climax. Probably the majority of women, however, do require some more direct stimulation than that provided by penile movement alone in order to reach climax on many occasions.

SUMMARY

Sexual functioning may be judged to be inadequate because it is accompanied by pain, vaginal spasm or anxiety, or because of some impairment of sexual motivation, arousal, climax or satisfaction. Such judgements of inadequacy are in part subjective, and more than one problem may co-exist in the same individual. The few surveys that have been conducted do not provide any reasonably precise estimate of the incidence of sexual inadequacy in general populations, but they do indicate that impairments of sexual performance are not necessarily accompanied by sexual dissatisfaction.

The causes of sexual inadequacy can be conceptualized in the general categories of organic factors, previous learning experiences and current conditions, operating singly or in combination in particular cases. The relevant organic factors include certain disease conditions, together with the side-effects of some types of medication or surgery. They may have an adverse effect on sexual functioning through physiological or psychological mechanisms. Among the previous learning experiences and current conditions, operating singly or in combination in particular cases. The relevant organic factors include certain diseases conditions, together with the side-effects of some types of medication or surgery. They may have an adverse effect on sexual functioning through physiological or psychological mechanisms. Among the previous learning experiences that are alleged to contribute to sexual inadequacy are an excessively restrictive upbringing and sexual victimization in childhood or adolescence. Although such previous experiences may have resulted in the acquisition of sexually inadequate responses, the performance of these responses is initiated and maintained by current conditions which include various psychological stresses and reactions, together with discord in the overall relationship between the partners.

Individualized treatment programmes for sexual inadequacy are constituted from a range of components including sexual assignments undertaken by patients in the privacy of their own homes, and various specific procedures designed to provide information, modify attitudes and beliefs, reduce stress, promote sexual stimulation and responses, and enhance overall relationships.

REFERENCES

Baisden, M. J., and Baisden, J. R. (1979). A profile of women who seek counseling for sexual dysfunction. *American Journal of Family Therapy*, 7, 68–76.

Barnett, D. M. (1973). Diabetic impotence unrelated to treatment. *Hospital Tribune*, 8 Oct. 1973.

Becker, J. V., Skinner, L. J., Abel, G. G., and Treacy, E. C. (1982). Incidence and types of sexual dysfunctions in rape and incest victims. *Journal of Sex and Marital Therapy*, 8, 65–74.

Bregman, S. (1975). *Sexuality and the Spinal Cord Injured Woman*. Minneapolis: Sister Kenney Institute.

Bregman, S. (1978). Sexual adjustment of spinal cord injured women. *Sexuality and Disability*, 1, 85–92.

British Medical Journal (1974). Editorial, Diabetic autonomic neuropathy. 2, 2–3.

Chesney, A. P., Blakeney, P. E., Cole, C. M., and Chan, F. A. (1981). A comparison of couples who have sought sex therapy with couples who have not. *Journal of Sex and Marital Therapy*, 7, 131–40.

Ellenberg, M. (1977). Sexual aspects of the female diabetic. *The Mount Sinai Journal of Medicine*, 44, 495–500.

Ferguson, K., and Figley, B. (1979). Sexuality and rheumatic disease: a study. *Sexuality and Disability*, 2, 130–8.

Finkelhor, D. (1979). *Sexually Victimized Children*. New York: Free Press.

Frank, D., Dornbush, R. L., Webster, S. K., and Kolodny, R. C. (1978). Mastectomy and sexual behavior: a pilot study. *Sexuality and Disability*, 1, 16–26.

Frank E., Anderson, C., and Rubenstein, D. (1978). Frequency of sexual dysfunction in 'normal' couples. *New England Journal of Medicine*, 299, 111–15.

Frank, E., Anderson, C., and Rubenstein, D. (1979). Marital role strain and sexual satisfaction. *Journal of Consulting and Clinical Psychology*, 47, 1096–1103.

Friedman, J. M. (1978). Sexual adjustment of the postcoronary male. In J. Lo Piccolo and L. Lo Piccolo (eds), *Handbook of Sex Therapy*, New York: Plenum.

Glasner, A. J. (1980). The incidence of adult sexual dysfunction in people who were sexually molested in childhood. (Doctoral dissertation, United States International University.) *Dissertation Abstracts International*, 41, 3159–B (University Microfilms No. 8103385).

Heiman, J., Lo Piccolo, L., and Lo Piccolo, J. (1976). *Becoming Orgasmic: A Sexual Growth Program for Women*. Englewood Cliffs, NJ: Prentice-Hall.

Hellerstein, J., and Friedman, E. J. (1970). Sexual activity and the postcoronary patient.

Archives of Internal Medicine, 125, 987–99.

Herman, J. L. (1981). *Father-Daughter Incest*. Cambridge, Mass: Harvard University Press.

Higgins, G. E. (1979). Sexual response in spinal cord injured adults: a review on the literature. *Archives of Sexual Behavior*, 8, 173–93.

Hudson, W. W., Harrison, D. F., and Crosscup, P. C. (1981). A short-form scale to measure sexual discord in dyadic relationships. *Journal of Sex Research*, 17, 157–74.

Jehu, D. (1979). *Sexual Dysfunction: A Behavioural Approach to Causation, Assessment, and Treatment*, Chichester: Wiley.

Jehu, D. (in press). Clinical practice in behavioral treatment for sexual dysfunction: programs and procedures, In C. M. Franks and C. Diament (eds), *New Developments in Practical Behavior Therapy*, New York: Haworth.

Jensen, S. B. (1981). Diabetic sexual dysfunction: a comparative study of 160 insulin treated diabetic men and women and an age-matched control group. *Archives of Sexual Behaviour*, 10, 493–504.

Kaplan, H. S. (1974). *The New Sex Therapy: Active Treatment of Sexual Dysfunctions*, New York: Brunner/Mazel.

Kaplan, H. S. (1979). *Disorders of Sexual Desire: and Other New Concepts and Techniques in Sex Therapy* New York: Brunner/Mazel.

Kolodny, R. C. (1971). Sexual dysfunction in diabetic females. *Diabetes*, 20, 557–9.

Kolodny, R. C. (1981). Evaluating sex therapy: process and outcome at the Masters & Johnson Institute. *Journal of Sex Research*, 17, 301–18.

Kolodny, R. C., Masters, W. H., and Johnson, V. E. (1979). *Textbook of Sexual Medicine*, Boston: Little, Brown.

Krop, H., Hall., and Mehta, J. (1979). Sexual concerns after myocardial infarction. *Sexuality and Disability*, 2, 91–7.

Leiblum, S. R., and Pervin, L. A. (eds) (1980). *Principles and Practice of Sex Therapy*, New York: Plenum.

Lobitz, W. C., and Baker, E. L. (1979). Group treatment of single males with erectile dysfunction. *Archives of Sexual Behaviour*, 8, 127–38.

Lo Piccolo, J., and Lo Piccolo, L. (eds) (1978). *Handbook of Sex Therapy*, New York: Plenum.

Maguire, P. (1978). Psychiatric problems after mastectomy. In P. C. Brand and P. A. van Keep (eds), *Breast Cancer: Psychological Aspects of Early Detection and Treatment*. Baltimore, Md: University Park Press.

Massie, E., Rose, E., Rupp, J., and Whelton, R. (1969). Sudden death during coitus – fact or fiction? *Medical Aspects of Human Sexuality*, 3, 22–6.

Masters, W. H., and Johnson, V. E. (1970). *Human Sexual Inadequacy*, Boston: Little, Brown.

Masur, R. T. (1979). Resumption of sexual activity following myocardial infarction. *Sexuality and Disability*, 2, 115–21.

Meiselman, K. C. (1978). *Incest: A Psychological Study of Causes and Effects with Treatment Recommendations*, San Francisco: Jossey-Bass.

Meyerowitz, B. E. (1980). Psychosocial correlates of breast cancer and its treatments. *Psychological Bulletin*, 87, 108–31.

Mills, K. H., and Kilmann, P. R. (1982). Group treatment of sexual dysfunctions: a methodological review of the outcome literature. *Journal of Sex and Marital Therapy*, 8, 259–96.

Mooney, T. O., Cole, T. M., and Chilgen, R. A. (1975). *Sexual Options for Paraplegics and Quadriplegics*, Boston: Little, Brown.

Nettelbladt, P., and Uddenberg, N. (1979). Sexual dysfunction and sexual satisfaction in 58 married Swedish men. *Journal of Psychosomatic Research*, 23, 141–7.

Papadopoulos, C. (1978). A survey of sexual activity after myocardial infarction, *Cardiovascular Medicine*, 3, 821–6.

Perlman, S. D., and Abramson, P. R. (1982). Sexual satisfaction among married and cohabiting individuals. *Journal of Consulting and Clinical Psychology*, 50, 458–60.

Polivy, J. (1977). Psychological effects of mastectomy on a woman's feminine self-concept. *Journal of Nervous and Mental Disease*, 164, 77–87.

Price, S. C., Reynolds, B. S., Cohen, B. D., Anderson, A. J., and Schochet, B. V. (1981). Group treatment of erectile dysfunction for men without partners: a controlled evaluation. *Archives of Sexual Behavior*, 10, 253–68.

Rachman, S. J., and Wilson, G. T. (1980). *The Effects of Psychological Therapy* (2nd edn), Oxford: Pergamon.

Reynolds, B. S., Cohen, B. D., Schochet, B. V., Price, S. C., and Anderson, A. J. (1981). Dating skills training in the group treatment of erectile dysfunction for men without partners. *Journal of Sex and Marital Therapy*, 7, 184–94.

Richards, J. S. (1980). Sex and arthritis, *Sexuality and Disability*, 3, 97–104.

Rubin, A., and Babbott, D. (1958). Impotence and diabetes mellitus. *Journal of the American Medical Association*, 168, 498–500.

Schover, L. R., Friedman, J. M., Weiler, S. J., Heiman, J. R., and Lo Piccolo, J. (1982). Multi-axial problem-oriented system for sexual dysfunctions: an alternative to DSM-III. *Archives of General Psychiatry*, 39. 614–19.

Stein, R. A. (1977). The effect of exercise training on heart rate during coitus in the post-myocardial patient. *Circulation*, 55, 738–40.

Tsai, M., Feldman-Summers, S., and Edgar, M., (1979). Childhood molestation: variables related to differential impacts of psychosexual functioning in adult women. *Journal of Abnormal Psychology*, 88, 407–17.

Tsai, M., and Wagner, N. N. (1978). Therapy groups for women sexually molested as children. *Archives of Sexual Behavior*, 7, 417–27.

Ueno, M. (1963). The so-called coition death. *Japanese Journal of Legal Medicine*, 17, 535.

Wabrek. A. J., and Burchell, R. C. (1980). Male sexual dysfunction associated with coronary heart disease. *Archives of Sexual Behavior*, 9, 69–75.

Wellisch, D. K., Jamison, K. R., and Pasnau, R. O. (1978). Psychosocial aspects of mastectomy: II The man's perspective. *American Journal of Psychiatry*, 135, 543–6.

Zilbergeld, B. (1975). Group treatment of sexual dysfunction in men without partners. *Journal of Sex and Marital Therapy*, 1, 204–14.

Zilbergeld, B. (1978). *Male Sexuality: A Guide to Sexual fulfillment*, New York: Bantam.

Zilbergeld, B. (1980). Alternatives to couples counseling for sex problems: group and individual therapy. *Journal of Sex and Marital Therapy*, 6. 3–18.

Zilbergeld, B., and Evans, M. (1980). The inadequacy of Masters and Johnson. *Psychology Today*, 14, 29–43.

7

Impairment of Sexual Behaviour in Non-human Primates

Derek Jehu

The non-human primates discussed in this chapter are the ape, including the chimpanzee, gorilla, orangutan and gibbon, the Old World monkeys, such as the baboon and the macaque or rhesus monkey, together with the New World howler and spider monkeys. In evolutionary terms, the most closely related to man are the apes, followed by the Old World monkeys, and most distantly by the New World monkeys.

There are considerable interspecies differences in sexual behaviour among the non-human primates, but the successive phases of sexual attraction, appetitive behaviour, consummatory behaviour and post-consummatory behaviour (Beach 1976) can be applied across species.

PHASES OF SEXUAL BEHAVIOUR

Sexual attraction

This refers to the value one animal has as a sexual stimulus for a potential mate. The degree of attraction is inferred from the appetitive behaviour of the animals concerned, such as a male's attempts to copulate. The process of attraction is mutual and reciprocal between males and females, and it occurs in response to specific characteristics of the potential mate. For example, there are certain somatic and behavioural features that serve to attract males to females. The somatic features include the swelling or heightened colour of the 'sex skin' adjacent to the vulva when the female is in oestrus, together with the smell and taste of her vaginal secretions. Among the relevant behavioural features are the grooming of the male by the female, and presentation of herself to the male for copulation. Such features do not automatically or inevitably elicit sexual attraction in potential partners. Many non-human primates appear to be selective in their choice of mates on the basis of individual preferences, and this is discussed further below.

Appetitive behaviour

Appetitive, invitational or proceptive behaviour serves to elicit sexual attraction from a potential partner, to enhance sexual arousal in both partners, and to co-ordinate their actions, thus preparing them for the consummatory phase. The initiation of such behaviour is fairly evenly distributed between males and females, and it is displayed selectively to different potential partners according to the individual preferences of the animal concerned.

Male appetitive behaviour towards females includes pursuit, manual and oral stimulation of the partner's genitals, and attempts to mount. Sexual approaches to males and manual and oral stimulation of their genitals also feature in female appetitive behaviour, but this is especially characterized by sexual 'presentations' in which the female adopts the copulatory position directly in front of the male while exposing her vaginal area.

The appetitive behaviour of both males and females also includes grooming of the partner's body, and vocalizations such as those produced by rhythmic tongue movements in howler monkeys, 'smacking of the lips' in macaques, and dental 'clicks' in baboons.

Consummatory behaviour

The most prevalent form of consummatory behaviour is copulation. For the male, this involves mounting, erection, intromission, thrusting and ejaculating. For the female, it requires adoption and adjustment of the mating position in order to facilitate male intromission, and the maintenance of this position until intravaginal ejaculation occurs. These acts are referred to as the female's receptive behaviour, in contrast to her proceptive attempts to attract and arouse the male.

The mode of copulation is influenced by the structure of the genital organs and this varies considerably among the non-human primates. For instance, the penis of the gorilla most resembles the human penis, but it is much smaller, while that of the chimpanzee is a long slender shaft without a glans. Female gorillas have outer and inner lips, together with a fairly prominent clitoris, similar to women. In adult chimpanzees, the outer lips are rudimentary, so that the inner lips and clitoris are constantly exposed. In non-human primates the vagina is directed more towards the rear than in women.

This may account for the overwhelmingly most frequent adoption of rear-entry positions for copulation among all non-human primates, although face-to-face positions are sometimes used by gorillas, chimpanzees and orangutans.

There are wide differences between species in the number of mounts and thrusts required before a male can ejaculate. In a study by Nadler (1976), gorillas generally ejaculated on a single copulation during which between 14 and 346 thrusts were executed in a continuous or discontinuous pattern, and these animals were capable of multiple copulations and ejaculations within a half-hour testing period. Yerkes (1939) found that chimpanzees usually ejaculate during one copulation, of less than 15 seconds' duration, with between 12 and 20 thrusts. Among free-living macaques, Carpenter (1942) reported that the time from first mount to discontinuation of sexual activity was 40 minutes. The male mounted 37 times and thrust 161 times, with a total intromission period of 6.9 minutes, and an average intromission of 11 seconds. As orgasm approached, the intervals between copulations decreased and the number of thrusts increased, culminating in 22 rapid thrusts when ejaculation occurred.

Male orgasm is fairly readily recognizable from the cessation of thrusting, muscular tension throughout the body, and often a visible ejaculate. There are a few comparable signs of female orgasm and whether this occurs in non-human primates is still not clear (Lancaster 1979).

Post-consummatory behaviour

As in man, there is a refractory period after ejaculation in male non-human primates during which they cannot obtain another erection and do not show any appetitive behaviour. The length of this refractory period varies across species as well as between individuals, according to the number of previous ejaculations in the same sexual encounter, the age of the animal, and other characteristics.

Female non-human primates generally remain sexually receptive and are capable of many more matings than the male, although there is some evidence of reduced appetitive behaviour immediately after copulation.

Impairments of sexual behaviour can occur in any one or more of the four phases outlined above, as a result of a variety of adverse influences that are discussed below in the general categories of organic factors, early experiences and current conditions.

ORGANIC FACTORS

The main adverse organic influences on sexual behaviour are various hormonal and neural factors which are outlined below. This discussion reflects the fact that much more is known about hormonal impairments, evidence on the adverse effects of neural factors being extremely sparse.

Hormonal factors

There is a growing body of evidence on the adverse effects of certain hormonal factors on the different phases of sexual behaviour in both male and female non-human primates (Herbert 1977, 1978).

Hormonal impairments in females. The sexual attractiveness of the female to the male is impaired by any deficiency of oestrogen, arising perhaps from the removal of the ovaries or the antagonistic action of progesterone. The adverse effect occurs because it is oestrogen that produces the swelling and colour changes in the sex skin, together with the accompanying taste and smell of the vaginal secretions, that are sexually attractive to a male.

The role of oestrogen in female appetitive behaviour is not yet clear, but this may be decreased as an indirect effect of progesterone. Because this hormone reduces the female's attractiveness, the male does not display appetitive behaviour, which in turn will diminish this behaviour in the female.

Female appetitive behaviour is depressed by a deficiency of androgens, as occurs when both the ovaries and the adrenal glands are removed. This adverse effect remains even though the animals are given corticoid replacement therapy to keep them healthy, and oestrogen to maintain their attractiveness to the male. The site of action for androgens appears to be on the neural mechanisms subserving appetitive behaviour. An insufficiency of androgens also reduces the receptivity of females, although the effects are more varied than on appetitive behaviour. There is still considerable dispute over the influence of progesterone on receptivity.

These hormonal factors influence the levels of sexual activity throughout the menstrual cycle, although there are substantial differences across species, individuals and situations in this respect. Copulation usually peaks at mid-cycle when ovulation occurs, and it is least probable during the luteal phase immediately after ovulation, often with some resurgence just before menstruation. Most of this fluctuation is probably due to variation in the female's attractiveness to the male. At mid-cycle, oestrogen levels are maximal and the sexually stimulating vaginal changes are evident. In contrast, during the luteal phase the newly formed corpus luteum secretes increasing amounts of progesterone with its antagonistic action on oestrogen. The corpus luteum and progesterone levels wane just before menstruation. Androgen levels are also elevated during mid-cycle, so that appetitive behaviour is generally more frequent at this time. Receptivity usually remains high throughout the cycle.

Hormonal impairments in males. The reduction of androgens through castration does have adverse effects on the consummatory behaviour of male non-human primates, although there are wide individual differences and the effects are often not apparent for a long time. The ability of some animals to achieve intromission and ejaculation is lost rapidly, and later they show decreased mounting behaviour. Other males continue to perform these functions for years after castration, although often at reduced frequency, and this persistence of sexual activity is not related to residual plasma testosterone levels.

Neural factors

In general terms it is clear that lesions of the relevant neural mechanisms will impair sexual behaviour, but very little is known at present about the specific sites of such lesions in non-human primates. Indeed, there is virtually no information available in respect of female animals (Herbert 1977).

Receptors on the surface of the glans penis in male monkeys are covered by spines, and these disappear if the animal is castrated. The function of these spines is not clear, though they may serve to increase sensory input to the male and/or the female.

Afferent sensory input is disrupted by lesions of the penile dorsal nerve in male monkeys. Complete lesions lead to loss of ejaculation, and thrusting becomes uncoordinated and irregular, while mounting and intromission are less affected.

Mounting and copulation in male monkeys are reported to be reduced markedly by lesions of the medial preoptic hypothalamus, although testosterone levels are unaffected (Slimp 1976). Interestingly, masturbation to ejaculation remained at preoperative levels in these animals, which suggests that their sexual motivation is not entirely a function of hypothalamic mechanisms.

EARLY EXPERIENCES

It is very clear that lack of early experience in mixed-sex groups of both adult and juvenile members of the same species does have a serious detrimental effect on later sexual and social behaviour. This has been demonstrated for several non-human primate species, including rhesus monkeys, chimpanzees and gorillas (Goldfoot 1977; Hanby 1977).

In mixed groups, infant animals normally engage in genital play, presenting, mounting, erection, intromission and thrusting. In fact, every aspect of copulation except ejaculation is practised during the first year of life. Adult females, including the mother, permit and encourage the young males to mount them and to insert, and mounting and dismounting behaviour is faciliated by the carriage of the infants on the backs of the females. These activities occur long before puberty, for menstruation usually commences between ages two and a half and three and a half years in rhesus monkeys, and it is accompanied by an increase in the female's participation in sexual activity. The male of this species starts to ejaculate at about age four and a half years. The equivalent ages for chimpanzees are several years later.

Adverse early experiences

Complete social isolation in infancy, even if a terry-cloth-covered surrogate 'mother' is made available, has devastating effects on the later sexual and social behaviour of rhesus monkeys (Harlow and Harlow 1966). Male animals reared in these conditions either do not attempt to mount, and often engage in pelvic thrusting without mounting, or they may mount in totally ineffective and inappropriate ways. These copulatory deficiencies are only partially remediated by subsequent experiences as juveniles or adults with either younger non-threatening partners, or with very patient and experienced partners, and the more general adverse effects on social interactions are even more intractable. Female monkeys are less severely affected, although receptive behaviour is sometimes impaired, and any adverse effects are more easily reversed by appropriate later experiences.

Goldfoot (1977) and his associates have demonstrated that less extreme social deprivation produces more moderate and partially reversible impairments of sexual and social behaviour. More than 90 per cent of male rhesus monkeys reared in communal pens with their mother and peers develop adequate mounting patterns prior to 12 months of age. One group of males was permanently separated from their mothers at 3 to 6 months of age, after which they were allowed access to peers for half an hour each day. Only 30 per cent of these animals developed adequate mounting behaviour, and usually with some delay up to 18 to 24 months of age. These males also copulated in adulthood, although not with the proficiency of feral-reared animals. The remaining 70 per cent did not acquire adequate mounting behaviour in the first two or three years of life, and they failed to copulate as adults. If access to peers for half an hour a day was followed by 24-hour access in the second year, this increased the probability of the animals developing adequate mounting behaviour. Thus suitable experiences before puberty did correct the adverse effects of moderate earlier deprivation in some male monkeys.

The same group of investigators examined the respective contributions of the mother and peers to the sexual development of rhesus monkeys. During the first year of life each animal had continuous access to its mother, and either half an hour's and/or 24 hours' access to peers each day. None of the males allowed half an hour's access to peers in the first year ever became proficient in mounting behaviour, whereas all the males allowed 24 hours' access did become competent mounters. Thus continuous access to the mother in the first year is not a sufficient condition for the acquisition of satisfatory mounting patterns with peers later in life.

Social interactions

Deficiencies in copulatory behaviour with peers in completely isolated or less deprived monkeys are not due to lack of sexual motivation, because these animals are observed to masturbate frequently. Nor are these deficiencies caused by an inability to perform the necessary motor actions, for the males have been observed to mount their mothers or a cloth dummy female without difficulty.

Rather the impediment to copulation appears to be in the social interactions of the deprived animals with their peers, which are characterized by high levels of threat, aggression and withdrawal, together with low levels of grooming and other signs of positive affect. These features may be the result of lack of opportunity to experience trusting and anxiety-free relationships with peers in infancy. More particularly, satisfactory mounting requires the co-operation of the male and female, and if this is lacking because of fear or hostility then mounting is unlikely to be achieved. Thus it is suggested that copulation may be impaired as a result of discordant social interactions with potential partners, which in turn are the result of social deprivation in infancy.

CURRENT CONDITIONS

This leads to consideration of some sexual and social conditions in the current situation that may impair sexual behaviour in non-human primates. Important among these conditions are deficient sexual stimulation and low social status.

Deficient sexual stimulation

In the first section of this chapter a number of stimuli that evoke sexual behaviour between partners are noted, including (1) sex-skin changes, (2) smell and taste of vaginal secretions, (3) grooming, (4) vocalizations, (5) pursuit, (6) manual and oral stimulation of the partner's genitals, (7) presentation, (8) attempts to mount, (9) intromission and (10) thrusting. It follows that any deficiencies in these stimuli in the current situation may be accompanied by corresponding impairments of sexual attraction, arousal and copulation.

One example of such deficiency is the absence of olfactory stimuli or pheromones from the vagina, with consequent adverse effects on sexual attraction (Rogel 1978). Michael and Keverne (1970) required male rhesus monkeys to press a lever repeatedly in order to gain access to a female partner that they could see and smell. The males rarely performed this task for females whose ovaries had been removed and who had not been treated with the oestrogen necessary for pheromone production. Similarly, if the males were temporarily deprived of their sense of smell they failed to respond to female pheromones.

It is important to appreciate that these olfactory stimuli evoke varied rather than fixed responses in non-human primates. Males will respond to pheromones from some females but not others, and the nature of the responses ranges from a reduction in aggressive behaviour, through to grooming, masturbation to ejaculation, and copulation.

Finally, satiation to sexual stimuli from a particular partner is reported among non-human primates. Michael and Zumpe (1978) found that mounting latencies increased and ejaculations decreased in male rhesus monkeys over a three-and-half-year period, during which each male was repeatedly mated with one female whose ovaries had been removed and who was given daily injections of oestrogen to maintain a receptive state. The introduction of a novel, similarly treated female was accompanied by an abrupt and complete reversal of the decrements in male performance.

Low social status

Ranking systems are common in groups of non-human primates and an animal's status in the hierarchy may affect his or her sexual behaviour. Among males, high status seems to be a function of age, integration and familiarity in the group, and to a much lesser extent fighting ability or aggressiveness. For females, high status is associated with the number of offspring or kin she has in the group, and animals who have not had an infant tend to be of low rank. Status hierarchies are relatively much more stable among females, whereas there is considerable fluctuation in male hierarchies as animals leave the group or become older (Hanby 1977; Lancaster 1979).

Male status.   Low-status males tend to copulate less than those higher in the hierarchy. One possible reason for this is that the presence of more dominant males will inhibit or disrupt sexual activity by the less dominant. Another factor is that females often prefer high-status, though not extremely aggressive, males as partners. An exception is that chimpanzees are reported by Tutin (1976) to prefer males who spend more time grooming the female and who are generous in sharing food with her, rather than those who are most dominant. Access to females can also affect frequency of copulation. When receptive females are plentiful low-ranking males are very active sexually, but they participate less as the number of females is reduced.

Female status. Male non-human primates tend to prefer high-status females as sexual partners. For example, when Perachio et al. (1973) introduced a male rhesus monkey to two oestrogen-treated females, copulation occurred most frequently with the more dominant female. This preference persisted even if oestrogen was withdrawn from the more dominant partner, for the male would still not mount the less dominant, oestrogen-treated female unless she was only slightly subordinate to the other.

High-status females tend to direct more sexual behaviour to males, as well as to receive more sexual attention from them. In a study by Goldfoot (1971), the more dominant females showed the highest frequencies of sexual behaviour at all phases of the menstrual cycle, and they also displayed increases in this behaviour during the peak preovulatory period, whereas the less dominant did not do so.

HUMAN SEXUAL DYSFUNCTION

Many behavioural scientists and clinicians are interested primarily in the understanding and treatment of human sexual dysfunctions. For them, knowledge about sexual impairments in non-human primates is likely to be relevant not because of any direct generalizations from animals to man, but rather for the relatively fresh perspectives on human dysfunctions derived from issues raised or highlighted in the animal work. A few selected examples of these issues are outlined below.

Sexual attraction

One sharp discrepancy between the relevant literature on animals and man is the amount of attention paid to sexual attraction. This topic is almost totally overlooked in texts on sexual dysfunction (e.g. Jehu 1979; Kaplan 1974, 1979; Leiblum and Pervin 1980; Lo Piccolo and Lo Piccolo 1978; Masters and Johnson 1970). Nevertheless, patients do sometimes complain that they are not sexually attracted to their partner, although other aspects of the relationship such as companionship or support may still be highly valued, and sexual attraction to other possible partners may still be experienced. Thus some patients could be failing to transmit and/or receive signals of sexual attraction and this might be contributing to impairments of their sexual motivation, arousal or performance.

Much of the literature on interpersonal attraction concerns more general relationships of liking, friendship and love between people rather than sexual attraction particularly, and little information is available on the specific cues that serve to attract potential partners. An exception is the work of Cook and his colleagues (Cook 1977; Cook and McHenry 1978; Cook and Wilson 1979). There are considerable cross-cultural differences in sexual cues at different times and places, but Cook (1977) gives some indications of the non-verbal cues used in some contemporary western cultures. When talking to men they like, women tend to adopt an 'open' posture with arms and legs uncrossed. Men who are about to make advances to a woman tend to display a 'courtship readiness' pattern involving a general stiffening of the muscles resulting in a more upright posture, pulling back the shoulders, holding in the stomach. Courting couples generally sit side by side in bars and restaurants, and usually turn inward towards each other so that other people are excluded. A glance can convey sexual interest, and holding a gaze even more so, especially if the gaze is then broken to wander down the other person's body in frank sexual invitation. In contrast, not looking at a partner can also be a revealing signal of sexual attraction. Large dilated pupils may be very appealing to a member of the opposite sex, perhaps because they communicate strong interest which could be sexual. Touching is a particularly important way of displaying sexual interest, especially while dancing. Cook suggests that the relative vagueness of such non-verbal signals compared to explicit verbal invitations is advantageous because indirect communications can be withdrawn or rejected without confrontation or insult. A disadvantage of vagueness is that some individuals are unable to recognize or use body language, with adverse consequences for their sexual relationships.

Verbal behaviour is of course also used to attract a partner. In a questionnaire study of coitally experienced US college students, Jesser (1978) reported that more than 70 per cent of both male and female respondents used touching (snuggling, kissing, allowing hands to wander) to signal their desire, while 58 per cent of the females and 56 per cent of the males asked directly for sex. In another study Brown and Auberback (1981) administered questionnaires to 50 well-educated, middle-class couples in the San Francisco area. They were aged from 21 to 63 years and had been married to each other for between two and thirty-five years. In initiating sex 60 per cent of this group used non-verbal techniques and only 40 per cent verbal messages, the latter being used more by women possibly because men are more afraid of being rejected. The non-verbal techniques included use of music, a fire in the fireplace, reading sexually explicit material, the consumption of alcohol, touching, kissing and genital fondling. Verbal messages included phrases like 'Let's make love', 'I want to make love to you', 'You sure look sexy to me', and 'Are you in the mood?' A high-priority component of the ideal approach for both men and women was being touched or caressed by their spouses. Women also attached considerable importance to gentleness or tenderness, and to verbal appreciation. Other important aspects for men included initiations by their spouses in verbally direct and free and abandoned ways, making it clear that they passionately desired their husbands. Again it is clear that inability to display or perceive appropriate verbal and non-verbal cues may impede sexual attraction, possibly with more widespread adverse repercussions on other aspects of sexual functioning.

A related issue arises from the recognition of individual preferences between potential sexual partners among non-human primates. This casts further doubt on one of the commonest myths about male sexuality, that any man worthy of the name should always want and always be ready to have sex with any available woman (Zilbergeld 1978). Many sexually dysfunctional males impose this unrealistic prescription on themselves, and expect to be able to function like sex machines regardless of their feelings towards the partner. Not surprisingly, anxiety and failure is often experienced in these circumstances.

Appetitive behaviour

Among the functions of appetitive behaviour in non-human primates is the preparation of the partners for the consummatory phase. The earlier stages of this transition process is another relatively neglected aspect of human sexual dysfunction, much more attention being devoted to deficiencies in specific techniques for sexual arousal at later stages in the encounter (Knoepfler 1981). Some patients complaining of a lack of sexual motivation, however, appear to have difficulty in making the transition from a non-sexual to a sexual state; consequently they fail to experience sexual desire. Often these patients seem to expect intense sexual urges to arise quite spontaneously 'out of the blue', rather than requiring the establishment of suitable conditions for their emergence.

In general, these are conditions that are relaxing and which focus attention on the pleasure being experienced at the time rather than the attainment of some performance goal. They might include a shared meal, a small amount of alcohol, sensual rather than sexual touching, and a bath or shower. In the course of such activities there is a progressive shift towards the sexual aspects of the interaction, perhaps by sensual caressing moving into more explicitly sexual tactile stimulation, or by the introduction or erotic fantasies or materials. This increasing sexualization may be problematic for certain dysfunctional patients, including those who fear pleasure or loss of control in sexual encounters.

Problems can also arise at an earlier stage of the transition from a non-sexual to a sexual state, for individuals need to be willing to embark upon this process. They may know that certain conditions will evoke sexual desire in them, but be reluctant to arrange or enter these conditions because they anticipate that the resulting encounter will be disappointing, unpleasant, accompanied by guilt or distracting from other occupational or leisure activities that have greater salience at the time. Thus some dysfunctional patients will avoid or escape from transitional activities that would otherwise facilitate sexual desire.

Consummatory behaviour

To the clinician, one of the most striking things about copulation in some non-human primate species is its discontinuous nature; thrusting is often interrupted, numerous mounts may occur with intervals between them, and the whole mating can occupy a quite lengthy period. This pattern is markedly different from the prescription for intercourse that many dysfunctional men impose upon themselves (Zilbergeld 1978).

They commonly believe that sex should be a process of continuously increasing excitement and movement, during which any slowing down or stopping is unacceptable to themselves and their partners. Any such temporary interruption may be thought to signify a loss of ardour to the partner or to be disruptive of her arousal, whereas in fact they may be more likely to facilitate high levels of arousal and the achievement of climax. If an interruption is accompanied by loss of erection, then panic is often experienced in case it cannot be recovered, and this anxiety may in fact prevent recovery. Similarly, voluntary control over the ejaculatory reflexes may be impaired because the premature ejaculator does not feel able to stop, slow down or alter his thrusting, all of which are techniques used by most men in order to exercise effective control. Thus greater tolerance of more leisurely, spaced-out sexual encounters is important in the alleviation of problems such as erectile dysfunction and premature ejaculation, as well as facilitating the enjoyment of sexual encounters by both partners.

Early experience

Another marked difference between the animal and human literature is the extent of the information available on the contribution of early experience to sexual impairment later in life. For instance, in respect of rhesus monkeys a substantial body of knowledge exists on the effects of certain conditions of social deprivation in infancy on later capacity to mount and copulate. In contrast, relatively little is known about the conditions in human childhood that may influence sexual development, or about the specific aspects of sexual functioning that may be adversely affected by these conditions. This topic is not pursued further at this point because it is discussed at greater length in chapter 6.

Current conditions

A related topic emphasized in the animal literature is the close connection between sexual functioning and current social conditions. The impairments of mounting and copulation mentioned above may be due to the adverse effects of early social deprivation on later capacity to co-operate harmoniously with a partner. Likewise, the influence of social status on sexual behaviour is well demonstrated in non-human primates. The contributions of similar current social conditions, such as marital discord and occupational stresses, to human sexual dysfunctions are recognized by professionals, but dysfunctional patients are often convinced that they should still be interested and able to perform sexually whatever else is happening in their lives. Thus a wife who is resentful and angry towards her husband may not connect this with her loss of interest in having sex with him, or a man who is threatened with unemployment may regard this as quite irrelevant to his concomitant inability to obtain or maintain an erection. The role of such stressful life events in the aetiology of sexual dysfunction is discussed further in chapter 6.

SUMMARY

The successive phases of sexual attraction, and appetitive, consummatory and post-consummatory behaviour are applicable across non-human primate species, despite considerable interspecies differences in sexual behaviour. Sexual attraction refers to the value that an animal has as a sexual stimulus for a potential mate. This stimulus value is a function of somatic and behavioural features such as sex-skin changes, the smell and taste of vaginal secretions, grooming and presentation, that serve to attract a partner. Appetitive behaviour elicits sexual attraction from a potential partner, enhances sexual arousal in both partners, and co-ordinates their actions in preparation for the consummatory phase. This behaviour includes pursuit, grooming, vocalizations, manual and oral stimulation of the partner's genitals, sexual presentations and attempts to mount. The most prevalent form of consummatory behaviour is copulation, involving mounting, erection, intromission, thrusting and ejaculation for the male, and the adoption, adjustment and maintenance of the mating position for the female. Post-consummatory behaviour includes a refractory period for males, But not females. Any one or more of these phases can be impaired by a variety of organic factors, early experiences and/or current conditions.

The main organic factors are hormonal or neural in nature. In female animals, sexual attractiveness is impaired by any deficiency of oestrogen, and both appetitive behaviour and receptivity are impaired by a deficiency of androgens. In males, androgen deficiencies are accompanied by impairments of copulatory behaviour. Little is known about neural factors that may adversely affect sexual behaviour, especially in female animals. In males, sensory input may be diminished by loss of the spines on the glans penis by lesions of the penile dorsal nerve. These lesions or others in the medial preoptic hypothalamus can also result in impaired copulatory behaviour.

Lack of early experience in mixed-sex groups of both adult and juvenile members of the same species has a serious detrimental effect on later sexual and social behaviour. Complete social isolation is followed by copulatory deficiencies and disturbed social interactions in males which are only partially remediated by more appropriate later experiences, and similar though lesser effects are reported in females. Less extreme social deprivation produces more moderate and less intractable impairments of sexual and social behaviour. The sexual difficulties following adverse early experiences appear to be a function of the associated social difficulties, in that the interactions of deprived animals with their peers are characterized by high levels of threat, aggression and withdrawal, together with low levels of grooming and other signs of positive affect.

Among the current conditions that may impair sexual behaviour in non-human primates are deficient stimulation and low social status. Sexual attraction, arousal and copulation may be impaired by any deficiencies in the stimulation provided by sex-skin changes, smell and taste of vaginal secretions, grooming, vocalization, pursuit, manual or oral stimulation of the partner's genitals, presentation, attempts to mount, intromission or thrusting. As far as social status is concerned, males that are low in a hierarchy tend to copulate less than those who are more dominant, and both males and females show preferences for high-status animals as partners.

Some fresh perspectives or emphases on human sexual dysfunction can be derived from knowledge of sexual impairment in non-human primates. The role of sexual attraction is an important gap in the human literature. Similarly, the function of appetitive behaviour as a preparation for the consummatory phase in animals highlights the lack of attention to the difficulties in this transition process that are experienced by some human patients. The discontinuous nature of copulation in some non-human primates contrasts with the prescription for intercourse and ejaculatory control that many men impose upon themselves. There is a marked discrepancy in the amount of information available about the influence of early experience on later sexual behaviour in non-human primates and man. Lastly, the potential for adverse effects from current social conditions on sexual functioning is readily apparent in the animal literature, but less well recognized by many human patients. These are just some selected instances of the relatively new light that may be cast on human sexual dysfunction by the study of similar impairments in non-human primates.

REFERENCES

Beach, F. A. (1976). Cross-species comparisons and the human heritage. *Archives of Sexual Behavior.* 5, 469–85.

Brown, M., and Auerback, A. (1981). Communication patterns in initiation of marital sex. *Medical Aspects of Human Sexuality*, 15, 101–117.

Carpenter, C. R. (1942). Sexual behavior of free-ranging rhesus monkeys (*Macaca Mulatta*) 1: Specimens, procedures and behavioral characteristics of estrus. *Journal of Comparative psychology*, 33, 113–42.

Cook, M. (1977). Sex and body language. *Medical Aspects of Human Sexuality*, 11, 118–34.

Cook, M., and McHenry, R. (1978). *Sexual Attraction*. Oxford: Pergamon.

Cook, M., and Wilson, G. (1979). *Love and Attraction: An International Conference.* Oxford: Pergamon.

Goldfoot, D. (1971). Hormonal and social determinants of sexual behaviour in the pig-tail monkey (*Macaca nemistrina*). In G. Stoelinger and J. v. d. Werff Ten-Bosch (eds), *Normal and Abnormal Development of Brain and Behaviour*, Leiden: Leiden University Press.

Goldfoot, D. A. (1977). Sociosexual behaviors of nonhuman primates during development and maturity: social and hormonal relationships. In A. M. Schrier (ed.), *Behavioral Primatology: Advances in Research and Theory*, 1, New York: Wiley.

Hanby, J. P. (1977). Social factors affecting primate reproduction, In J. Money and H. Musaph (eds), *Handbook of Sexology*, Amsterdam: Excerpta Medica.

Harlow, H. F., and Harlow, M. K. (1966). Learning to love. *American Scientist*, 54, 244–72.

Herbert, J. (1977). Neuroendocrine basis of sexual behavior in primates. In J. Money and H. Musaph (eds), *Handbook of Sexology*, Amsterdam: Excerpta Medica.

Herbert, J. (1978). Neuro-hormonal integration of sexual behaviour in female primates. In J. B. Hutchinson (ed.), *Biological Determinants of Sexual Behaviour*, Chichester: Wiley.

Jehu, D. (1979). *Sexual Dysfunction: A Behavioural Approach to Causation Assessment, and Treatment*, Chichester: Wiley.

Jesser, C. J. (1978). Male responses to direct verbal sexual initiatives of females. *Journal of Sex Research*, 14, 118–28

Kaplan, H. S. (1974). *The New Sex Therapy: Active Treatment of Sexual Dysfunctions*, New York: Brunner/Mazel.

Kaplan, H. S. (1979). *Disorders of Sexual Desire: and Other New Concepts and Techniques in Sex Therapy*, New York: Brunner/Mazel.

Knoefler, P. (1981). Transition: a prephase of the human sexual response cycle. *Journal of Sex Education and Therapy*, 7 15–17.

Lancaster, J. B. (1979). Sex and gender in evolutionary perspective. In H. A.

Katchadourian (ed.), *Human Sexuality: A Comparative and Developmental Perspective*, Berkeley: University of California Press.

Leiblum, S. R., and Pervin, P. A. (eds) (1980). *Principles and Practice of Sex Therapy*, New York: Guildford.

Lo Piccolo, J., and Lo Piccolo, L. (eds) (1978). *Handbook of Sex Therapy*, New York: Plenum.

Masters, W. H., and Johnson, V. E. (1970). *Human Sexual Inadequacy*, London: Churchill.

Michael, R. P., and Keverne, E. B. (1970). Primate sex pheromones of vaginal origin. *Nature*, 225, 84–5.

Michael, R. P., and Zumpe, D. (1978). Potency in male rhesus monkeys. Effect of continuously receptive females. *Science*, 200, 451–3.

Nadler, R. D. (1976). Sexual behavior of captive lowland gorillas. *Archives of Sexual Behavior*, 5, 487–502.

Perachio, A. A., Alexander, M., and Marr, L. D. (1973). Hormonal and social factors affecting evoked sexual behaviour in rhesus monkeys. *American Journal of Physical Anthropology*, 38, 227–32.

Rogel, M. J. (1978). A critical evaluation of the possibility of higher primate reproductive and sexual pheromones. *Psychological Bulletin*, 85, 810–30.

Slimp, J. C. (1976). Effects of medial proptic-anterior hypothalamic lesions on heterosexual behavior, masturbation, and social behavior of male rhesus monkeys. Unpublished doctoral thesis, University of Wisconsin-Madison.

Tutin, C. E. G. (1976). Exceptions to promiscuity in a feral chimpanzee community. PhD thesis, University of Edinburgh.

Yerkes, R. M. (1939). Sexual behavior in the chimpanzee. *Human Biology*, 2, 78–110.

Zilbergeld, B. (1978). *Male Sexuality: A Guide to Sexual Fulfillment*, Boston: Little, Brown.

8

The Assessment of Diverse Sexual Behaviour

D. R. Laws

INTRODUCTION

The importance of investigating human sexual diversity lies primarily in the fact that there is virtually no aspect of our personal and social lives, even economic and political lives, upon which our sexuality does not impinge. The pioneer American sex researcher Kinsey believed that this aspect of human behaviour had to be studied because 'It is desperately strategic that our civilization realize something of the diversity in human sex behavior, and acquire some sympathetic understanding of that which is different from one's own' (cited in Pomeroy 1972, p. 78). With isolated and albeit very significant exceptions, this is almost exactly what has not happened. Throughout a century of study there has been, and continues to be, a persistent reluctance on the part of medical and social science forthrightly to study human sexual behaviour, particularly its more unusual forms. Infrequently writers have urged that science pay the price of negative public and professional opinion and 'issue succinct statistics and physiologic summaries of what we find to be average and what we believe to be normal' (Dickenson and Pierson 1925, cited in Masters and Johnson 1966, p. v). No one was willing to pay the price until Kinsey and his colleagues began their large sex-research project in 1938. The study of human sexual diversity properly begins with Kinsey and these researches. The Kinsey data, despite any shortcomings, remain to this day the largest body of empirical information on human sexual diversity ever compiled, and to a large extent remain the standard against which most subsequent work is to be compared.

Kinsey and his colleagues knew what they faced.

Although . . . scientists have largely avoided investigations of human sexuality, leaving this one of the most poorly explored fields in biology, psychology, or sociology, it should be emphasized that there is no aspect of human behavior about which there has been more thought, more talk, and more books written. . . .

> The printed literature is tremendous. . . . It is, at once, an interesting reflection of man's absorbing interest in sex, and his astounding ignorance of it; his desire to know and his unwillingness to face the facts; his respect for an objective, scientific approach to the problems involved, and his overwhelming urge to be poetic, pornographic, literary, philosophic, traditional, and moral. (Kinsey et al. 1948, pp. 21–2)

They proposed to cut through this mass of previously inhibiting problems and produce a taxonomic picture of human sexual diversity, an ordered classification by experiences, behaviours, preferences and the like. And all of this was to be demystified and deromanticized by statistical presentation.

By the use of direct and forthright interviewing of ordinary American citizens, Kinsey broke the mould of previous human sex research, then still largely dominated by the thought of Freud and Havelock Ellis. Writing of the social impact of sex research, Gagnon (1975) notes that the intellectual roots of Kinsey's work lay in earlier statistical case-studies and in his own prior research in biological taxonomy. Thus the final form of his work were large numbers of case-histories, cross-classified on taxonomic variables, the data expressed as statistical summaries. Gagnon (1975) characterizes this procedure as 'social bookkeeping' and terms it revolutionary. 'Despite methodological carping,' he writes, 'there existed for the first time an accountancy for sexual behaviour' (p. 129). In a single blow, as Kinsey had intended, the research cut a wide swath through the pre-existing poetic, literary, philosophic and moral traditions, a not entirely welcome event. 'The contest between imaginative-literate and the scientific-numerate traditions was rejoined . . . it was the canons of proof that were unacceptable, the movement from imagination to science, from literary to numeracy that was unpalatable' (Gagnon 1975, p. 131).

Why study sexual diversity? Precisely because we still need the sort of accountancy for sexual behaviour begun by Kinsey. Research in sexual diversity did not die with him, but the pace has slowed and even become regressive, as if no one has again dared be so bold. In reviewing methods of assessing sexual diversity one is frequently struck with a sense of *déjà vu* – researchers shying away from controversial topics, or asking the wrong questions, or the same inadequate questions over and over again, with the result that a comprehensive picture of human sexuality remains elusive. If our goal is to be a sort of social bookkeeeping of sexual behaviour, we must conclude that, since 1948, we have been remiss in keeping the books.

Part of the problem in assessing sexual diversity, it seems to me, lies in the absence of agreement on what the words 'sexual diversity' mean as an object of research. In reviewing the assessment literature one finds that sexual diversity from this viewpoint could be defined as any or all of the following:

1   Values expressed toward various types of sexual activity.

2 A diversity of opinion toward various sexual behaviours.

3 Awareness that certain sexual behaviours occur.

4 Classification of persons of known behavioural disposition by psychological, typological or physiological measures.

5 A disposition towards or preference for various sexual behaviours.

6 A diversity of interest in various sexual activities.

7 A diversity in performance or variety of sexual activities.

8 A diversity of performance within specific sexual activities.

These, of course, do not exhaust the possibilities. Review of the assessment literature reveals that much of the research focus has been on the first four points: values, opinions, awareness and classification. Researchers seemingly never tire of asking respondents what they think about premarital sex, extramarital sex, whether homosexuality is right or wrong; attempting to demonstrate that homosexuals or other sexual nonconformists show personality traits different from heterosexuals; or laboriously fitting subjects into classificatory pigeon-holes. Over the past 50 years this has been an area of appallingly low empirical yield. While it is undeniably important that we should know people's awareness of sexual behaviours, what their opinions are, what they value, and how their personalities are reflected in their sexuality, these are less important than knowing what their actual behavioural dispositions are, what interests them sexually, what they prefer, what their personal sexual behaviour is like. In short, what is it that people *do* when they are being sexually diverse? We are heirs to a fine tradition initiated by the Kinsey researches. It is a behaviourist tradition, numerate rather than literate, scientific rather than imaginative, and the empirical yield has always been greatest when we have followed this tradition.

In what follows I will review the major methods which have been used to assess human sexual diversity and give representative examples of each. These methods will be evaluated for the extent to which they contribute to informing us about what people do when they behave sexually, or provide valid mesures of sexual interest, preference or disposition, and the extent to which that method assists us to understand human sexual diversity.

METHODS OF ASSESSMENT

Over the years the most popular methods of assessing sexual behaviour in males and females have been varieties of subjective report. These have included structured interview, including personal in-depth interviewing as well as brief, survey research interviews; psychometric testing, usually of the personality assessment variety, but sometimes shading over into well-constructed and psychometrically sound self-report inventories, questionnaires and rating scales; specific tests of sexual interest and preference; typological classification; and little-used methods such as direct participant and non-participant observation of sexual behaviour. Within the past 30 years these methods have been supplemented by direct measurement of sexual arousal through genital plethysmography and other psychophysiological methods.

There are several sources of error in all these procedures. Any technique dependent upon subjective report is clearly open to influence. Sources of error here include faulty recall, deliberate falsification, and refusal to report pertinent data. Any classification scheme or typology requiring judgement by examining professionals is heavily influenced by clinical impression, experience and theoretical persuasion of the examiner. The physiological methods, while hardly perfect, are the most objective of the procedures. Some of these are minimally open to subject influence while others seem to be relatively independent of subject control.

The Kinsey interview

For the assessment of individuals or of population characteristics in very large samples, the Kinsey interview would be a major procedure of choice. Even after the elapse of 45 years, no better procedure for eliciting sexual diversity data by interview has been developed. Although Kinsey et al. (1948, pp. 35–62) go into considerable detail about interviewing techniques, they do not describe how the interview was actually conducted. Perhaps this is understandable, given the social and scientific attitude toward sex in America during the 1930s and 1940s, but not least due to Kinsey's concern for confidentiality of data and protection of his respondents (Pomeroy 1972). Although Pomeroy (1972) gives some details of the technique in his biography of Kinsey, it was only recently that he finally published the full details of the interview procedure and its coding techniques (Pomeroy et al. 1982).

The Kinsey interview is a face-to-face, highly personalized, structured interview. The interviewer follows a predetermined sequence in the questioning and each question requires only a brief and explicit response. There are 521 items in the full history although a basic minimum history contains 350. Many items are supplemented by additional questions where necessary, and unlike a fixed questionnaire this permits the interviewer to pursue details and still record data.

There are two important features of this procedure which are often absent in the typical taking of sexual histories. First, while all the usual amenities of establishing rapport, non-judgemental attitude, respect for the client, etc., are observed, the interviewer commands and controls the procedure, administering the questions rapid fire, forcing the pace, and thus not permitting time for extensive reflection by the client and possible omission or falsification of responses. To facilitate this, questions of the 'have you ever' variety are never asked. The assumption underlying this is 'assume everybody does everything' (Pomeroy et al. 1982, p. 10). For example, the question would not be 'Have you ever had a homosexual experience?' but rather 'How old were you when you first had a homosexual experience?' This still permits the respondent to deny but lessons the likelihood by communicating that the interviewer is making no value judgement about it.

Second, all data obtained are expressed as abbreviations or symbols in what is called a 'position code'. This allows economy in recording and relatively easy retrieval and transformation of data. Responses are recorded on a single sheet of paper divided into blocks representing the 24 areas covered in the interview. It has been estimated that the amount of data so recorded would occupy 25 typed pages if expressed as text (Pomeroy 1972). The 'position' code refers to the placement of a particular symbol or abbreviation within different blocks. For example, the abbreviation 'C' could mean 'Catholic', 'confirmation', 'coitus', 'companion', or 'city', while the symbol '√√√' could mean 'alcoholic', 'excessive' or 'abusive'. For the uninitiated, the code is impossible to break, ensuring confidentiality. Pomeroy reports (1982) that it takes about 20 hours to train an interviewer by means of a tape-recorded programme. On the negative side, unlike a fixed questionnaire, this is a personalized procedure and must be administered by a trained interviewer, may not be given to groups, and so is less cost-efficient than simpler methods. For all this, in terms of breadth and richness of data, the Kinsey interview has no peer in the sexual diversity literature.

Survey research by interview

One of the primary objections lodged against all survey research on sexual behaviour is that samples interviewed are unrepresentative of the population about whom generalizations are likely to be made. The cost of obtaining representative nationwide samples is quite high, and the best examples of these surveys are those usually undertaken by a national polling or survey research organization who interview a large probability sample throughout the United States. The results are sometimes, but rarely, published in detailed format (e.g. Abelson et al. 1971; Kant et al. 1971). More often sections are abstracted and published as journal reports (e.g. Wilson 1975; Merritt et al. 1975; Glenn and Weaver 1979). Frequently the data of these reports are compared to the original Kinsey data (Wilson 1975).

A typical sample of this process may be seen in a study by Merritt et al. (1975) on attitudes toward pornography. A probability sample of 2486 adults, aged 20–80, in 14 sampling units in 43 of the 48 contiguous United States were interviewed about their attitudes towards 12 statements about visual and textual 'sexual materials'. The questions appeared to state the conventional wisdom about pornography, e.g. 'Sexual materials make people sex crazy' or 'Sexual materials lead people to commit rape' or 'Sexual materials lead to a breakdown of morals'. What makes this study interesting, and typical of this genre, is not its major finding that people view pornography more negatively as they grow older, but rather the striking absence of the questions that were *not* asked. For example, more direct and unequivocal questions might have been posed, such as 'Do you become sexually aroused when you look at pornographic pictures?' or 'Do you masturbate when you look at pornographic pictures?' This emphasis is rather crucial as this investigation was commissioned by the famous President's Commission on Obscenity and Pornography whose charge it was to determine the effect of pornography on sex crimes and societal values, yet there were only two questions relevant to those areas, the cited ones on rape and morality. The remaining questions were rather general in nature. The respondents could state only that sexual materials did or did not produce the stated effect, and whether they had this effect on them, someone they knew or neither. This type of procedural imprecision of asking the wrong questions or not enough of the right questions is unfortunately rather common in survey sex research. Much of the problem appears to lie in the researchers' 'anxiety about asking sexual questions of a representative unselected sample of people' (Wilson 1975, p. 46), although a substantial body of data has existed for nearly half a century which clearly indicates that unselected interviewees are not reluctant to provide quite intimate details on their sexual beliefs and practices (Kinsey et al. 1948, 1953).

A second example reveals much the same difficulties. Glenn and Weaver (1979) describe the use of the General Social Surveys, conducted by the National Opinion Research Center, to sample trends in attitudes and behaviour. These authors report on attitudes toward premarital, extramarital and homosexual relations in the US between 1972 and 1978 obtained by interviewers from seven independently drawn probability samples of 1500 each (N = 10,500). With a sample of that size, over such a period of time, the survey designers saw fit to include only one question for each of the behaviours of interest. For example, 'What about sexual relations between two *adults* of the same sex – do you think it is always wrong, almost always wrong, wrong only sometimes, or not wrong at all?' While the graded response options are superior to yes/no, note that the respondent is forced to choose between three varieties of wrongness or endorsing homosexuality as completely acceptable. Thus, despite the methodological rigour in subject selection it is hardly surprising that highly similar studies, whether employing a large N (30,018) (Levitt and Klassen 1974) or a small N (1197) (Nyberg and Alston 1976–7) find 'confirmation' in their data that 'most white Americans disapprove of homosexual relations' (Nyberg and Alston 1976–7, p. 99).

The cited studies were not chosen as particularly poor examples of interview survey research; indeed they are rather good examples. Interview survey research with respect to sexual diversity is, more than anything else, a literature of lost opportunities. First, it does not study sexual diversity *per se*, but rather what people say about diversity, i.e., attitudes, beliefs, opinions. Second, the use of extremely careful sampling techniques to ensure representativeness in the research population is often vitiated by the fact that researchers ask irrelevant, tangential or unnecessarily general questions and, when they ask the right questions, they fail to elicit sufficient detail to make the data more than modestly informative.

A rather better example of large-scale interview survey research is Hunt's *Sexual Behavior in the 1970s* (1974), compiled from a lengthy questionnaire designed by a market survey and research organization. The questionnaire, of 1000–1200 items, was prepared in four versions (male, female, married, unmarried) and was administered to 2026 persons (982 males and 1044 females) in 24 cities. Public opinion survey terms randomly contacted persons over 18 by telephone and invited them to participate in small, private panel discussions on current trends in American sexual behaviour. Those who agreed (about 20 per cent of those contacted) met in groups of 16 for the discussion, then were asked to complete the questionnaire. A small subsample of persons under 18 were also contacted and an additional group of 100 males and 100 females participated in in-depth interviews. Hunt admits that this was not a probability sample but efforts were made to ensure that major demographic variables were represented. Although often hailed as such, the report is in no sense a replication of Kinsey et al. (1948, 1953). However, Hunt did extend those earlier findings by including data on anal eroticism sadomasochism, incest, mate swapping and group sex. This report has gained considerable respectability over the years and the data are frequently compared with the Kinsey data and later work.

Other studies in the interview survey research literature show how less ambition, but careful and relevant procedure, can yield useful information on sexual diversity. White (1982) reviewed the small literature on effects of ageing on sexuality and concluded that, while increasing age affects performance and there is some decline in sexual activity, there are no known limits to sexuality in older persons, and sexual attitudes and behaviours in old age are a continuation of previous patterns. White's interest was in the institutionalized aged, an understudied group. Using a portion of a sexual knowledge and attitudes questionnaire, 250 males and females, residents of a stratified sample of nursing homes in one state, were interviewed. Data on current and past sexual behaviour were obtained in response to the following questions: (1) 'In your whole life prior to entering the nursing home, how sexually active have you been?' (on a scale of 1–7, 1=inactive, 7=very active); (2) 'How often in the past month did you masturbate?'; (3) 'How often in the past month did you engage in sexual activity with another person?' and (4) 'How often in the past month did you feel sexually aroused?' (White 1982, p. 18). The data indicated that institutionalization did not rule out sexual activity in the aged, so extending previous findings. The important point is, while the sampling procedure may leave something to be desired, these were simple, straightforward questions which elicited relevant, useful data on diversity. People either are or are not sexually active, and if they become sexually aroused, masturbate or have sexual relations, they do so at some frequency. By removing the words 'prior to entering the nursing home', these questions could be put to a cross-section of age groups, and so develop a longitudinal picture of ageing and sexuality. This type of study, unfortunately, remains the exception but it demonstrates that simple and direct interview survey techniques can be a useful assessment procedure.

Typologies

Classification schemes such as typologies share in common with some psychometric instruments the goal of categorizing persons on the basis of possession of some behavioural characteristic, attitude, opinion, etc. In the area of sexual diversity, typological classification has most often been used to classify sexual deviants. All typologies are to some extent faulted. Being essentially definitional models they share a certain rigidity that classification implies. Many are weakened by the fact that they lack empirical foundation and are based on the practical experience and theoretical assumption of their authors.

There are basically three types of typology in the sexual diversity research literature: (1) impressionistic, based almost wholly upon the speculations and experience of the authors; (2) physiologically based classification by differential amplitudes of sexual response; and (3) psychometric, a classification produced by statistical manipulation. Impressionistic typologies are treated elsewhere in this volume, and sex response typologies below in the section on genital plethysmography. Here we will be concerned only with the psychometric method.

Psychometric typologies.　This variety of typological classification uses statistical methods, usually factor analysis or cluster analysis, to derive categories based on subject responses to a pool of items. Such typologies require great effort to produce, thus it is essential that basic premises be such that the resulting product contributes to our understanding of sexual diversity. Two high-quality examples follow.

Bell and Weinberg's *Homosexualities: A Study of Diversity Among Men and Women* (1978) is an oft-cited work that is an outstanding example of the psychometric typology. Using a 528-item schedule the authors did face-to-face interviews with 979 homosexuals and 477 heterosexuals, white and black males and females. Although the study has invited criticism, both methodological and political (e.g. Suppe 1981), it is an impressive and well-conceived piece of work. Bell and Weinberg state their intent to concentrate upon 'diversity – the ways in which homosexuals differ from each other' (p. 25). They properly title their book *Homosexualities* because 'there are "homosexualities" and "heterosexualities", each involving a variety of interrelated dimensions' (p. 219). To examine these diversities they subjected their interview data to a multivariate factor and cluster analysis to produce a typology of homosexual experience, which revealed the following groups:

1 Close coupled. Same-sex partner in quasi-marriage; few sex problems or other partners; little cruising.
2 Open coupled. Same-sex partner in close living arrangement; increased number of sex problems, other partners, or cruising.
3 Functional. Not coupled; many sex partners; high sex activity; little regret, few sex problems.
4 Dysfunctional. Not coupled; many sex partners *or* high sex activity; regretful, many sex problems.
5 Asexual. Not coupled; little sex activity; few partners, little cruising.

Even if we acknowledge, as Suppe (1981) maintains, that the methodology is faulted, the sampling unrepresentative, important variables not investigated, and that the respondents do not fall neatly into one of the resulting five taxa, the Bell and Weinberg typology is, heuristically speaking, a step forward. It defines diversity in behavioural terms and encourages us to examine these categories in a more detailed fashion. The major fault of the study was the failure to generate a heterosexual typology, which would probably have revealed a very similar breakdown, permitting a cross-preference look at two major types and subtypes of sexually diverse behaviour.

In a follow-up work, *Sexual Preferences: Its Development in Men and Women*, Bell et al. (1981) examined the acquisition of heterosexual and homosexual behaviours although, again, the former is slighted in favour of the latter. This work has also received methodological criticism for use of retrospective data and misuse of path analysis (Gagnon 1981). However, once again Bell et al. (1981) have produced data which give weight to social learning theories of sexual preference acquisition, an area about which almost nothing is known. Suppe's (1981) and Gagnon's (1981) criticisms are relevant and deserve attention, but they possibly focus too much on what is not there to the exclusion of what is.

Psychological tests

The basic problem with almost all traditional psychological tests is that the obtained data are at some remove from the behaviour of interest, i.e. responses in one domain are used to identify people in another. In the sexual area let us say that well-adjusted normals are known to endorse certain clusters of items on a personality inventory. Later it is discovered that paedophiles, exhibitionists or sexual aggressives seem to endorse other sets of items, so deviance subscales are derived for that instrument. This is inefficient as more direct and reliable information could be gathered in a less obtuse way. The subscales derived from traditional instruments may on occasion differentiate sexually conventional from unconventional persons, but they tell us little or nothing beyond that about sexual diversity. We will consider two types here.

Projective methods

These procedures, due to the deliberate use of ambiguous, often non-sexual stimuli, are the least informative methods for assessing sexual interests. Most of the data on the use of these techniques have been obtained from homosexuals. They are most often used for categorical, diagnostic purposes with no attempt to obtain more qualitative information. Therefore, if one assumes their validity, they make only gross differentiation between various sexual persuasions, and then rarely. Following are some typical examples.

The Rorschach inkblot test has seen considerable service in the search for 'homosexual signs', content responses predominantly produced by homosexual testees. Early research (Bergmann 1945) identified some of these which included a high number of sex responses, human movement responses with homoerotic content, or heterophobia. The industry standard was presented a few years later in what have come to be known as the 'Wheeler signs', 20 typical responses of homosexuals which are either specific responses to areas of particular Rorschach cards, or certain general responses to any card (Wheeler 1949). Such data as these techniques yield are at best mixed and in general not very useful. Reviewing this literature, and once more seeking evidence for the signs in a reasonably controlled study, Hendlin (1976) could find no evidence for this index in two groups of educated, well-adusted homosexual and heterosexual males. He recommended that clinicians cease using the Rorschach to assess male homosexuality.

Nor have the Rorschach or other classical projective techniques such as the Thematic Apperception Test or the Draw-A-Person test fared better with another important clinical population, female homosexuals. Reviewing this literature, Reiss et al. (1974) state that lesbian protocols 'cannot be easily distinguished from those of heterosexual women. . . . There is little from the projective literature to suggest that female homosexuality is a specifiable clinical entity' (p. 77). And of the projective techniques themselves 'One of the problems in reviewing the literature on projective approaches . . . is the absence of consistency or commonality in the studies. Each researcher has defined the problem independently and developed hypotheses and methodologies with little reference to previous findings' (p. 77). It is in the supposed strength of the projective techniques – the use of ambiguous stimuli and the independent skill, expertise and experience of the examining clinician – that their actual weakness lies. Grounded in psychoanalytic theory, they focus on purported unconscious processes and intrapsychic dynamics rather than ongoing cognitions and overt behaviour, thus actually inhibiting rather than facilitating our understanding of sexual diversity.

Objective methods

In this group are those usually called personality tests or inventories, included here as they fit the definition above that responses in one domain, i.e. reports on moods, feelings, attitudes, are used to make inferences in another domain, e.g. mental states, motivation, sexual deviation, etc. When an examiner is involved, his or her role is usually formal and follows a predetermined pattern.

By far the most popular personality instrument for these purposes has been the MMPI. Typically a particular group of sexual deviants is found to show elevations on one or more of the scales, or items are abstracted from various scales to form a subscale which identifies a group of deviants. For example, Marsh et al. (1955) developed a Sexual Deviation (Sd) scale in the attempt to separate child molesters, psychotics, neurotics and college students. The subscale differentiated the molesters from the students but not from the other two clinical groups, a finding very typical of this literature. Toobert et al. (1959) developed a 24-item Pedophile (Pe) scale and found that child molesters could not be differentiated from each other by their responses to this scale, but as a group they could be separated from normals and criminal offenders, another typical finding. Studying personality features of paedophiles, McCreary (1975) was able to differentiate molesters on four of the clinical scales. Similarly Ohlson and Wilson (1974) found that three of the MMPI scales separated heterosexual from homosexual females. An item analysis showed that 38 items could be used to form a subscale for this purpose, but only four of those were related to overt homosexuality. An analogous study by Adelman (1977) also found differences between lesbians and heterosexuals on two scales, the homosexuals showing elevations on

Masculinity–Feminity (Mf) and Schizophrenia (Sc). Item analysis showed that the Sc elevations were related to the social alienation items but not to the pathological ones. Finally, Husted and Edwards (1976) had normal subjects keep daily records of sexual behaviours including number of sexual partners, frequency of sexual arousal, and total sexual outlet (as measured by the total number of ejaculations through either masturbation or coitus in a one-month period). These data were then correlated with the MMPI. Results showed that both Social Introversion (Si) and Depression (D) were positively and significantly related to autoerotic stimulation and arousal, but not with heterosexual activity.

These studies show how sophisticated personality tests such as the MMPI are most frequently used: to differentiate sexually unconventional groups from normals or non-sexual offenders. The issue of diversity beyond that point is usually not pursued. Only the Husted and Edwards (1976) study examined the relationship of personality variables to a range of specific male sexual behaviours, and then in a limited correlational fashion.

Even in cases where personality tests are constructed specifically with sexual interest assessment in mind, the reported problems persist. One of the most extensively researched instruments in this area is The Sex Inventory (Thorne 1966a), a 200-item self-report inventory using a combination of direct and projective questions to assess sexual interest and a variety of psychoanalytically based personality factors. It is psychometrically sound (Allen and Haupt 1966; Thorne 1966b) and has been shown, not surprisingly, to discriminate sexual deviants from normals (Haupt and Allen 1966; Thorne and Haupt 1966) but not from each other. Using only two of the Sex Inventory scales (29 items) Cowden and Pacht (1969) found that it could be used in a correctional setting to screen sexual deviants from other inmates. Using the same 29 items but expanding the response options Johnston and Anderson (1981) showed that this version could differentiate paedophiles, rapists and exhibitionists from college students but, again, not from each other. The Sex Inventory seems useful for limited purposes but fails to differentiate sexually deviant persons from one another and provides no information on history, type or frequency of sexual practices.

The problem with traditional projective techniques and personality tests is that most of them were never intended to be used to assess sexual interests. Problems of inference persist in these instruments. Presenting ambiguous stimuli and asking no questions, or asking questions about one thing in order to make inferences about another are ineffective ways of gaining information. In my judgement the use of traditional psychological tests to assess sexual interests should be abandoned, especially in light of the fact that far more useful and direct methods are readily available.

Self-reports on sexual behaviour

The devices described in this section were either developed for research purposes, e.g. from general surveys of sexual knowledge, attitudes or behaviours to individual self-reports on specific sexual practices, or for purposes of assessing change resulting from sexual therapies. Even if we grant the potential unreliability of self-report, many of these methods provide data which are very useful for understanding sexual diversity. As in the areas already reviewed the methods and data are variable in quality. Despite their faults, use of the better self-report methods begins the move away from the theoretical, speculative and anecdotal, and towards the sounder empirical traditions of sex research.

Questionnaires

The questionnaire approach, as we will define it here, is often devoted to larger social issues rather than the specifics of behaviour. These studies inform us in a general way about structural changes in the social milieu; they are most often uninformative about the specifics of sexuality. Several examples will demonstrate this approach.

The use of standardized instruments such as the Sex Knowledge and Attitude Test (SKAT) provides such general information. The SKAT has four subscales: heterosexual relations (HR), sexual myths (SM), autoeroticism (M), and abortion (A). The test was standardized on a broad population of 850 students and has been administered to very large groups since. Norms exist for all subscales.

Miller and Lief (1976) studied the responses of 556 males and females to the SKAT items dealing with masturbation: the masturbation attitude score (MA), the masturbation knowledge score (MK), and the masturbation experience score (ME), all of which increase with increasing liberal attitude, knowledge and experience. Specifically these authors were interested in whether attitude, knowledge and experience were related to sexual intercourse. Predictably, non-virgins were found to be more likely to endorse liberal attitudes about masturbation and be more knowledgeable about it than virgins. Other representative results were also of the broad brush variety and agree with earlier findings. Seventy six per cent of Miller and Lief's sample believed masturbation to be healthy; Hunt (1974) found 80 per cent endorsing this position. Miller and Lief found the cumulative incidence of masturbation to be 97 per cent for males and 78 per cent for females; Kinsey et al. (1948, 1953) found 92 per cent and 62 per cent; Hunt (1974), 94 per cent and 63 per cent. In Miller and Lief's sample attitudes, knowledge and experience were correlated, the strongest relationship being between attitudes and knowledge. This study is highly representative of the general information approach to sexual diversity.

Noting that premarital sexual attitudes of unmarried university students underwent gradual change between 1940 and the mid-1960s, Bauman and Wilson (1976) sampled attitudes of this population in 1968 and again in 1972. Informing the male and female respondents that they were interested in their personal values and standards, they administered the Premarital Sexual Permissiveness Scale to the two samples. The items were of the following variety:

3 Sexual intercourse is acceptable for the male before marriage when he is in love.
5 Sexual intercourse is acceptable for the male before marriage even if he does not feel particularly affectionate toward his partner.

The items were then repeated with the female as referent. In comparing the 1972 student sample with that of 1968, Bauman and Wilson found more permissive attitudes toward premarital sex, fewer differences in attitude between men and women, and less adherence to the double standard. These results generally supported earlier studies (Christensen and Gregg 1970; Bell and Chaskes 1970). Although something of an elaboration of the obvious, this is an investigation highly typical of the genre.

A much more ambitious study along similar lines was undertaken by Schmidt and Sigusch (1972) in which they assessed changes in sexual behaviour among males and females between 1960 and 1970. These studies were made of 4568 men and women in 1966, 1968 and 1970, using a combination of self-report questionnaire and questionnaire-based interviews. Items were directed at sexuality in childhood, sexual development since puberty, masturbatory and coital behaviour in the preceding 12 months, first coitus, coital abstinence and attitudes towards sexuality. Respondents were 3666 university students (1966), 300 unskilled and semi-skilled workers (1968), and 602 teenagers. The results give an example of indications of structural changes in the social milieu: (1) age at first masturbation dropped slightly for boys of high and low education levels, markedly for girls of high educational level, and not at all for girls of low educational level; (2) age at first coitus decreased markedly; (3) age at initiation of sociosexual activities decreased markedly among the less educated; (4) ability to experience sex free from conflict increased for the less educated; and interestingly, (5) none of the above was due to extreme changes in sexual standards or philosophy. The Schmidt and Sigusch study is an excellent example of questionnaire research which provides information at a molar level, in this case complete with sociological analysis of results.

Smaller in scope but similar in intent is an investigation of the convergence of male and female sexual arousal after exposure to sexually explicit stimuli (Schmidt 1975). In a series of five studies, 1124 men and women were exposed to slides, films and narrative descriptions of kissing and caressing, fondling, coitus, masturbation and sexual aggression. Following each study, each participant completed a questionnaire immediately and again 24 hours later. Schmidt's interest was in investigating the stereotype of the female as one whose sexuality finds expression only in the context of an emotional and personal relationship. In general he found more similarities than differences between men and women in terms of actual coital and masturbatory activity and fantasies following exposure to erotic stimuli. Although of narrower focus, these are molar data similar to those of Schmidt and Sigusch (1972). They would have been strengthened had the questionnaire data been supplemented by direct measurement of sexual arousal to the stimuli, possibly yielding quite different results.

Finally, an example of even narrower focus, the perceptions of a random sample of adults in a medium-sized midwestern American community of a particular deviant sexual behaviour; consensual wife swapping, or swinging. Spanier and Cole (1975) note that swinging is a form of sexual diversity which redefines a formerly proscribed behaviour, extramarital sex, as positive and acceptable. A stratified area probability sample was contacted and 597 married adults were given a self-administered questionnaire. The questions were rather mild, e.g. 'Have you ever been approached about engaging in this sort of activity?', and did not ask for specific information about the participants' sexual activities in this context. Nonetheless, the results were illuminating in providing information on the awareness of a peculiar social phenomenon by rather ordinary citizens. Fifty-six per cent of the sample had heard of swinging, 7 per cent had direct knowledge of persons who had participated, 3 per cent had been directly approached, and although fewer than 2 per cent had actually participated, 7 per cent stated that they would if given the opportunity. The authors conclude that if these percentages found in a medium-sized conservative community are consistent with the extent of swinging behaviour elsewhere in the US, a substantial number of fairly conventional people are actively involved in a structured and very unconventional sexual practice.

These examples are very interesting if one seeks information on general trends in social and sexual life. Of the examples given the more interesting ones for heuristic purposes are those of Schmidt (1975) and Spanier and Cole (1975), and especially Schmidt's, as they point the way toward accumulation of data on what people do when they behave diversely, rather than what they know about some phenomenon or believe other people know.

Rating scales

These devices are used to assess human sexual interests or behaviours often both in research and as part of a therapeutic activity. Several examples are presented here where rating scales have been used to assess deviant and non-deviant populations.

Sexual attitudes are a measure of sexual interest and shifts in those attitudes could be one measure of therapeutic progress. Marks and Sartorius (1968) used the semantic differential procedure to examine concepts held by sexual deviants undergoing treatment. Four bipolar scales were constructed to assess the dimension of sexual attraction, e.g. 'seductive–repulsive', 'sexy–sexless', 'exciting–dull' and 'erotic–frigid'; six of a general evaluative nature, e.g. 'approachable–distant'; and three relating to anxiety, e.g. 'relaxed–tense'. These adjectives were placed at opposite ends of a 7-point scale along with concepts to be judged, for a total of 10 concepts on 13 scales. Both sexual and non-sexual concepts were judged. General sexual concepts included 'sexual intercourse', 'women' or 'my wife', while specific concepts were items such as 'panties'. Administered to a group of sexual deviants being treated by electrical aversion, Marks and Sartorius showed that conceptual changes occurred during treatment, e.g. fetish objects were devalued and reported to be unpleasant and sexless post-treatment.

A similar investigation was reported by Feldman et al. (1966). These authors developed a technique called the Sexual Orientation Method (SOM) to assess levels of heterosexual and homosexual orientation to evaluate response to treatment for homosexuality by aversive conditioning. Like Marks and Sartorius (1968) they also used a semantic differential, taking six adjectives from the original Osgood et al. (1957) list as sexually relevant: 'Interesting', 'attractive', 'handsome', 'hot', 'pleasurable' and 'exciting'. Scores were derived for two concepts: 'Women (or men) are sexually to me' and the respondent chose one of five scale positions: (1) very exciting, (2) quite exciting, (3) neither exciting or unexciting, (4) quite unexciting, and (5) very unexciting. Feldman et al. present impressive psychometric data on the procedure and show that it was a good index of treatment change between a patient group which improved in treatment and one which did not. The authors state that the SOM is not intended to replace clinical interview but to provide concurrent qualitative data.

These two studies are unique in their approach to assaying concepts about sexuality. The Marks and Sartorius (1968) is the more fruitful in that it deals with highly specific concepts, e.g. 'panties', and makes useful comparisons by means of a repertory grid technique (Slater 1965).

A variation of the Sexual Orientation Method was developed by Harbison et al. (1974) to measure the degree of interest a male or female shows in particular heterosexual or homosexual behaviour. The four sexual evaluation scales of Marks and Sartorius (1968) were used, and the respondent rated them on the five scale positions of Feldman et al. (1966). Five behaviours relating to kissing, touching and sexual intercourse were used. Like Feldman et al. the adjectives were presented as pairs:

> quite exciting—
>
> 71 Touching my partner is sexually to me
>
> very exciting—

Harbison et al. tested the procedure with both normal and deviant groups and demonstrated that their version of the SOM had acceptable internal consistency, test–retest reliability and criterion-related validity. The authors argue that the technique is sensitive and reliable in measuring changes in particular symptoms and attitudes, allows examination of the respondent's consistency of response, permits investigation of various areas of sexual behaviour, and yields a range of scores large enough to assess change within treatment. The move from the concepts of Feldman et al. (1966) to specific behaviours in the Harbison et al. revision is a step up in sexual behaviour assessment of this sort. It would be further improved by the addition of more behaviours to be rated.

Bentler (1968a) also found fault with the Feldman et al. (1966) approach in that it failed to report changes in behaviour. He designed a Guttman-type scale to assess the extent to which a male respondent had engaged in various forms of heterosexual behaviour. This was useful, Bentler argued, to serve as a therapeutic adjunct in cases of heterosexually anxious and inhibited males, and for assessing the degree to which homosexuals in treatment were orienting towards heterosexual involvement. He initially constructed a set of 56 items dealing with various forms of heterosexual behaviour and administered it to 175 normal males. Bentler sought a Guttman ordinal scale, i.e. a person endorsing an item midway on the scale is in effect endorsing all previous, presumably 'easier', items, and is assumed to have engaged in those behaviours. A form of factor analysis produced a final subset of 21 items. Examples follow, progressing from 'easy' to more 'difficult' items:

1 One minute continuous lip kissing.
5 Kissing nipples of female breasts.
10 Manual manipulation of female genitals.
15 Mutual manual manipulation of genitals to mutual orgasm.
21 Mutual oral manipulation of genitals to mutual orgasm.

The data supported the scaling work of previous investigations and, importantly, the speculations of Kinsey et al. (1948) that a standard sequencing of behaviours occurs in the acquisition of heterosexual experiences. Bentler (1968b) reasoned that the existence of a male hierarchy implied an equivalent hierarchy for females which would be useful in treatment of low sexual desire and to evaluate the sexual experiences of women. Use of the same scaling techniques did produce an equivalent hierarchy of 21 items describing exactly the same behaviours from a female viewpoint, although the order differed slightly. Zuckerman (1973) also developed Guttman scales for male and female sexual experiences. He produced two 12-item scales but did not describe the method of derivation. Although these scales contain fewer items, they are highly similar in content to those of Bentler (1968a, 1968b). Such data provide an important validation of earlier work (Kinsey et al. (1948, 1953) and serve as sound models for one type of assessment of sexual behaviour.

Rating scales have also been used in non-therapeutic research investigations which also bear upon past and present findings on sexual diversity. For example, Kinsey et al. (1953) reported differences in male and female response to erotic stimuli, males reporting greater arousal to visual and narrative stimuli. More recent research has indicated that the differences are not as great as previously thought. Investigating these differences Steele and Walker (1974) presented 20 slides with heterosexual, homosexual and sadomasochistic content to 100 male and 100 female college students who rated them on 50-point Likert scales in terms of: sexual stimulation, liking for the slide, and extremeness of the behaviour portrayed. Somewhat contrary to prior results they found that both males and females report minimal liking for the slides and minimal stimulation, males reporting more liking and stimulation than females. This is another investigation which could have been considerably strengthened by concurrent measure of sexual arousal.

Wishnoff (1978) was interested in whether less or more sexually explicit stimuli elicit extreme sexual anxiety. As a potential adjunctive therapy procedure he presented 45 women, preselected as virginal and anxious, with videotapes showing either explicit or non-explicit sexual activities. They then completed post-test instruments, two anxiety scales and Zuckerman's (1973) scale of sexual experience. Results indicated that anxious, sexually inexperienced women exposed to explicit erotic stimuli in a laboratory situation reported lowered general and specific sexual anxiety levels, and also more willingness to participate in a variety of sexual experiences than women exposed to non-explicit stimuli. Wishoff discussed these data as supporting Bandura's (1977) statements on vicarious and symbolic social learning and suggested the use of media aids in education and therapy;

Bentler and Peeler (1979) and Newcomb and Bentler (1982) recently performed an elegant pair of studies investigating dimensions of female orgasmic responsiveness. The argument which persists in this area is that female orgasm is a physiologically unidimensional process which all women experience to a greater or lesser extent , irrespective of stimulatory source (Masters and Johnson 1966) *versus* the view that there is a demarcation between masturbatory and coital orgasm which is subjectively perceived by females (Robertiello 1970; Singer and Singer 1972; Butler 1976). Bentler and Peeler (1979) constructed a 38-item Orgasm Questionnaire by principal components anlysis which was presented to 281 female college students who rated the items on a 7-point scale. The items was highly specific as the following examples show:

How fast does your orgasm build once it starts?
Do you experience sucking sensations in your vagina during orgasm?
How fast is your heartbeat right after orgasm?

The results failed to support the unidimensional orgasm process; separate coital and masturbatory facts of orgasmic experience were identified. The results, however, were questionable as only 23 (8 per cent) of the subjects had had both masturbatory and coital experience, 131 (47 per cent) had experienced only masturbatory orgasms, and 127 (45 per cent) had experienced neither. To remedy this embarassing selection problem, Newcomb and Bentler (1982) replicated the study with sexually experienced women. One sample (N=115) was given the two-dimensional questionnaire of Bentler and Peeler (1979) and the data replicated the earlier finding of the distinction between coital and masturbatory orgasm. The earlier study's questions had failed to distinguish between solitary masturbation and stimulation by a partner, so a second sample (n=101) was administered a questionnaire which was three-dimensional. Data analysis substantiated the existence of three dimensions. Interestingly, responsiveness was highly correlated across the three dimensions and Newcomb and Bentler were able to isolate a second-order factor of general orgasmic responsiveness, consistent with Masters and Johnson's (1966) concept of a unitary physiological process. Using statistical modelling, Newcomb and Bentler went on to show that masturbatory responsiveness predicted coital responsiveness, which predicted non-coital partner responsiveness. This is consistent with current practice for treating female orgasmic dysfunction (e.g. Kaplan 1974, 1979) and agrees with prior findings (Bentler 1968a, 1968b) of the sequential ordering of sexual experience, i.e. partner- produced non-coital orgasms are more sophisticated than coital orgasms, which are in turn more sophisticated than masturbatory orgasms.

Inventories specific to sexual interest and preference

These inventories deal with highly specific aspects of sexual behaviour and request a qualitative response from the subject. In so doing they expand the data base afforded by the better questionnaires such as the SKAT, or superior rating scales such as those of Bentler (1968a, 1968b) or Zuckerman (1973).

One of the superior inventories is the Clarke Sexual History Questionnaire (Paitich et al. 1977). This 225-item instrument samples the frequency of, desire for and disgust for a broad range of sexual behaviours and has been shown to discriminate clinically various groups of sexual deviants (N=454) from non-deviant controls. The 24 scales of the questionnaire were derived by factor analysis and have been shown to have adequate discriminant and criterion-related validity. The SHQ can differentiate exhibitionists, hetero- and homosexual paedophiles, incest offenders, transsexuals and multiple deviants (more than one deviation) from each other. Additionally, it provides information on preferences for various sexual activities and frequencies of engaging in certain activities, unusual for this kind of instrument and useful for understanding diversity. The original SHQ has been revised (Langevin 1982) but the new version is not a substantial improvement (Langevin et al. 1982).

Although it is primarily used as a categorical diagnostic instrument, analysis of an individual's response to various items yields extremely detailed and useful data. A brief sampling of representative items provides a feel for the explicit content of this instrument:

88 Have you ever put your penis in the rear end (rectum) of a boy 12 or younger since the age of 16? How many times?

122 Since you were 16, have you ever secretly and intentionally tried to see women undressing by looking in windows or by other means? (not counting movies or sex shows) How many times?

134 Have you ever been sexually aroused by someone hurting you physically, humiliating or embarassing you? How many times?

157 Have you ever taken part in group sex? How many times?

While items 88 and 134 above are clearly meant to apply to sexual deviants, that is not necessarily true for items 122 or 157. Item analysis of the responses of self-labelled normals would definitely expand our understanding of the extent to which their preferences, fantasies and overt behaviours diverge from the supposed conventional norms.

Recognizing the need for an instrument which could assess the actual sexual functioning and satifaction of heterosexual couples, Lo Piccolo and Steger (1974) developed a paper-and-pencil self-report inventory. Modelled after Bentler's (1968a, 1968b) Guttman scale, it covers the range of marital heterosexual behaviours in a 17-item list. For each of the 17 behaviours, husband and wife answer six questions on a 6-point rating scale with verbal labels. These six questions are presented on three dimensions: frequency of occurrence, degree of pleasure, and response of self and mate. For example:

14 The female caressing the male's genitals with her mouth (lips and tongue)

When you and your mate engage in sexual behaviour, does this particular activity occur? How often would you like this activity to occur?

1 Currently occurs:
   1—Never
   2—Rarely (10% of the time)
   3—Occasionally (25% of the time)
   4—Fairly often (50% of the time)
   5—Usually (75% of the time)
   6—Always

The remaining scales have similar response options. The data are then plotted on 11 scales in an MMPI-like format, providing information on dissatisfaction with frequency and range of behaviours engaged in, self-acceptance, pleasure obtained from sexual activity, accurate knowledge of partner preferences, and acceptance of partner. Norms for the various scales were established with 124 volunteer couples who reported a satisfactory sexual relationship. Reliability and validity studies were conducted with an additional 191 couples, 28 of whom were undergoing sexual dysfunction treatment. The authors report that the Sexual Interaction Inventory (SII) is generally internally consistent, reliable on retest, able to discriminate clinical from non-clinical groups, reactive to treatment, and correlated with self-report of sexual adjustment. It has diagnostic advantages in that the scale elevations can pinpoint which aspects of sexual behaviour are most dysfunctional and thus changes in the elevations during or after treatment serve as a symptom-specific outcome measure. It is conceivable that this approach could be profitably modified for assessment and treatment of less conventional behaviours such as adult homosexual dysfunction.

A very similar instrument is the Sexual Arousal Inventory (SAI) (Hoon et al. 1976a), designed to measure the construct of sexual arousability in women. This was intended for assessment of sexual dysfunction in females, and to collect information on sexual experience and activity, satisfaction with sexual responsivity, and awareness of physiological changes during sexual arousal. The authors constructed a pool of 131 items which they presented to 151 females for rating on 7-point Likert scale. Factor analysis narrowed this pool to a 28-item set. Although examining another dimension of experience, a sample item shows that the SAI is not unlike the procedures of Bentler (1968a, 1968b), Zuckerman (1973) and Lo Piccolo and Steger (1974):

17 When you hear sounds of pleasure during sex.
   −1 adversely affects arousal; unthinkable, repulsive, distracting

0 doesn't affect sexual arousal
1 possibly causes sexual arousal
2 sometimes causes sexual arousal; slightly arousing
3 usually causes sexual arousal; moderately arousing
4 almost always causes sexual arousal; very arousing
5 always causes sexual arousal; extremely arousing

A second sample completed the 28-item set. Data analysis showed that the SAI had concurrent validity with respect to sexual experience, activity and satisfaction, and could separate clinical from non-clinical groups. Importantly it may be used in different formats with single, married, or homosexual women. Like the SII (Lo Piccolo and Steger 1974) the SAI may be used for diagnosing sexual dysfunction in specific areas of behaviour and experience, and for assessing change in sexual dysfunction therapy.

The PopPsych alternative

Thus far I have criticized interviewers and instruments for asking questions that are insufficiently precise or for asking an insufficient number of the right questions. As we have seen in some of the cited studies, extraordinary care was taken to obtain a random, stratified probability sample of the US population (e.g. Merritt et al. 1975) only to have respondents presented with questionable items such as 'Sexual materials make people sex crazy.'

There is an alternative to this approach and we find it in the popular psychology literature, what I have termed the 'PopPsych alternative'. PopPsych data do not appear in refereed, archival journals or scholarly texts; they are intended for mass consumption and they are found most frequently in the mass market paperback display at the newsagent's shop or the supermarket. It is not my intent to disparage this literature; indeed, within it lies a curious irony which is something of a bad joke on traditional social science. PopPsych researchers generally make no effort to obtain random, stratified probability samples and their respondents are usually the readers of newspapers and mass consumption periodicals. Ironically, what they do properly is ask relevant and detailed questions. Several recent examples will illustrate this approach.

On the first page of *The Kahn Report on Sexual Preferences* (Kahn and Davis 1981) appears the following: 'Marsha yearned for the natural wetness that she felt when she read Rosemary Rogers' novels or when she fantasized or masturbated' (p. 3). The intrepid reader who persists to p. 45 and beyond will find here an interesting replication of the Levitt and Brady (1965) study on sexual preferences in males. Kahn's study is worthy of consideration, even though she used a highly biased sample of upper-middle-class, educated males and females, in that it provides an interesting look at the expressed preferences of a rather select group. Levitt and Brady (1965) had constructed a list of 19 themes, mostly common heterosexual and homosexual behaviours, selected 57 photographs (three per theme) as representative of these behaviours, then had college males rate them on a 0–5 scale in terms of their potential for sexual stimulation. From an original pool of 280 subjects Kahn selected 200 in the age-range 27–49. All were Caucasian, self-admitted heterosexuals, from professional, academic and social organizations, of varied ethnic background, all Chicago-area urbanites. The arbitrariness of the selection procedure was perhaps serendipitous, as this is the sort of subject rarely studied in sex research. The subjects were first required to rate the randomly presented photographs in terms of their own sexual preferences. As a second task they were asked to rate the themes (e.g. homosexual cunnilingus) in terms of (1) how other persons of their sex would rate them, and (2) how persons of the opposite sex would rate them.

Following is a sample of the expressed preferences obtained:

Activities women prefer for themselves
1 Heterosexual cunnilingus; male on female.
2 Triad: two males, one female, coitus and oral-genital.
3 Heterosexual petting, both nude.
4 Heterosexual intercourse, female superior.
5 Heterosexual petting, both partially clad.

Activities men prefer for themselves
1 Heterosexual fellatio; female on male.
2 Nude female.
3 Heterosexual intercourse, female superior.
4 Heterosexual petting, both nude.
5 Partially clad female.

Since Kahn's subjects were older, better educated and presumably more sexually sophisticated, their data differ from Levitt and Brady's (1965) college males. The samples shown indicate that there is nothing irreconcilable in the expressed preferences; there is similarity but the order of preference differs. The only really unusual finding is the expressed female preference for the threesome. The balance of the report is concerned with a fairly exhaustive and careful discussion of the data and their relation to other work. Kahn's study should receive more attention than it will probably get as it is filled with (albeit inadvertent) suggestions for other research and deserves replication with other populations, particularly lower-middle-class, blue-collar males and females.

Seemingly more in the PopPsych tradition is *The Hite Report* on female sexuality (Hite 1981). Replete with detailed self-reports ('I prefer the tongue because it's smaller and more versatile than the penis' (p. 377)), the data of this investigation at first appear to be considerably less than they are. It is in fact a formidable study, a more complete account of what 1844 females actually *do* sexually than any other source presently available. It is a true study of sexual diversity.

Hite prepared three different versions of a simple questionnaire which required detailed, written replies. They were distributed under the aegis of the National Organization of Women (NOW) and were sent to chapters of NOW, abortion rights groups, women's centres and women's newsletters; notices were placed in newspapers and women's magazines for write-in requests; *Oui* magazine ran the questionnaire and it appeared in a book available since 1974 as well as in the *Report*. One hundred thousand questionnaires were eventually distributed (72,000 by mail) and 3019 replies were received. *The Hite Report* is based on 1844 of those replies from women aged 14–78 received from 49 of the 50 United States and from Canada, and a few received from outside North America. Occupational status of the respondents was broad, from professional to unskilled to unemployed.

The questionnaire was divided into five parts: orgasm, sexual activities, relationships, life stages, and a section of general questions. The great virtue of the *Report*, as in most good social science, is its very simplicity and the total directness of its approach:

> 8 Please give a graphic description or drawing of how your body could best be stimulated to orgasm. (p. 580)
> 15 How do you masturbate? What is the sequence of physical events which occur? Please give a detailed description. (p. 580)

Much of the text is composed of the edited replies to these questions and lengthy tabular summarizations. As a singular example of how the data were treated, Hite was able to identify six general masturbation types (or styles) and 13 subtypes (pp. 591–7), a variety of finding rare in the professional literature (e.g. Newcomb and Bentler 1982).

Perhaps this sort of information, at least for the present, may only be available to us through mass-market channels for, as we have seen, establishment researchers are rarely so frank in approaching their respondents. *The Hite Report* therefore has something to teach us methodologically and, heuristically, much to offer in suggesting follow up studies.

A similar but less impressive study is *The Cosmo Report* (Wolfe 1981). In early 1980 the editors of *Cosmopolitan* magazine, a periodical directed at young, upper-middle-class women, published a 79-item survey on female sexual practices. A sample item:

> 25 How long do you like foreplay to last?

Less than 5 minutes —
5 to 10 minutes —
Up to 20 minutes —
Up to half an hour —
Up to an hour or more —

To their surprise they received 106,000 replies. In late 1980 they published 'The Sexual Profile of That *Cosmopolitan* Girl', based on 15,000 replies which met their criteria of the 'typical' reader: a woman between the ages of 18–34 who lives in a city of over one million and earns her own living, hardly a representative sample of American women. Wolfe was invited to examine all the data as 86 per cent of the replies had failed to meet the inclusionary criteria for the original survey. The age-range of the respondents was very broad, they were from all occupational levels, were married, single, cohabiting, divorced or lesbian, and many had included letters, comments, elaborations, reminiscences, or scraps from diaries and journals. Realizing what the sex survey had actually tapped, Wolfe wrote *The Cosmo Report*.

This is not as elaborate nor as rich a study as *The Hite Report*. The data are in the nature of flat reports of survey findings supplemented by many individual reports and some discussion. Two examples:

2 *Marital infidelity*
MAJOR FINDINGS:
Fifty-four per cent of the women who were married had one or more sexual experiences with partners other than their husbands since marrying. (p. 189)

3 *Father–daughter incest*
MAJOR FINDINGS:
Three per cent of the women had experienced father–daughter incest. (p. 220)

This portion of the literature is not trash, as many professionals presuppose, but I hasten to add that neither is it treasure. In the end, for all their imperfections, these reports provide a window on human sexuality rarely seen in the professional literature. One cannot read them and fail to recognize that what is being described are frank and often quite touching accounts of human experience, what people actually *do* sexually, and that this has immense potential value for our efforts to understand sexual diversity. The PopPsych reports suggest more questions than they answer and perhaps therein is their utility. In their fashion they provide us a rich lode of information which has yet to be mined.

A minor genre: The thrilling escape

These are usually studies of some sexual phenomenon performed by amateur social scientists and occasionally by professionals who behave like amateurs. Reading them it is difficult to discern whether they are intended to titillate, inform, or both. Bartell's (1971) ostensibly serious account of swinging is of the thrilling escape genre. In these studies the investigator usually gathers as much information as possible about a particular practice, finds out how it is socially structured, then gains the confidence of one or more participants. To this point the procedure resembles the participant-observer approach, to be discussed below. Inevitably, sooner or later an invitation to participate is forthcoming. At this point the investigator performs a deft escape in order to avoid having to 'do anything'. Example:

> When we asked him to invite us to some of these exciting parties he said that he first had to determine how sexually talented we were. We asked him how he intended to decide this, and he had a simple solution: 'Why, we rent a motel room right now and I go with your wife.' A bit taken aback, I inquired: 'What do I do in the meantime?' Jerry shrugged, 'Well, you can watch if you want to.' I replied I would have to leave it up to my wife. She said she wasn't quite up to it, and we took our leave. (Bartell 1971, p. 75)

This type of report should never be trusted without proper cross-validation by persons who did participate.

Direct observation

It is often said that human sex research will not permit direct observation because (1) people will not perform sexually in front of observers and, anyway, (2) it is unethical to ask them to do so, or (3) participant observers will (a) alter the event being studied by their presence, or (b) become so mentally and physiologically incapacitated if they personally participate that they will be unable to report reliably on the event. This latter objection is probably accurate but the others are not. There are two types of direct observation: participant and non-participant.

Participant observation. In this variety of investigation the researcher participates to some degree in the sexual activity under study and then reports on it from that perspective. There is the real objection of reactivity here, that the presence of the observer alters the event being observed and therefore no data so obtained will be an accurate account of it. This may to some extent be so but the only options are not participating (which ensures that no data will be collected from this unique perspective) or non-participant observation.

Humphreys' *Tearoom Trade: Impersonal Sex in Public Places* (1970) is the classic participant-observation study in the sexual diversity literature. His interest was in the patterns of social interaction and brief, impersonal, uncommitted sexual encounters of males in public toilets ('tearooms'). The tearooms 'are accessible, easily recognized by the initiate, and provide little public visibility' (p. 3) of these encounters. The participants engage in homosexual acts but few are active in the homosexual subculture and many deny homosexual identity; as the author puts it, the research concerns participants in homosexual acts rather than homosexuality itself. Ingratiating himself with the tearoom trade, Humphreys passed as a deviant, a tearoom voyeur or 'watchqueen.' In this role, which doubles as participant voyeur and police lookout, Humphreys distributed his observations throughout any day, and observed and meticulously recorded the dynamics of fifty such encounters. His technique was to observe an encounter in the toilet, then depart to complete a systematic observation sheet on which he recorded time and place involved, a description of the actors, a diagram on which their movements could be plotted, locations of the encounter within the tearoom, a description of the progress of the action, and his reactions. Following is a sample of an encounter description:

> by then, Y (principal passive recipient) had an erection – X (principal aggressor) reached over and began to masturbate him with right hand, himself with left. I moved over to the far window. A (other participant) looked at me. I smiled and nodded. X and Y walked to stall 1. X lowered pants and sat down. Y, standing in front with pants still unzipped and erection showing, continued to masturbate for another minute, then he inserted penis in X's mouth. He reached climax in about 3 minutes . . . He then went to basin, washed hands and left. (p. 35).

Aside from this rather remarkable observation technique, there are two other features of the study that distinguish it. By noting car licence numbers he was able, with police co-operation, to trace a large number of tearoom participants to their home neighbourhoods. Since he did not wish to approach them directly, in the context of other research involving the interviewing of males for a large health survey, he included a large sample of the tearoom deviants as interviewees and so was able to compare them with a large group of non-deviants on a number of variables. Finally, through familiarity and relationships struck in the tearooms he was able to confide his real motives and secure a small group he called the 'intensive dozen' who permitted interviews regarding their participation as tearoom trade. A sample: 'Sex is something I have with my wife in bed. It's not as if I were committing adultery by getting my rocks off – or going down on some guy – in a tearoom. Some of my friends go out for handball. I'd rather cruise the park. Does that sound perverse to you?' (p. 119). In terms of careful methodology and richness of description of a highly unique form of human interaction the like of *Tearoom Trade* is seldom seen. The comparison of Humphreys' work with Bartell's *Group Sex* (1971) is inevitable and the latter cannot touch the former in quality.

There is another form of participant-observer approach, not empirical but not entirely testimonial either, definitely not of the thrilling escape variety. An examples is Talese's *Thy Neighbor's Wife* (1980). A product of eight years' research and hundreds of interviews by a professional journalist, the book is at once an account of a man's journey through the American sexual revolution and coming to terms with his own sexuality, and a social history of that revolution. In its way it is a quite remarkable, often touching and absorbing work, inviting comparison with Gagnon's (1975) conclusions in his more scholarly account of sex research and social change.

Non-participant observation. In this approach researchers or therapists observe and/or record sexual behaviour being performed by one or more persons. Here the problem of reactivity is omnipresent as one can never be certain that the event observed is the same as it would be were the observers absent. Use of one-way observation windows or videotape cameras probably does not alter this basic problem. Nonetheless data obtained in this fashion have provided a view of sexual diversity unavailable by other means.

Pomeroy (1966, 1972) reports that the Kinsey researchers were able to observe heterosexual and homosexual behavior directly as well as view it on film. There is a long section in the second report (Kinsey et al. 1953, pp. 574–641) where precise details of anatomy and physiology of sexual response in both males and females are rather exhaustively described. Pomeroy (1966) notes that this information was compiled from observations made during the early stages of setting up what was to become a physiological laboratory, planned but unfortunately uncompleted at the time of Kinsey's death in 1955.

At about the same time Masters and Johnson began the work which would become *Human Sexual Response* (1966). While they praised Kinsey's work as 'a landmark of sociologic investigation' (p. 3), they ignored the previous observational data. They would replicate much of it and improve upon it. The Masters and Johnson method was one of direct laboratory observation by the researchers as well as 'techniques of physiologic measurement and the frequent use of color cinematographic recording in all phases of the sexual response cycle' (p. 4). The primary research aim was 'concentrated quite literally upon what men and women do in response to effective stimulation, and why they do it, rather than on what people say they do or even think their sexual reactions and experiences might be' (p. 20). Behaviours studied included male and female masturbation, natural coition with the female partner in various positions, and artificial coition by females with a plastic penis through which photographs of physiological changes could be made, and which could be adjusted by the subject for rate and depth of thrust. Over 11 years they obtained over 7500 complete cycles of female sexual response and over 2500 male ejaculatory experiences. The major finding was, of course, the four stages of sexual response: excitement, plateau, orgasm and resolution. Recently, Seeley et al. (1980) have independently confirmed the existence and physiological patterning of these phases by external thermographic measurement. The Masters and Johnson work is an undisputed classic which has been reviewed, criticized and discussed many times elsewhere. It is worthy of note here primarily because of the frankness of its aim and directness of approach, and because of the objectivity of its methodology, about which far too little is revealed in *Human Sexual Response* (1966). If the work has a failing it is probably that it tells us too much about convergency of human sexual response rather than divergency.

Physiological assessment of human sexual response

This mode of assessment as we will consider it here refers to direct measurement of physiological change in the male and female genitals. In terms of assessing human sexual interests and preferences, these methods presently appear to offer the best objective avenue to that goal, although it must be emphasized that the data produced are measures of sexual arousal, not overt sexual behaviour. Although they require modest instrumentation and the attendant inconvenience, the methods have distinct advantages available in no other methodology. They are unequivocal – sexual response either occurs or it does not. They are specific in that responses occur in the presence of effective sexual stimuli and not in their absence or to neutral or non-sexual stimuli. They are superior to other physiological measures directed to the same ends, e.g. GSR, heart rate, blood pressure, respiration. They are valid in that they have been shown to be related to past history, present sexual interests, and self-reports. Finally they are objective and only partially amenable to control by the responding subject.

Beginnings. Genital plethysmography, the measurement of genital vasocongestion, is a relative newcomer to the fields of psychophysiology and sex research. Specifically, the responses measured are, in males, the circumferential changes occurring in penile erection and, in females, (1) vaginal pulse pressure, (2) vaginal blood volume, or (3) temperature change in the labia minora.

Devices for measuring erection responses have been available for 35 years. Ohlmeyer and Brilmayer (1947) and Ohlmeyer et al. (1947) developed a binary gauge to detect frequency and duration of noctural erections but this was rejected by sex researchers as it could record only occurrence or nonoccurrence of erection and gave no information on degree of tumescence. Volumetric plethysmographs, which measure volume disaplacement in a small air-filled chamber (Freund et al. 1965; McConaghy 1967) have been used for assessment purposes, but these are limited by the bulk of the transducer, high expense and methodological problems in use, e.g. movement artefacts. The most popular devices are the circumferential penile trans- ducers which may be either a thin metal ring open at one end to which strain gauges are attached (Barlow et. al. 1970; Laws and Bow 1976), or a loop of silicone tubing filled with mercury and plugged at both ends by electrodes (Fisher et al. 1965; Bancroft et al. 1966; Karacan 1969). Both circumferential devices measure the expansion of the penis during the erection cycle from flaccidity to full erection. Of the two the mercury gauge is least expensive, subject to the fewest problems, and is the most popular.

Genital plethysmographs for females are of more recent origin and are of two types, the vaginal photoplethysmograph and the labial thermistor. The photoplethysmograph (Sintchak and Geer 1975) is a photoelectric transducer which measures changes in the optical density of tissue being supplied with blood, i.e. indirect light passes through vaginal wall tissue and is reflected to the photocell surface which is in contact with the vaginal wall. Two measures are possible with this unit (Hatch 1979): (1) vaginal pulse pressure (VPP; sometimes valled VPA, vaginal pulse amplitude), the arrival of the pulse wave at the photocell on each cardiac cycle; or (2) vaginal blood volume (VBV), the pooling of blood in the vaginal wall. The labial thermistor (Henson et al. 1977) uses a highly sensitive thermistor to measure minute temperature changes in the labia minora during sexual arousal.

Can we physiologically assess sexual diversity?   The state of the art permits a very affirmative answer but there is at present far more data on males than females, and more on sexually deviant than normal males. In males there have been essentially two types of studies. One type uses erection measurement to assess nocturnal penile tumescence as an aid to diagnosing psychogenic impotence (e.g. Karacan 1969, 1970) in normal subjects. The other application has been in the assessment (e.g. Abel 1976; Abel and Blanchard 1976) or treatment (e.g. Van Deventer and Laws 1978; Laws and O'Neil 1981) of sexual deviants, primarily rapists and paedophiles. Normals have been infrequently studied as objects of primary research interest. They most often appear as subjects in very basic research investigations (e.g. Laws and Rubin 1969; Henson and Rubin 1971; Rosen 1973; Rosen et al. 1975) or as comparison groups in research on deviants (e.g. Barbaree et al. 1979). Although males sometimes appear in inter-sex comparative studies (e.g. Heiman 1977), they have for the most part not received attention as a group who are interesting because they are supposedly normal.

An example of the diagnostic use of male sexual response data is the construction of physiologically based typologies. The basic idea underlying this approach is quite simple. Stimuli which either depict or describe sexual activities are constructed and presented as slides, videotapes or audiotapes while the subject's sexual response is concurrently measured. The obtained differential amplitudes of these responses are typically compared to the various stimulus categories employed and judgements made about the subject's sexual interests and preferences.

The categories in these sexual response typologies are usually not empirically generated but are products of the author's experience and speculations. The relatively objective sexual response data are then used to confirm the validity of those speculations. For example, Abel et al. (1977) constructed two-minute audiotaped descriptions of mutually consenting intercourse, a rape attack, and a physical assault without sexual contact. In this procedure the sexually oriented rapist would likely respond to the rape and consenting intercourse descriptions, the aggressive rapists to rape and assault and possibly consenting, and the sadistic rapist to the assault description and considerably less if at all to the other two. In general, the data supported these speculations and were further confirmed by examination of previous offence history.

A similar study by Avery-Clark and Laws (1983) showed that a similar typological classification could differentiate paedophiles with a history of violence from those not having that history. The behavioural dimension examined was formed by a series of five audiotapes describing fondling, consenting intercourse with a child, mild verbal and physical force to accomplish intercourse, rape and sadism. The erection responses clearly demarcated the groups during the two most violent descriptions.

Use of sexual responses for categorization seems the least subjective method, although it is the most expensive. Analogous to item analysis of inventory data, one may also examine sexual response tracings in comparison to portions of audiotaped descriptions in order to determine what specific stimuli produce the greatest responsiveness (Laws 1984). This still emerging technology promises to be an effective way of getting at the core of specific sexual interests.

Some of these methods have been tested with normal males. Such evidence as we have indicates that normals are responsibe to paedophilic stimuli (Freund et al. 1972; Quinsey et al. 1975), as well as to rape and physical assault (Barbaree et al. 1979; Quinsey et al. 1981; Murphy 1982; Malamuth 1982), but ordinarily not to the same magnitude observed in experienced sex offenders. More qualitative analysis (e.g. Laws 1984) will be required to sort out these differences.

Most of the research on females employs normal subjects, usually college students. This is a relatively thin literature due to the brief period that measurement apparatus has been available and most of the data on female sexual diversity remain in the literature on rating scales and self-report, although on occasion such measures are combined with arousal measures (Heiman 1977; Osborn and Pollack 1977).

In general the sexual diversity literature on female arousal is limited to establishing what sorts of stimuli produce sexual excitement, and in this sense it resembles the early work in the male literature. Vaginal blood volume (VBV) changes have been observed when females viewed erotic stimulus films (Geer et al. 1974; Hoon et al. 1976b, 1977; Henson and Rubin 1978; Henson et al. 1979a, 1979b; van Dam et al. 1976; Wincze et al. 1976, 1977), listened to erotic audiotapes or fantasized (Heiman 1977), or masturbated (Geer and Quartararo 1976; van Dam et al. 1976). Vaginal pulse pressure (VPP) changes have also been observed when females saw erotic films (Geer et al. 1974; Henson et al. 1979a, 1979b; Wilson and Lawson 1976), heard audiotapes or fantasized (Heiman 1977), or masturbated (Geer and Quartararo 1976; Gillan 1976). To my knowledge Henson and Rubin (1978) and Henson et al. (1977, 1979a, 1979b) are the only researchers to have used the labial thermistor and they have exclusively assessed response to erotic films.

Interpretive problems.   There are essentially no interpretive problems in evaluating data from the male sexual response. The erection response has a 0 per cent and 100 per cent state and the most convenient way to treat the data is to assume linear distribution along the scale and report any unit as some percentage of the maximum. That penile erection is a valid measure of sexual arousal, related to interests, preferences and history, is no longer in doubt (Freund 1963; Masters and Johnson 1966; Zuckerman 1971; Bancroft and Mathews 1971; Abel 1976; Barlow 1977; Rosen and Keefe 1978). Still, on an interpretive level, it is best employed with complementary measures of cognitions and overt behaviours where possible (Heiman 1976).

There are unsolved problems in interpreting vaginal blood volume and vaginal pulse pressure data. No reliable method for quantifying the response has been developed (Hatch 1979) and there is a persistent problem in shifting baselines (Heiman 1976; Henson et al. 1979a). The baseline problem can be solved by single-stimulus presentations, but the non-quantifiability issue remains and the data are most often reported as millimetres of pen deflection on a polygraph tracing and correlated with subject self-report of arousal, correlations falling in the moderate to strong range (Heiman 1977; Henson et al. 1979a). Inability to scale the response makes inter-subject comparisons difficult, unlike the method used with males.

Use of the labial thermistor (Henson et al. 1977) appears to solve the quantification problem. Although these authors measured a range of response from only 0.10°C to 1.38°C, this is an interval scale and easily interpretable. The labial measures also correlate strongly with self-report. Possibly the most interesting feature of these tracings is how closely they resemble the male sexual response tracings, which is not true of VBV and VPP. If they are equivalent in that they accelerate to subjectively erotic portions of presented stimuli and decelerate to non-erotic portions, we are in a position to make finer analyses of female sexual response, then compare these to similar procedures used with males (Abel et al. 1975; Laws 1984).

Do the genitals lie? Since physiological assessment appears to be the most promising assessment procedure, we must examine the issue of subject influence on the response. At this writing there is no evidence that females can exert voluntary control over vasocongestion, i.e. no one has conducted a study of female faking.

Suppression of the erection response, the ability to fake, has been repeatedly demonstrated (Laws and Rubin 1969; Henson and Rubin 1971; Abel and Blanchard 1976; Laws and Holmen 1978). This has been of concern as most subjects studied and evaluated have been sex offenders. In our have examined assessment data from a large group of rapists (N = 49), persons laboratory we have examined assessment data from a large group of rapists (N = 49), persons highly likely to fake, and found close agreement between measured levels of response and subjects' estimates of those levels. Evaluation of the faking literature shows that hardly anyone can fully suppress all the time and most subjects have difficulty in suppressing at all. Subject dissimulation certainly occurs, but the evidence is unpersuasive that it has a serious biasing effect.

Improving assessment by eliminating opportunity to fake. Until such time as it can be shown that cognitive manipulation can reduce or eliminate genital vasocongestion in females, we must assume that it is beyond voluntary control.

In recent works Earls and Marshall (1982) have demonstrated that erection responses below 10 per cent of full erection may have significant diagnostic value. Following up observations of McConaghy (1974) and Laws (1977), Earls and Marshall showed that the first component of the erection response is a lengthening of the penis as the cavernosa fill. During the period of time that it takes the penis to expand circumferentially to about 10 per cent of full erection, it has lengthened to about 35 per cent of the total it will achieve at full erection. The circumferential response at values above 10 per cent is the response commonly monitored which is to some extent under voluntary control. The lengthening response, conversely, appears to be involuntary, although subjects report awareness of its occurrence. If it could be shown that these lengthening responses below 10 per cent show the same topographical characteristics as the larger responses usually measured, we would then have a highly sensitive index of sexual arousal not open to client influence, greatly increasing the validity of assessment.

Pupillography, a much understudied area, also provides an alternative as well as a correlative measure of sexual arousal in both males and females. Although very expensive and requiring tight control of potential confounding artefacts, this technology has great potential in sex research. The best of these devices not only record pupillary dilation to various stimuli, but produce a record of how the eye tracks the stimulus, and give a measure of dwell time. Abel et al. (1981) have reported on its use in the assessment of sexual deviants.

Conclusion.   Obviously it is my belief that physiological assessment provides the best approach to evaluation of human sexual interests. It is, however, necessary once again to stress that these are measures of sexual arousal and that the relation of such data to overt sexual behaviour and its current or subsequent probability is, at best, imperfectly understood at present. Nonetheless, the combination of genital measures with other valid physiological measures, e.g. pupillography, supplemented by subjective reports and/or ratings, plus observational data on overt sexual behaviour, currently provide the best available package for assessing human sexual diversity. What is clearly needed is more work on normal males and more qualitative data on female sexual interests.

WHITHER ASSESSMENT OF SEXUAL DIVERSITY?

If nothing else the preceding brief sampling of the methods of assessing human sexual interests and behaviours leads rather inexorably to the conclusion that it is truly appalling that we know so little about human sexuality, especially in the areas of expressed interests, inclinations, predispositions and the specific behaviours in which people engage. It is equally clear that there is no excuse whatever for this as we have never lacked the methodology to accomplish the task. A short recapitulation of the major methodologies may give some indication of directions we may see in the future.

The individual structured interview will remain effective for normative purposes and useful in individual evaluation and treatment, but we may no longer be able to subsidize interview projects such as the Kinsey researches. However useful and intriguing they may be, they cannot be made cost-efficient. Interview survey research remains useful, albeit expensive, but will not prove fruitful until investigators relinquish their shyness and preconceptions about their respondents and begin asking direct and detailed questions. This area has much to learn from the PopPsych approaches and a combination of the two would be a leap forward.

Psychometrically derived typologies and sex-response typologies have produced useful information. These approaches, however, risk becoming static and institutionalized unless their proponents move to expand their variety and comprehensiveness, as well as broaden and deepen their data base.

The standard psychometric tests, be they projective or objective, have performed very poorly in advancing our knowledge of human sexuality. For these purposes they may safely be laid to rest.

The best of the self-report devices, whether in the form of questionnaires, rating scales, self-report inventories, or combinations of all three, have proven to be the most widely applicable, the least expensive, and so represent the best single alternative to actually observing sexual behaviour *in vivo* or analogue observation by direct measurement of sexual response. It is clear that these methodologies continue to move forward and this deserves encouragement and support.

High-quality direct-participant observation by trained researchers is almost certain to remain a low-rate activity. It is an intensive, expensive labour of love and is unlikely to find much support. I count this a shame as much of the best of sociology resides in these methods. Non-participant observation, on the other hand, was lent enormous credibility by Masters and Johnson and will likely increase in the future.

If we scan the handful of journals publishing sex research in Europe and America we can see that physiological assessment of sex response is a major emergent technology in the field today. I see no other area where knowledge is growing so rapidly and, in my brief account of this work, I have tried to suggest how far we have yet to go. While I am myself a proponent of this approach, it is apparent to me that it is but a single, though very useful, methodology which must be used carefully and concurrently with other measures of cognition and behaviour, supplemented as much as possible by observation of overt behavior.

Quite contrary to the conventional wisdom, males and females have proven almost astonishingly co-operative in assisting us to understand human sexual behaviour. It is equally clear that detailed and comprehensive assessment is possible. If we have a problem that is retarding our research efforts, it is very likely our apparent embarrassed reluctance to look at what we must see and to ask the very questions to which we must have the answers.

REFERENCES

Abel, G. G. (1976). Assessment of sexual deviation in the male. In M. Hersen and A. S. Bellack (eds), *Behavioral Assessment: A Practical Handbook*, Elmsford, New York: Pergamon.

Abel, G. G., Becker, J. V., Skinner, L. J., and Hakarem, G. (1981). Determining sexual preference in sexual deviates using pupillary responses. Paper presented at Third National Conference on the Evaluation and Treatment of Sexual Aggressives, Avila Beach, Ca., 18 Mar. 1981.

Abel, G. G., and Blanchard, E. B. (1976). The measurement and generation of sexual arousal in male sexual deviates. In M. Hersen, R. M. Eisler and P. M. Miller (eds), *Progress in Behavior Modificaiton*, 2. New York: Academic Press.

Abel, G. G., Blanchard, E. B., Barlow, D. H., and Guild, D. (1977). The components of rapists' sexual arousal. *Archives of General Psychiatry*, 34, 895–903.

Abel, G. G., Blanchard, E. B., Barlow, D. H., and Mavissakalian, M. (1975). Identifying specific erotic cues in sexual deviation by audio-taped descriptions. *Journal of Applied Behavior Analysis*, 8, 247–60.

Abelson, H., Cohen, R., Heaton, E., and Studer, C. (1971). National survey of public attitudes toward and experience with erotic materials: findings. In US Commission on Obscenity and Pornography. *Technical Reports*, 6, Washington: Government Printing Office.

Adelman, M. R. (1977). A comparison of professionally employed lesbians and heterosexual women on the MMPI. *Archives of Sexual Behavior*, 6, 193–201.

Allen, R. M., and Haupt, T. D. (1966). The Sex Inventory: Test–retest reliabilities of scale scores and items. *Journal of Clinical Psychology*, 22, 375–8.

Avery-Clark, C. A., and Laws, D. R. (1984). Differential erection response patterns of sexual child abusers to stimuli describing activities with children. *Behavior Therapy*, 15, 71–83.

Bancroft, J., Jones, H. G., and Pullan, B. R. (1966). A simple transducer for measuring penile erection, with comments on its use in the treatment of sexual disorders. *Behaviour Research and Therapy*, 4, 239–41.

Bancroft, J., and Mathews, A. (1971). Autonomic correlates of penile erection. *Journal of Psychosomatic Research*, 15, 159–67.

Bandura, A. (1977). *Social Learning Theory*. Englewood Cliffs, NJ: Prentice-Hall.

Barbaree, H. E., Marshall, W. L., and Lanthier, R. P. (1979). Deviant sexual arousal in rapists. *Behaviour Research and Therapy*, 17, 215–22.

Barlow, D. H. (1977). Assessment of sexual behavior. In A. R. Ciminero, H. E. Adams and K. S. Calhoun (eds), *Handbook of Behavioral Assessment*, New York: Wiley.

Barlow, D. H., Becker, J., Leitenberg, H., and Agras, S. (1970). A mechanical strain gauge for recording penile circumference change. *Journal of Applied Behavior Analysis*, 3, 73–6.

Bartell, J. D. (1971). *Group Sex*, New York: Wyden.

Bauman, K. E., and Wilson, R. R. (1976). Premarital sexual attitudes of unmarried university students: 1968 vs. 1972. *Archives of Sexual Behavior*, 5, 29–37.

Bell, A. P., and Weinberg, M. S. (1978). *Homosexualities: A Study of Diversity Among Men and Women*, New York: Simon & Schuster.

Bell, A. P., Weinberg, M. S., and Hammersmith, S. K. (1981). *Sexual Preference: Its Development in Men and Women*, Bloomington, Indiana: Indiana University Press.

Bell, R. R., and Chaskes, J. B. (1970). Premarital sexual experience among coeds, 1958 and 1968. *Journal of Marriage and the Family*, 32, 81–4.

Bentler, P. M. (1968a). Heterosexual behavior assessment I: males. *Behaviour Research and Therapy*, 6, 21–5.

Bentler, P. M. (1968b). Heterosexual behavior assessment II: females. *Behaviour Research and Therapy*, 6, 27–30.

Bentler, P. M., and Peeler, W. H. (1979). Models of female orgasm. *Archives of Sexual*

Behavior, 8, 405–23.

Bergmann, M. S. (1945). Homosexuality in the Rorschach test. *Bulletin of the Menninger Clinic*, 9, 78–84.

Butler, C. A. (1976). New data about female sexual response. *Journal of Sex and Marital Therapy*, 2, 40–6.

Christensen, H. T., and Gregg, C. F. (1970). Changing sex norms in America and Scandinavia. *Journal of Marriage and the Family*, 32, 616–27.

Cowden, J. E., and Pacht, A. R. (1969). The Sex Inventory as a classification instrument for sex offenders. *Journal of Clinical Psychology*, 23, 53–7.

Earls, C. M., and Marshall, W. L. (1982). The simultaneous and independent measurement of penile circumference and length. *Behavior Research Methods and Instrumentation*, 14, 447–50.

Feldman, M. P., MacCulloch, M. J., Mellor, V., and Pinschof, J. M. (1966). The application of anticipatory avoidance learning to the treatment of homosexuality III: The sexual orientation method. *Behaviour Research and Therapy*, 4, 289–99.

Fisher, C., Gross, J., and Zuch, J. (1965). Cycle of penile erection synchronous with dreaming (REM) sleep. *Archives of General Psychiatry*, 12, 27–45.

Freund, K. (1963). A laboratory method for diagnosing predominance of homo- or heteroerotic interest in the male. *Behaviour Research and Therapy*, 1, 85–93.

Freund, K., McKnight, C. K., Langevin, R., and Cibiri, S. (1972). The female child as a surrogate object. *Archives of Sexual Behavior*, 2, 119–33.

Freund, K., Sedlacek, F., and Knob, K. (1965). A simple transducer for mechanical plethysmography of the male genital. *Journal of the Experimental Analysis of Behavior*, 8, 169–70.

Gagnon, J. H. (1975). Sex research and social change. *Archives of Sexual Behavior*, 4, 111–41.

Gagnon, J. H. (1981). Searching for the childhood of Eros. *New York Times Book Review*, 13 Dec. 1981, 10.

Geer, J. H., Morokoff, P., and Greenwood, P. (1974). Sexual arousal in women: The development of a measurement device for vaginal blood volume. *Archives of Sexual Behavior*, 3, 559–64.

Geer, J. H., and Quartararo, J. D. (1976). Vaginal blood volume responses during masturbation. *Archives of Sexual Behavior*, 5, 403–13.

Gillan, P. (1976). Objective measures of female sexual arousal. *Journal of Physiology*, 260, 64P–65P.

Glenn, N. D., and Weaver, C. N. (1979). Attitudes toward premarital, extramarital, and homosexual relations in the U.S. in the 1970s. *Journal of Sex Research*, 15, 108–18.

Harbison, J. J., Graham, P. J., Quinn, J. T., McAllister, H., and Woodward, R. A. (1974). A questionnaire measure of sexual interest. *Archives of Sexual Behavior*, 3, 357–66.

Hatch, J. P. (1979). Vaginal photoplethysmography: Methodological considerations. *Archives of Sexual Behavior*, 8, 357–73.

Haupt, T. D., and Allen, R. M. (1966). A multivariate analysis of variance of scale scores on The Sex Inventory, Male Form. *Journal of Clinical Psychology*, 22, 387–95.

Heiman, J. R. (1976). Issues in the use of psychophysiology to assess female sexual dysfunction. *Journal of Sex and Marital Therapy*, 2, 197–204.

Heiman, J. R. (1977). A psychophysiological exploration of sexual arousal patterns in females and males. *Psychophysiology*, 14, 266–74.

Hendlin, S. J. (1976). Homosexuality in the Rorschach: A new look at the old signs. *Journal of Homosexuality*, 1, 303–12.

Henson, D. E., and Rubin, H. B. (1971). Voluntary control of eroticism. *Journal of Applied Behavior Analysis*, 4, 37–44.

Henson, D. E., and Rubin, H. B. (1978). A comparison of two objective measures of sexual arousal in women. *Behaviour Research and Therapy*, 16, 143–51.

Henson, D. E., Rubin, H. B., and Henson, C. (1979a). Analysis of the consistency of objective measures of sexual arousal in women. *Journal of Applied Behavior Analysis*, 12, 701–11.

Henson, C., Rubin, H. B., and Henson, D. E. (1979b). Women's sexual arousal concurrently assessed by three genital measures. *Archives of Sexual Behavior*, 8, 459–69.

Henson, D. E., Rubin, H. B., Henson, C., and Williams, J. R. (1977). Temperature change of the labia minora as an objective measure of female eroticism. *Journal of Behavior Therapy and Experimental Psychiatry*, 8, 401–10.

Hite, S. (1981). *The Hite Report*, New York: Dell.

Hoon, E. F., Hoon, P. W., and Wincze, J. P. (1976a). An inventory for the measurement of female sexual arousability: The SAI. *Archives of Sexual Behavior*, 5, 291–300.

Hoon, P. W., Wincze, J. P., and Hoon, E. F. (1976b). Physiological assessment of sexual arousal in women. *Psychophysiology*, 13, 196–204.

Hoon, P. W., Wincze, J. P., and Hoon, E. F. (1977). The effects of biofeedback and cognitive mediation upon vaginal blood volume. *Behavior Therapy*, 8, 694–702.

Humphreys, L. (1970). *Tearoom Trade: Impersonal Sex in Public Places*, Chicago: Aldine.

Hunt, M. (1974). *Sexual Behavior in the 1970s*, Chicago: Playboy Press.

Husted, J. R., and Edwards, A. E. (1976). Personality correlates of male sexual arousal and behavior. *Archives of Sexual Behavior*, 5, 149–56.

Johnston, S., and Anderson, R. E. (1981). Development of scales to measure sexual psychopathology. Paper presented at Third National Conference on the Evaluation and Treatment of Sexual Aggressives, Avila Beach, Ca., 18 Mar. 1981.

Kahn, S. S., and Davis, J. (1981). *The Kahn Report on Sexual Preferences*, New York: Avon.

Kant, H. S., Goldstein, M. J., and Lepper, D. J. (1971). A pilot comparison of two research instruments measuring exposure to pornography. In US Commission on Obscenity and Pornography. *Technical Reports*, 7, Washington: Government Printing Office.

Kaplan, H. S. (1974). *The New Sex Therapy*, New York: Brunner/Mazel.

Kaplan, H. S. (1979). *Disorders of Sexual Desire*, New York: Brunner/Mazel.

Karacan, I. (1969). A simple and inexpensive transducer for quantitative measurements of penile erection during sleep. *Behavior Research Methods and Instrumentation*, 1, 251–2.

Karacan, I. (1970). The clinical value of nocturnal erection in the prognoses and diagnoses of impotence. *Human Sexuality*, 4, 27–34.

Kinsey, A. C., Pomeroy, W. B., and Martin, C. E. (1948). *Sexual Behavior in the Human Male*, Philadelphia: Saunders.

Kinsey, A. C., Pomeroy, W. B., Martin, C. E., and Gebhard, C. E. (1953). *Sexual*

Behavior in the Human Female, Philadelphia: Saunders.

Langevin, R. (1982). *Sexual Strands: Understanding and Treating Sexual Anomalies in Men*, Hillsdale, NJ: Erlbaum.

Langevin, R., Paitich, D., Handy, L., and Russon, A. (1982). A new version of the Clarke Sexual History Questionnaire for Males. Unpublished manuscript, Clarke Institute of Psychiatry, Toronto.

Laws, D. R. (1977). A comparison of the measurement characteristics of two circumferential penile transducers. *Archives of Sexual Behavior*, 6, 45–51.

Laws, D. R. (1984). Assessment of dangerous sexual behavior in males. *Medicine and Law*, 3, 127–40.

Laws, D. R., and Bow, R. A. (1976). An improved mechanical strain gauge for recording penile circumference change. *Psychophysiology*, 13, 596–9.

Laws, D. R., and Holmen, M. L. (1978). Sexual response faking by pedophiles. *Criminal Justice and Behavior*, 5, 343–56.

Laws, D. R., and O'Neil, J. A. (1981). Variations on masturbatory conditioning. *Behavioural Psychotherapy*, 9, 111–36.

Laws, D. R., and Rubin, H. B. (1969). Instructional control of an autonomic sexual response. *Journal of Applied Behavior Analysis*, 2, 93–9.

Levitt, E. E., and Brady, J. P. (1965). Sexual preferences in young adult males and some correlates. *Journal of Clinical Psychology*, 21, 347–54.

Levitt, E. E., and Klassen, A. D. (1974). Public attitudes toward homosexuality. *Journal of Homosexuality*, 1, 29–43.

Lo Piccolo, J., and Steger, J. C. (1974). The Sexual Interaction Inventory: A new instrument for assessment of sexual dysfunction. *Archives of Sexual Behavior*, 3, 585–95.

McConaghy, N. (1967). Penile volume changes to moving pictures of male and female nudes in heterosexual and homosexual males. *Behaviour Research and Therapy*, 5, 43–8.

McConaghy, N. (1974). Measurements of change in penile dimensions. *Archives of Sexual Behavior*, 3, 381–8.

McCreary, C. P. (1975). Personality differences among child molesters. *Journal of Personality Assessment*, 39, 591–3.

Malamuth, N. (1982). Cultural factors related to sexual violence. Lecture presented at Fourth National Conference and Workshops on Sexual Aggression, Denver, Co., 18 Apr. 1982.

Marks, I. M., and Sartorius, N. H. (1968). A contribution to the measurement of sexual attitude. *Journal of Nervous and Mental Diseases*, 145, 441–51.

Marsh, J. J., Hilliard, J., and Liechti, R. (1955). A sexual deviation scale for the MMPI. *Journal of Consulting Psychology*, 19, 55–9.

Masters, W. H., and Johnson, V. E. (1966). *Human Sexual Response*, Boston: Little, Brown.

Merritt, C. G., Gerstl, J. E., and LoSciuto, L. A. (1975). Age and perceived effects of erotica-pornography. *Archives of Sexual Behavior*, 4, 605–21.

Miller, W. R., and Lief, H. I. (1976). Masturbatory attitudes, knowledge and experience: Data from the Sex Knowledge and Attitude Test (SKAT). *Archives of Sexual Behavior*, 5, 447–67.

Murphy, W. (1982). New assessment methods for sex offenders. Lecture presented at Fourth National Conference and Workshops on Sexual Aggression, Denver, Co., 17 Apr. 1982.

Newcomb, M. D., and Bentler, P. M. (1982). The dimensions of subjective female orgasmic responsiveness. Unpublished manuscript.

Nyberg, K. L., and Alston, J. P. (1976–7). Analysis of public attitudes toward homosexual behavior. *Journal of Homosexuality*, 2, 99–107.

Ohlmeyer, P., and Brilmayer, H. (1947). Periodische Vorgange im Schlaf. *Pfleugers Archive Gesamte Physiologie*, 248, 559–60.

Ohlmeyer, P., Brilmayer, H., and Hullstrung, H. (1947). Periodische Vorgange im Schlaf II. *Pfluegers Archive Gesamte Physiologie*, 249, 50–5.

Ohlson, E. L., and Wilson, M. (1974). Differentiating female homosexuals from female heterosexuals by use of the MMPI. *Journal of Sex Research*, 10, 308–15.

Osborn, C. A., and Pollack, R. H. (1977). The effects of two types of erotic literature on physiological and verbal measures of female sexual arousal. *Journal of Sex Research*, 13, 250–6.

Paitich, D., Langevin, R., Freeman, R., Mann, I., and Handy, L. (1977). The Clarke SHQ: A clinical sex history questionnaire for males. *Archives of Sexual Behavior*, 6, 421–36.

Pomeroy, W. B. (1966). The Masters–Johnson report and the Kinsey tradition. In R. Brecher and E. Brecher (eds), *An analysis of 'Human Sexual Response'*, New York: New American Library.

Pomeroy, W. B. (1972). *Dr. Kinsey and the Institute for Sex Research*, New York: Harper & Row.

Pomeroy, W. B. (1982). Personal communication, 1 Oct. 1982.

Pomeroy, W. B., Flax, C. C. and Wheeler, C. C. (1982). *Taking a Sex History*, New York: Free Press.

Quinsey, V. L., Chaplin, T. C., and Varney, G. (1981). A comparison of rapists' and non-sex offenders' sexual preferences for mutually consenting sex, rape, and physical abuse of women. *Behavioral Assessment*, 3, 127–35.

Quinsey, V. L., Steinman, C. M., Bergerson, S. G., and Holmes, T. F. (1975). Penile circumference, skin conductance, and ranking responses of child molesters and 'normals' to sexual and nonsexual stimuli. *Behavior Therapy*, 6, 213–19.

Reiss, B. F., Safer, M. A., and Yotive, W. (1974). Psychological test data on female homosexuality: A review of the literature. *Journal of Homosexuality*, 1, 71–85.

Robertiello, R. C. (1970). The 'clitoral vs. vaginal orgasm' controversy and some of its ramifications. *Journal of Sex Research*, 6, 307–11.

Rosen, R. C. (1973). Suppression of penile tumescence by instrumental conditioning. *Psychosomatic Medicine*, 35, 509–13.

Rosen, R. C., and Keefe, F. J. (1978). The measurement of human penile tumescence. *Psychophysiology*, 15, 366–76.

Rosen, R. C., Shapiro, D., and Schwartz, G. E. (1975). Voluntary control of penile tumescence. *Psychosomatic Medicine*, 37, 479–83.

Schmidt, G. (1975). Male–female differences in sexual arousal and behavior during and after exposure to sexually explicit stimuli. *Archives of Sexual Behavior*, 4, 353–64.

Schmidt, G., and Sigusch, V. (1972). Changes in sexual behavior among young males and females between 1960–1970. *Archives of Sexual Behavior*, 2, 27–45.

Seeley, T. T., Abramson, P. R., Perry, L. B., Rothblatt, A. B., and Seeley, D. M. (1980). Thermographic measurement of sexual arousal: A methodological note. *Archives of Sexual Behavior*, 9, 77–85.

Singer, J., and Singer, I. (1972). Types of female orgasm. *Journal of Sex Research*, 8, 255–67.

Sintchak, G., and Geer, J. H. (1975). A vaginal photoplethysmograph system. *Psychophysiology*, 12, 113–15.

Slater, P. (1965). The use of the repertory grid technique in the individual case. *British Journal of Psychiatry*, 111, 965–75.

Spanier, G. B., and Cole, C. L. (1975). Mate swapping: Perceptions, value orientations, and participation in a midwestern community. *Archives of Sexual Behavior*, 4, 143–59.

Steele, D. G., and Walker, C. E. (1974). Male and female differences in reaction to erotic stimuli as related to sexual adjustment. *Archives of Sexual Behavior*, 3, 459–70.

Suppe, F. (1981). The Bell and Weinberg study: Future priorities for research on homosexuality. *Journal of Homosexuality*, 6, 69–97.

Talese, G. (1980). *Thy Neighbor's Wife*, New York: Doubleday.

Thorne, F. C. (1966a). The Sex Inventory. *Journal of Clinical Psychology*, 22, 367–74.

Thorne, F. C. (1966b). A factorial study of sexuality in adult males. *Journal of Clinical Psychology*, 22, 378–86.

Thorne, F. C., and Haupt, T. D. (1966). The objective measurement of sex attitudes and behavior in adult males. *Journal of Clinical Psychology*, 22, 395–403.

Toobert, S., Bartelme, K. F., and Jones, E. S. (1959). Some factors related to pedophilia. *International Journal of Social Psychiatry*, 4, 272–9.

van Dam, F. S. A. M., Honnebler, W. J., van Zalinge, E. A., and Barendregt, J. T. (1976). Sexual arousal measured by photoplethysmography. *Behavioral Engineering*, 3, 97–101.

VanDeventer, A. D., and Laws, D. R. (1978). Orgasmic reconditioning to redirect sexual arousal in pedophiles. *Behavior Therapy*, 9, 748–65.

Wheeler, W. M. (1949). An analysis of Rorschach indices of male homosexuality. *Rorschach Research Exchange and Journal of Projective Techniques*, 13, 97–126.

White, C. B. (1982). Sexual interest, attitudes, knowledge, and sexual history in relation to sexual behavior in the institutionalized aged. *Archives of Sexual Behavior*, 11, 11–21.

Wilson, W. C. (1975). The distribution of selected sexual attitudes and behaviors among the adult population of the United States. *Journal of Sex Research*, 11, 46–64.

Wilson, G. T., and Lawson, D. M. (1976). Effects of alcohol on sexual arousal in women. *Journal of Abnormal Psychology*, 85, 489–97.

Wincze, J. P., Hoon, E. F., and Hoon, P. W. (1976). Physiological responsivity of normal and sexually dysfunctional women during erotic stimulus exposure. *Journal of Psychosomatic Research*, 20, 445–57.

Wincze, J. P., Hoon, P. W., and Hoon, E. F. (1977). Sexual arousal in women: A comparison of cognitive and physiological responses by continuous measurement.

Archives of Sexual Behavior, 6, 121–33.

Wishnoff, R. (1978). Modeling effects of explicit and nonexplicit sexual stimuli on the sexual anxiety and behavior of women. *Archives of Sexual Behavior*, 7, 455–61.

Wolfe, L. (1981). *Women and Sex in the 80s: The Cosmo Report*, New York: Bantam.

Zuckerman, M. (1971). Physiological measures of sexual arousal in the human. *Psychological Bulletin*, 75, 297–329.

Zuckerman, M. (1973). Scales for sex experience for males and females. *Journal of Consulting and Clinical Psychology*, 41, 27–9.

9

Sexual Diversity: A Sociological Perspective

Ken Plummer

For the past century, much of the research and thinking about sexual diversity has been within the psychological, biological and medical sciences; all the contributors to this volume work within these fields, and the value of such work has been clearly demonstrated in their reviews. As the sole sociological contributor, my task of redressing the balance requires a reviewing of issues rather than a summary of findings. There is now a substantial corpus of social and political writing which is perhaps alien to the clinical mode of thought, and I intend merely to signpost some central debates rather that to perform the impossible task of detailing this literature. My central themes, now almost taken for granted by sociologists, will be dual. First, human sexuality is overwhelmingly a matter of symbolism: other animals just do not inhabit the eerie erotic worlds that humans make for themselves. Human sexuality is thought about, fantasized about, talked about, written about and scripted into action. It is enmeshed in the dialogues of theology, philosophy, medicine, literature, law, morality, psychiatry and the sciences. However biological and 'animal-like' its foundations may be, human sexuality is assembled and comes to life through these languages. Thus I will suggest the need to examine the assumptions we make about sexuality – especially its being a natural essence geared to normal procreation; the need to examine how specific historical cultures come to construct their notions of the normal and the pathological; and the need to examine how the sexual diversities are fashioned out of such notions.

My second theme will be to suggest, and here I am on more treacherous ground, that however neutral and objective talk about sexual diversity appears to be, it is also talk about *power*. Every culture has to establish – through both formal and informal political processes – the range and scope of the diversities that will be outlawed or banned. No culture could function with a sexual free-for-all, but the pattern of these constraints is exceedingly variable across time and space. Thus, I will suggest the need to examine the very different ways in which political definitions separate male and female diversities; the ways in which sexual taboos can symbolize the boundaries of a particular culture; the critical function that medicine has played politically in our culture in recent times; and the modes in which the sexually diverse organize to 'fight back' and modify these political constructions. I shall conclude by briefly highlighting an emerging political debate – between the politics of desire and the politics of sexism – which could well work to reconstruct diversity as we move into the twenty-first century.

It has long been recognized that although the human mammal may have a great deal in common with other mammals a most important difference lies in the extent to which humans display wider variations both within and across cultures. In the field of sexuality this is no exception: anthropologists and historians have substantially documented the degree of cross-cultural variety (e.g. Ford and Beach 1952; Marshall and Suggs 1971; Bloch 1965; Bullough 1976), while clinicians and social researchers have indicated the degree of diversity within a culture (Krafft-Ebing 1886; Kinsey et al. 1948, 1953). That human eroticism and gender experience have displayed substantial diversity across time and space is now something of a commonplace – though it remains a curiosity as to why such a commonplace is frequently ignored.

In this chapter I shall review the broad social processes through which such diversities are handled in a society. Two main sets are involved: those which enable the society to mark boundaries of the acceptable and the unacceptable, and those which enable the members of a society to handle their own diverse sexualities. I call the first the *regulative* processes and the latter the *reactive* processes; both work together in constructing specific patterns of sexualities. My discussion is only a provisional one, and in the main I focus upon the construction of diverse sexualities in western societies in recent times. Much of what I say may actually only be applicable to a limited range of diversities but it is my hope that ultimately an extension of such reasoning may lead to a much wider and deeper analysis.

I shall also attempt to place research into sexual diversity within a wider framework by signposting some of the assumptions that usually underpin such work. This is absolutely necessary since, I suggest, all discussions of sexuality come from a point of view, whether acknowledged or not. Too frequently such preconceptions are nothing more than the commonsense wisdoms embedded in the wider culture of the researcher. Thus this chapter will start with an analysis of some such assumptions and indicate potential sources of inevitable bias.

ASSUMPTIONS ABOUT HUMAN SEXUAL DIVERSITY

All discussions about human sexuality must proceed from a bedrock of assumptions, whether articulated or not. Gone are the days when social scientists could research as if they were simply neutral, objective, value-free students with neither meta assumptions informing their studies nor social consequences arising from them.[1] Even the so-called sexual gurus of the modern day – Freud, Kinsey, Masters and Johnson – have been shown to be entangled with hidden assumptions and ideological bias (cf. Robinson 1976); while the sudden and dramatic reversal of the American Psychiatric Association's classification of homosexuality as a non-sickness in 1973 suggests that psychiatry is at least as much politics as science (cf. Bayer 1981; Spector and Kitsuse 1977). Indeed, the title of this very book suggests assumptions: two decades ago it would have used more negative words like perversion, disorder or deviation:[2] the notion of diversity attempts to capture a more benign and tolerant mood which has recently emerged in pockets of western culture. Without elaborating my case, it must be acknowledged that all writing on sexuality contains assumptions, including this chapter and all the others in this book, and since, as Kenneth Burke once remarked, 'every way of seeing is a way of not seeing', to analyse those assumptions can help generate alternative ways of thinking.

From 'nature' to the 'symbol'

In recent history, thinking about human sexual diversity has been largely the province of medical and psychological science; it is, perhaps, of note that collections of the sort comprised in this volume are often composed primarily by those interested in medicine, psychology and zoology – anthropologists, historians, sociologists and the broader humanities are often conspicuously absent. We cannot think about sexuality, it seems, without evoking the imagery of natural bodies, powerful drives, dysfunctioning organs and clinical nomenclature. The field of enquiry has been thoroughly medicalized and individualized (cf. Foucault 1979; Szasz 1981). Such biological and medical imagery, however, can harness the mind away from the central feature of distinctively human life: that it is symbolic and utterly dependent upon historically specific cultures for its existence. Kenneth Burke has meditated on this problem at length and it will help to cite him here:

[We are] The 'symbol-using animal', yes, obviously. But can we bring ourselves to realise just what that formula implies, just how overwhelmingly much of what we mean by 'reality' has been built up through us by nothing but our symbol system? Take away our books, and what little do we know about history, biography, even something down to earth as the relative position of seas and continents? What is our 'reality' for today (beyond the paper thin line of our own particular lives) but all this clutter of symbols about the past combined with whatever things we know through maps, magazines, newspapers and the like about the present? In school, as they go from class, students turn from one idiom to another. The various courses in the curriculum are in effect but so many different terminologies. And however important to us is the tiny sliver of reality each of us has experienced first hand, the whole overall 'picture' is but a construct of our symbol systems. To meditate on the fact until one sees its full implications is much like peering over the edge of things into an ultimate abyss. And doubtless that's one reason why, though man is typically the symbol-using animal, he clings to a kind of naive verbal realism that refuses to realise the full extent of the role played by symbolicity in his notions of reality. (Burke 1966, p. 5).

This refusal to acknowledge 'symbolicity', as Burke calls it, seems particularly strong in the domain of the sexual. Try and imagine what human sexuality would be like if it did not exist in and through symbols. How could it be recognized? How could we do it? How could we feel it? How could we talk about it? Imagine, if you dare, a world where men have uncoordinated erections and women have uninterrupted lubrications; where sexuality existed devoid of rule or fantasy; of a constant inability to make sense of our feelings, our partners, our orgasms. Clearly none of these can announce themselves to us without symbols. It is a very basic precondition of human sexuality, and indeed it is because the world of symbolism is inherently ambiguous that the problem of diverse sexual meaning announces itself in all societies. We are the talking, thinking, symbolic sex; as Lawrence Stone remarks, 'Despite appearances, human sex takes place mostly in the head' (Stone 1977, p. 483). Symbols are the ghost in the machine, and to talk about human sexuality in terms derived from biology, medicine or nature is to talk about the less distinctive features of sexuality. Sexuality, for humans, is absolutely *unnatural*. For we are really quite removed from other species. They have little history (except their evolutionary programmes) to pass on from generation to generation; they have little language (except their elementary sign systems) to communicate with; and they have little concern with moral or political issues. This is not to deny that sexuality amongst humans has a clear biological substrata,[3] but it is to recognize that our essential human nature, although biologically based, is one that is grounded upon diverse, historically changing cultures, and, concomitantly, symbolism and language (cf. Leach 1982; Midgley 1979). Such a feature is indeed acknowledged by many prominent biologists. C. S. Beach, for example, comments: 'It is my present feeling that human sexuality is about as closely related to the mating behaviours of other species as human language is related to animal communication, a relationship that is distant indeed' (Beach 1974: p. 334). Understanding sexual diversity is dependent upon understanding the cultures that render us such a differentiated species, and most significantly the different patterns of symbolism and communication which enable such diversities to be fostered and transmitted.[4]

From 'essentialism' to 'phenomenalism'

The existence of both symbolism and diversity in all known cultures generates a second cluster of problem assumptions. Can we assume the diversities to display ultimately (after a great deal of scientific discovery) some clear, universal form? Or should we assume that specific forms of sexuality emerge under specific economic, religious, kinship and cultural conditions? Can we assume that the diversities exhibit definite and uniform constellations of experience? Or should we assume that people's lives are much less fixed, with a toing and froing of their sexualities across their life cycles?

The former view is *essentialist.* Thus, looking at history, prostitution can become the 'oldest profession', rape may be seen as the means by 'which all men keep all women in a state of fear' (Brownmiller 1975, p. 5), pornography becomes (universally) the 'depiction of whores' (Dworkin 1981), whilst homosexuality may be found just as readily in ancient Greece as in a modern sauna bath in New York. A common essence is found which transcends time and place. This view would also tend to see 'the family' as a given (cf. Thompson 1979), and, most supremely, sexuality is taken to be a universal constant – usually a powerful biological drive requiring control and directly linked to procreation and gender (cf. Gagnon and Simon 1973). This view, however, is open to the immediate accusation that it simply takes the assumptions of today and uses them to 'read' other cultures. It fails to recognize that the *meaning given the experiences in different cultures may be so at variance* that it does not help to see them unproblematically in the same terms. Is the experience of two men in a New York Leather Bar beating each other comparable to the fantasies of de Sade? Is the paternalistic tutorship of boy and adult in ancient Greece the same as the 'child molester' locked up in our modern prisons? Is the wearing of female costume by males in a modern Beaumont Society meeting in a provincial English town comparable to that of the Berdache? Of course there are similarities and tentative universals: but the actual meaning of the experience is organized so differently in each case that it is dangerous to render them too similar.[5]

As one clear instance, consider the young men of a small New Guinean community, fictitiously named the Sambia, who spend nearly ten years of their lives exclusively engaged in sexual relations with other men. This is not just a freak happening of a few; it is prescribed for all. More than this, intercourse with women is forbidden – indeed, the men are kept firmly away from women. In our culture it would be hard not to think of this as homosexuality – and indeed the anthropologist who studied this group does refer to it in such a fashion throughout his book (Herdt 1981). But as the author makes very clear, the rituals and meanings surrounding the experience are wildly at variance with those we associate with homosexuality in our culture.

In our culture (until recently) male–male fellatio was taboo – amongst the Sambia it was prescribed. In our culture it was linked to effeminacy and weakness – amongst the Sambia it was a sign of masculinity and strength. In our culture to engage in such acts for six or seven years exclusively, having no contact with women, would be seen as indicative of a fixed type of person (a homosexual man) who would have to be castigated, imprisoned or 'treated' – amongst the Sambia, it was a long experience in adolescence that prepared one for later-life heterosexual intercourse and marriage. In Sambia, male–male fellatio was one of a number of rituals in which older men and boys prepared younger boys for adulthood and masculinity – central to this was the idea that sperm from another man had to be built up in the younger man in order to meet women and procreate later in life. Fellatio was the cornerstone of masculinity; nothing could be further from the thoughts of all these young men that such activities were clinical disorders or evidence of homosexual types. To understand this experience it has to be placed in the wider context of Sambia interpretations of gender and Sambia explanations of procreation. If same-sex fellatio has a hormonal base then can it be the case that such hormones are activated for all males between the ages of seven and eighteen in Sambia culture? If same-sex fellatio is the result of behavioural conditioning, then something drastic must happen to transfer all these fellators to heterosexuality around the age of 18! If homosexuality is pathologic, then some cultures must have wholly pathological age-bands! Of course there are reasonable responses to such challenges, but the point I hope is made: it is not the case that other cultures make sense of diverse sexualities in the same way as we do and there are dangers to be found in interpreting the past through the lenses of the present, or other life experiences through our own.

Similar concerns emerge in comparing same-sex experiences amongst women (though there is the additional problem that until recently women have been so hidden from history that adequate data on which to build are hard to find). If an examination was made of same-sex experiences between women in the eighteenth century, women in the early twentieth century and women in the late 1970s (in England and America) there are clear signs of a radically different form of experience. Thus Lillian Faderman has documented the ubiquity and strength of 'romantic friendships' between women in the eighteenth century – a world accepted but ignored by men, a wholly different and powerful sphere of intimacy. Only if the women started to cross-dress and 'act like men' was it taken as a threat to the male world and hence reacted to with vengeance. Normally it was just an assumed untroubled part of the life of women (Faderman 1981). Not so, of course, by the twentieth century, when comparable relationships had become shrouded in a deep medical stigma – derived from a male model of pathology through which it was interpreted in roughly the same way as male homosexuality.[6] The lesbian became a new clinical type: the romantic relationships of a century earlier were banished and transformed totally in their significance and meaning. With the wake of the women's movement in the 1970s yet another shift in the meaning of lesbianism occurred: it was invested with a political meaning and became a central plank in feminist claims. The 'woman-identified-woman' was invented (Wolf 1979, p. 63). Again, it is a quite different phenomenon from the romance of the eighteenth century and the sickness of the early twentieth. It would hence be very dangerous and indeed foolish to read 'lesbianism' as if it was a clinical entity that transcended time and space; paradoxically this was but one mode of grasping such experiences and, as is now well understood, a highly damaging and destructive mode.

Such ideas led social scientists during the 1970s to develop a more relativistic and Constructionist view of sexuality. Padgug summarizes the general approach well:

> Sexual reality is variable, and it is so in several senses. It changes within individuals, within genders, and within societies just as it differs from gender to gender, class to class and from society to society. Even the very meaning and content of sexual arousal varies according to these categories. Above all, there is continuous *development and transformation* of its realities. . . . There do exist certain sexual forms which, at least at a high level of generality, are common to all human societies: live [sic], intercourse, kinship, can be understood universally on a very general level. But that . . . Greece, Medieval Europe and modern capitalist societies share general sexual forms, do[es] not make the contents and meaning of these forms identical or undifferentiated. They must be carefully distinguished and separately understood, since their inner structures and social meanings and articulations are very different. . . . The forms, contents and context of sexuality always differ. There is no abstract or universal category of 'the erotic' or 'the sexual' applicable without change to all societies. (Padgug 1979, pp. 10–11; my italics)

Although their problems differ, this new 'constructionist' understanding has united a number of differing theoretical postures towards the study of sexuality: symbolic interactionists (Gagnon and Simon 1973; Plummer 1975) find many similarities with discourse theorists (Foucault, 1979), while feminist theoreticians join hands with Marxists (Barrett 1980; Weeks 1982; Coward 1983).

From procreation to pluralism

Behind much writing on human sexuality the assumptions of both 'nature' and essentialism converge in a unitary view of the nature of sexuality: sex is for the reproduction of species. From this it follows *inter alia* that the ideal form of sexuality must be heterosexual coitus in which the male must be sufficiently aroused to penetrate and the woman must be capable of at least bearing the child (usually raising it too). Key images hence follow from this unitary conception of sexuality – images of heterosexuality, coital sex, male arousal, female nurturance, motherhood, procreation – and these certainly seem to have informed most of western thinking, no less in the past than in the present. I am not talking here simply of the more formal definitions of the perversions, most of which certainly make such criteria of normality very explicit; but rather of the more pervasive ideas which lie unstated throughout much other writing on sexuality, even much that aims to transcend such limitations (cf. Rich 1981).

The above assumptions of a unitary procreative model run very deep and have helped therefore to define the entire field of sexual diversity. The image of male activity and female receptivity helps us to understand why nearly all discussion of perverse sexuality are essentially discussions of male sexuality. Currently all the major sex offences (with the exception of prostitution) are aimed at male desire, while discussions of perversion invariably focus on men, since women's involvement seems to occur much less frequently. Where are all the women who cross-dress, who crave men's suede shoes, who steal underwear from clothes-lines, who seek out the young child or who find sexual excitement in obscene telephone calls? Where, indeed, is the pornography for women?[7] Of course there are exceptions, but generally the problem of perversion (diversity) has been established as a problem of men.

That sexual deviance is viewed this way is (in part at least) a consequence of the way we structure our expectations. Since it is men who need to be aroused in order to impregnate, it is when this desire is aroused by some non-procreative source that we have a problem. Since it is women who merely acquiesce in the sexual act, their sexuality can be for the most part ignored. They figure only in the background – servicing men (in prostitution, strip-tease, pornography, etc. – where the women's needs sexually are rarely the focus of attention), provoking men (as in many accounts of rape) and frequently, through denial, having their sexuality unconstructed – much lesbianism, historically, as we have seen from Faderman (1981) seems to have been ignored; and I have argued elsewhere that were a man to have a relationship comparable to a woman's sensuous relationship with a child it would lead the man directly into prison – the man is sexual whilst the woman is not (cf. Plummer 1981b, pp. 227–8). Until the advent of the recent women's movement, the issue of female sexuality has been a puzzlement to male social scientists and they have usually elected to ignore it. Arguably, then, the field of sexual deviation has been built out of the issue of male desire. Deviant women are likely to be those who break the 'virginity requirement' before marriage and the 'motherhood requirement' after it (cf. Edwards 1981).[8]

However necessary procreation may be for the survival of the species, it is increasingly recognized that human sexuality has more goals than this. And once this is accepted, the core assumptions of so many investigations begin to crumble. Singer calls this the pluralistic view of sex:

> By pluralism I mean the refusal to assume in advance that nature prescribes a unitary model for male and female response, that there is only one norm which could indicate how all men or women must behave in order to function properly, that there is a unique mode of consummation that satisfies male or female sexuality, that there is a universal condition which constitutes or structures sexual response in all people on all occasions, or that there is a single instinct or biological system basic to human sexuality. (Singer 1973, pp. 15–16)

Pluralism culturally is a growing feature of industrialized societies, and arguably sexuality is just one more instance of this awareness of pluralism. All manner of sexual activities may be engaged in for all manner of reasons; men and women can elect to follow their own patterns of sexuality (though, of course, within a broad culturally agreed framework: a sexual free-for-all is as unacceptable as any kind of free-for-all in a social order). Following on from this, there are some who see the sexual fringe (Rubin 1981) and most particularly same-sexers (homosexuals) as providing the experimental lead in diverse sexualities – working out patterns and establishing the trends that the rest of society may, at a later date, more cautiously follow (cf. Lee 1978; Altman 1982). Be this as it may, the important point for my discussion is the need to recognize just how deep the assumption of procreation (with all its accompanying unified imagery) has been in the study of sexual diversity. To move towards a pluralistic model is to unhinge the majority of work in this area during the past century. If, for example, pluralism was accepted, the debate would turn to such questions as: how flexible can sexuality be? Can men and women experience these forms in the same way? How can procreation be satisfactorily integrated with the other goals of human sexuality? Are there some goals of sexuality which should be recognized as socially and politically unacceptable (e.g. those in the services of power?) and others which should be fostered (e.g. those in the service of mutual play (affection? recreation?). A very different kind of analysis would proceed from this.

From perversity to diversity

Questions such as the above are couched in terms of human variety and to ask them requires breaking away from assumptions of a unitary or unilinear sexuality – notably ones geared to procreation. Much discussion of sexuality for the past century or so has been either with an explicit condemnation of diversity (through law and morality) or with an implicit attack (through the conversion of diversity into sickness and clinical problems by medicine and psychiatry). It has been impossible to think about patterns of non-procreative sexuality without evoking some sense of stigma: devaluation, dishonour, degradation. To read the purportedly objective studies of clinical science over the past century is, in effect, to read a catalogue of abuse – whether witting or unwitting. Minor sexual whims are placed side by side with monstrous murders; specific sexual experiences are seen to carry with them the seeds of the most general diseases and atrocities; causes are never found in the ordinary and mundane but are sought in the 'bad seed' and the 'bad home' – contaminating all who surround the experience; the small delight is turned into the worst excess.

Of course there are many exceptions as always; but the general trends are unmistakable. From Krafft-Ebing's blood-drinking, shit-eating, corpse-mutilating band of degenerates at the end of the nineteenth century to the modern unstable homosexuals, inadequate fetishists, dangerous child molesters and depraved prostitutes, the underlying imagery of stigma has not been far away. Accounts have become more benevolent, tolerant, humane: but the backdrop of stigma still looms large. It seems hard to write or look from a point of view which acknowledges that diversity of cultural experience is a central characteristic of human beings, and senses the extraordinarily limited images we have established of moral sexuality (the coital 'fuck'). It seems hard to grasp that the stigma which is assumed in so much writing may actually be the problem to be analyzed.

COPING WITH DIVERSITY IN MODERN SOCIETY: REGULATION AND CONSTRUCTION

There is no society where sexual experiences proceed untrammelled by social regulations – complete sexual freedom exists exclusively in the libertarian's dream and the moral reformer's nightmare. Of course, societies will differ in both the degree and the substance of such controls (cf. Brown 1952; Christensen 1966), but regulation of some form there always seems to be.

At the most general level, there are two main types of explanation of this regulation – those which focus on the regulations of desire, and those which focus upon the production of symbolic order. Each has many contradictory and competing adherents.

The regulation of diversity

Within this explanation, the problem is one ultimately of bodily control: of our bodily lust, instincts or desires being curtailed. People are assumed to be guided by a powerful set of urges pressing for constant satisfaction – though very often this is restricted to men alone, women's desires are seen as minimal. In most versions of this theory, this satisfaction can never be permitted because it is destructive of social life or personal character. In a few versions, its satisfaction is encouraged as a liberatory force. It is to be found no less in the writings of Christians than in those of Freudians, Marxists or feminists: despite enormous differences, a unity of belief in the powerful body binds them together.

Fornication and lust must be regulated, according to the writings of Christians, through virginity, denial – or, if one must, through careful control in marriage ('It is better to marry than to burn'). For Freud, the regulations of polymorphous perverse libido were a necessary concomitant of the advance of civilization – it was the very energy which needed to be rechannelled into cultural creations (Freud 1975). For Reich, capitalist organization held this desire in check, harnessing the needs of the system for work – a theory later amplified by Marcuse and Brown (cf. Robinson 1969). For some feminists, men established their supremacy over women by gaining control over their desires, which in earlier periods were much stronger than men's: becoming male sexual property is the cornerstone of many theories of patriarchy (cf. Sherfey 1972). First virginity and then motherhood are the only appropriate routes for the woman (cf. Edwards 1981).

Clearly, there are many divergent accounts of regulation subsumed here, but a broadly similar principle is at work. Lyman has expressed this unanimity:

> Lustful cravings are likely to arise anywhere, anytime, and toward any object – human, animal, or ideal. . . . lust, whether enobled by love or not, can assume the totality of interests, activities, energies of those overwhelmed by it. Once this has occurred, the contributions to society or to that part of it to which the parties are attached, are diminished by the loss of the lustful parties' services. In the most general sense the various methods of social control employed to curb or channel lust are directed towards securing society against the losses entailed by lustful withdrawal. (Lyman 1979, p. 77)

Within this argument, then, the sex drive is held constant and various patterns of regulation – religion, the state, the family, capitalism etc. – are grafted on to it, thereby transforming the patterns of sexual diversity. But there is another set of arguments which suggest that far from controlling sex, regulations may actually serve to construct it. Since this argument is much less well known and much less popular than the 'regulation of desire' view, I will elaborate it in more detail.

The construction of diversity

Once human sexuality ceases to be viewed as a powerful, natural drive universally pressing for release, then the argument about sexual repression is considerably weakened: if there is no drive, then there is nothing to be repressed. Such an argument thus comes to suggest that far from culture acting on a 'drive' and regulating it, culture actually constructs and assembles the 'drive' and all that comes with it. Human sexuality is not in conflict with society but is shaped by those very social definitions. There is a continuity between culture and personal experience. John Gagnon has put this position clearly:

> the kind of sexuality that members of a culture believe helps to create the kind of sexuality they get. If they believe that sex is an anarchic and powerful drive and teach that view to young people, then they will get at least some who will behave as if they were possessed by an anarchic powerful drive. If they offer sex as a calming and therapeutic truth . . . then the good learners will indeed find that sex is a calming and therapeutic experience. All of social life is part of a self-fulfilling prophecy – if we teach people to believe something and tell them that it is right, then they will tend to act in that direction. However, our control of learning is never complete; people behave reflexively and often choose not to do what we want them to. (Gagnon 1977, p. 34)

This broad cultural view renders the analysis of symbols especially important in looking at sexual diversity.

Symbols, despite their inherent ambiguity, always work to impose form upon formlessness. Both in the wider culture and in the personal mind, symbols suggest a sense of order upon what would otherwise be inchoate disorder – unmanageable, unstable, unpredictable. This sense of order means constructing a symbolic system of classification – the naming of parts and the labelling of the acceptable and the unacceptable. Such a process of symbolic constructions and hence selections seems necessary for human life. And this seems so at both the personal and public levels.

On the personal level the need for a certain amount of cognitive restriction keeps at bay the buzzing, booming confusion of the chaotic universe. However radical or free-thinking individuals seem to be, their views must always occur within deeply restricted sets of assumptions – what the phenomenologists call the 'world taken for granted' and more colloquially the 'OK World' (cf. Berger 1977). Roth has put the point nicely: 'People will not accept uncertainty. They will make an effort to structure it no matter how poor the materials they have to work with and no matter how much the experts try to discourage them' (Roth *the increased restrictions devised by concerned parents, in the [becoming] a self-fulfilling prophecy*

1963, p. 93). To attempt to get through a day without a deep sense of order guiding one's novelty of thought is to invite oneself to get no further than opening one's eyes in the morning. The existential world of human possibility would simply be paralysed. It behoves a few – like de Sade or Nietzche perhaps – to attempt such transcendence, but it is no basis for most people in most cultures to get through their day.

One part of this deeply assumed world will be our thoughts on sexuality: zombie-like most of the time, we will experience our classifications of sexuality only dimly, confronting ambiguities with fear and rage and attempting either to explain them to ourselves or else expelling them into the world of dirt and disorder, disease and decay, degeneracy and the devil. Such process of reinterpretation and expulsion will usually serve to strengthen our sense of security and order, our conviction that the way we believe is right. It is, of course, the process widely recognized as 'scapegoating' (cf. Becker 1973).

But it is not just on this psychological level that such processes of symbolic ordering work: societies are commonly analysed by anthropologists as elaborate classification systems containing their own internal logics and interconnections centring particularly around issues of purity and taboo. Cultures are made sense of through symbols, but such symbolic order always implies disorder: ambiguities will emerge, phenomena will not fit, new 'stuff' will emerge which threatens the purity of the existing symbolism. Disorder is symbiotic with order: indeed not only must the two coexist, the one (disorder) may actually serve to strengthen the other (order) by creating the need for tighter classifications, stronger boundaries, ritualistic denunciations. Far from disrupting social order, the anomalies – if handled correctly – can serve to enhance it. These are general points given articulation by Durkheim (1964) and amplified very effectively in the more recent work of Mary Douglas (1970), Kai T. Erickson (1966) and Robert Scott (1972). Classification of genders and sexualities will be part of any cultural classification system – at least for as long as such things are considered important enough to differentiate. (Arguably, some cultures make very weak distinctions in such matters, and some recent arguments have suggested that such distinctions could be abolished altogether (cf. Kessler and McKenna 1978).)

Such an analysis can be made much more concrete. Christie Davies (1982) has examined the origins of taboos against homosexuality, bestiality and transvestism – or phenomena resembling these – in such groups as the Old Testament Jews, the Parsees, the ancient Greek states, the early and medieval Christians and the modern British armed forces. From comparative materials, he argues that it is when the identity of a group is most at stake that it 'uses' sexual taboos to mark its cohesive boundaries. In talking of the Jews, for example, he suggests that 'The forces of the taboos lies less in their content than in their structure, in the way they insist on the separation of categories so that the keeping apart of like and unlike is an everyday reminder of God's setting apart the Jews, the chosen people, from the heathen, the lesser breeds without the law' (Davies 1982, p. 1034). But is not just the Jews and religion: he sees military cohesiveness as another domain where social boundaries need tightening. In sum, he concludes:

> A detailed examination of the history of a number of Western societies and institutions shows that the origins and maintenance of these taboos stem from the fact that these forms of behaviour have been perceived by religious and military leaders as a threat to crucial social boundaries. They have sought to punish the homosexual, the transvestite and to a lesser extent other sexual deviants both as a means of reinforcing the distinctive identity of a group by emphasising its boundaries and as the means of maintaining the boundaries between the different layers of a religious or military hierarchy. (Davies 1982, p. 1033)

I think this account of sexual taboos works well at the abstract and formal level: it is hard to imagine a society without layers of symbols, systems of classifications and thereby anomalies that do not fit. But the theory commits the very sin that I have described earlier: it is too general and lacks a specific historical analysis. Christie, for example, talks about homosexuality in all the cultures as if it were the same thing; such theories hold too much constant.

It is part of Foucault's recent and much discussed contribution to challenge this notion of continuity. Regulative theories (like Freud's) see a sexual essence (transhistorical and transcultural) that has to be acted upon; symbolic-order theorists stress the continuity across cultures of symbolic thresholds. Although Foucault is quite close to this latter position and places a great deal of importance upon symbolic controls, his prime aim is to break beyond the conventional modes of thinking which can only see continuity and unfolding rationality. For him, there is a significant rupture in the world with the onset of industrialization and capitalism; our modes of apprehending and grasping the universe significantly shifted. History cannot be written in a continuous line. Thus his most relevant study here – *The History of Sexuality* – is neither a history nor about sexuality as conventionally conceived. Instead, it is about the explosion of 'knowledge' and ideas which came to constitute our thinking about sexuality from (roughly) the eighteenth century onwards. Part of a much wider programme in which Foucault attempts to trace the geneology and archaeology of contemporary thought (about crime, about medicine, about madness), the burden of his argument seeks to show how such discourses are the modes through which we enact our life and through which power is ubiquitously engendered. Discourses about sexuality, Foucault argues, have proliferated since the eighteenth century and transformed the constitution of our sexualities. He conjectures an earlier period where sexuality seems relatively insignificant but routinely and enjoyably experienced, and contrasts that with the explosion of talk about sex: from the earliest confessionals, through the medical treatises and onwards to modern-day psychiatry and sexology. It has been a period which far from repressing sexualities has actually given it a shape, a coherence and – most vitally – an importance which it does not necessarily have in all societies. We have learnt to think differently about sexuality and in the same process we have come to organize our power relationships differently; they are everywhere enacted within a framework of sexuality. Bodily control has come through symbolic orderings.

Foucault's discussion is far removed from the orthodoxies which discuss sexual repression and regulation, and as such it is not always easy to follow. Certain parts are, however, clearer than others: he describes, for instance, four great mechanisms that have constructed sexualities in the recent epoch which have become 'especially dense transfer point(s) for relations of power: Between men and women, young people and old people, parents and offspring, teachers and students, priests and laity, an administration and a population' (Foucault 1979, p. 103). These mechanisms entailed the hysterization of women's bodies (with the creation of the hysterical woman), the pedagogization of children's sex (with the creation of the hysterical woman), the pedagogization of children's sex (with the creation of the Masturbating Child), the socialization of procreative behaviour (with the creation of the Malthusian couple) and the psychiatrization of perverse pleasure (with the creation of a gallery of modern perverts – from the homosexual to the sadomasochist). For Foucault, then, the modern categories surrounding diverse sexualities (produced largely by medical men) are not to be seen simply as the revelations of science. They are, in fact, new ways of constructing sexualities: and through them, new ways of reaching into the body politic. It is not diverse sexuality that is being controlled and regulated; rather diverse sexualities are being constructed, shaped, given a new form – and through this, our relationships are imbued with a dynamic of power.

The making of the modern perverts

Although roots can be traced back to at least the seventeenth century (cf. Diethelm 1750; McIntosh 1968; Bray 1982), it was distinctively during the nineteenth century that our contemporary modes of apprehending sexual diversity were consolidated. Partially this meant the increasing use of the law to construct sexuality, but more crucially it meant the rise of the medically defined expert. Human sexualities were progressively taken over from the domain of the explicit moralist to the domain of the presumedly objective and scientific medical men. It was 'female sexuality' and 'masturbatory insanity' that symbolized this medicalization of sex, and judged by today's standards the pejorative moralism and control disguised as benevolence is all too apparent.

Thus for women 'the act of sexual intercourse' was seen to become 'an absolute and positive source of disease' (cf. Edwards 1984, p. 82), while masturbation – for men and women – became a common cause of insanity. Esquirol in France, Acton in England and Rush in America converged on the centrality of the masturbatory hypothesis: at times it seemed as if masturbation was the greatest (evil) medical complaint in the world. As one commentator could write: 'neither plague, nor war, nor smallpox, nor a crowd of similar evils, have resulted more disastrously for humanity than the habit of masturbation: it is the destroying element of civilized society' (From the *New Orleans Medical and Surgical Journal*, quoted in Szasz 1981, p. 18). Along with such round condemnation emerged a whole cluster of implements and strategies for the containment of masturbation – well documented in Alex Comfort's *The Anxiety Makers* (Comfort 1968). Today this fear has been partially dissipated and the old medical treatises are a matter of amusement; but the basic structure of the argument still imbues the masturbatory experience with guilt and secrecy for many (Marcus and Francis 1975; Sarnoff and Sarnoff 1979).

It was particularly towards the end of the nineteenth century that the diverse sexualities became classified into a huge taxonomy of perversion: causes were sought, characteristics charted and treatments designated. Generic terms – such as nymphomania – were invented, and then subclassified – the nymphomaniac could be andromaniac, clitoromaniac or hypatomaniac (Cf. Acton 1857; Marcus 1981, p. 31). Elaborate classifications grew up designating the perversion of object choice and the perversions of aim; and case-study after case-study was introduced first to the medical profession and later to the general public through elaborate volumes such as Krafft-Ebing's *Psychopathia Sexualis* (1886). The 'homosexual' was literally born in 1869, when Benkert coined the term; the 'exhibitionist' was literally born in 1877, when Lasegue coined the term; and the fetishist came into being around 1887, when Binet coined the term. One by one, and in step with the more general developments in criminological science (cf. Mannheim 1966; Matza 1964), a rogues gallery of sexuality came into being. And it is this gallery which remained at the centre of contemporary modes of thinking about sexual diversity. It is true that over the past two decades there has been some shifting in these cultural constructions – most notably the women's movement has brought some change to the conceptions of female diversities (cf. Ehrenreich and English 1979; Banks 1981), and the gay movement managed to bring the American Psychiatric Association to remove homosexuality from the psychiatric nomenclature (cf. Bayer, 1981) – but the gallery of specific types (the homosexual, the paedophile, the transvestite) remain at the core of thinking about diversity. The point is that such categories construct diversities at least as much as reflecting them. A close look behind any one of these categories reveals enormous diversities of experience that are held together by a slender categorical device. Paedophilia, for instance, is an experience with so many levels and forms that the term obscures much more than it helps (cf. Rossman 1979; Plummer 1981b).

The classification and medicalization of diverse sexualities, however, needs to be seen against a much wider background. It is not just that medicine has constructed the perverse: it has also constructed the 'normal'. Masturbation, hysterical women, fetishists or homosexuals all stand in contrast to the assumed baseline that human sexuality has one natural goal – procreation. All sexualities should ultimately be harnessed to procreation and from this much of social life may be explained: the deep assumption of heterosexuality, since only heterosexuals can reproduce (cf. Plummer 1981b; Rich 1981); the deep assumption about the nature of men and women, since men impregnate and are thereby assertive and active, while, women 'merely' conceive and then are charged with the responsibilities of raising the child; and the deep assumption about the nuclear family, since this alone will provide the ideal stability for the procreative goal. It is this procreative assumption that becomes the key definer of contemporary sexuality. Even though, at the behavioural level, remarkably little sexuality is actually geared to a simple goal like procreation – sexuality is behaviourally pluralistic (cf. Singer 1973) – symbolically it is seen within this framework.

This image of 'procreation' not only serves to construct images of the 'perverse', it also serves to construct different sorts of perversities for men and women. The symbolism of procreation serves to play down the female's interest in sexuality (she does not have to experience orgasm in order to procreate) while playing up her interest in nurturing the child. Conversely, the symbolism serves to highlight the need for male orgasm through intercourse while minimizing his involvement with the nurturing of the child. And contained within such imagery is the notion of perversity for men and women. Thus a perverse woman is one who is either too sexual (nymphomania) or neglectful of motherhood. A perverse man is one whose sexual drives are not harnessed to reproductive intercourse. It is not the case that men are more perverse than women, as is so frequently suggested in clinical textbooks or criminal statistics. Rather, the perversities of men and women are assembled in different ways according to the image of their role in procreation.

COPING WITH DIVERSITY IN MODERN SOCIETY: REACTION AND CONSTRUCTION

To ban sexualities is not to eliminate them; rather, it is to give them a distinctive form. People who experience diversities are not simply the recipients of given biological or psychological needs; instead, they have to *construct* their sexuality as a response to the cultural definitions that surround them. In this section I propose to examine briefly three sets of responses to these cultural definitions: the personal, the collective and the political.[9] In each case, these responses can be seen as ways of handling a culturally induced set of problems; of access, guilt, secrecy and identity.

The problems of sexual stigma

A first key problem which confronts the sexually different is the feeling of guilt and the consequential desire for legitimacy. To apprehend that your diversity is taboo is to exist either in public shame or in private guilt. This problem manifests itself in different ways, but it is initially omnipresent. A person who seeks to cross-dress may be 'disgusted with himself'; a man who seeks sex with children may see this as a sign of 'weakness' or a sign of 'immaturity'; the person who wants to be urinated on may see this as a 'wicked thought'; the woman who wants to whip a man may fear she is a 'pervert'; the person who plans to sell their sexual wares may fear they are a 'whore'. Over and over again – in the stories of many diverse people – the tale of oddity, abnormality and wickedness is stressed. Yet such worries are not intrinsic to the experiences: all, at some time or place, could be acceptable. It is rather the stigma which generates them. Many may live with such guilt all their lives, but others may quickly overcome it. Crucial in this must be the gaining of legitimation which can transform the sense of wrong into a positive experience.[10]

A second problem centres around secrecy: stigma creates silence, ban breeds solitariness. If 'it' is spoken about, it will be in hushed tones, inadequate language, ridicule or horror. The struggle here is on to find the right words to use and the right person to approach. Homosexuals, for example, are brought up in families where the deep presumption is that the child will be heterosexual and marry, attend schools where sex education is strictly heterosexual and absorb a message from the mass media that excludes or ridicules the sexually different. The same holds, even more strongly, for the paedophile, the transvestite, the fetishist: who can imagine the child that asks its parents where to go for eroticized spankings or leather fetishism? Many will harbour this 'secret' till the day they die; others might broach the subject with a few, while some others may come to realize that there are whole worlds where such things are spoken about.

A third problem is that of access and availability. Once an experience becomes the subject of ban, it is clearly rendered unavailable to all except the active seeker – it cannot be a simple matter of 'drift' as marital sexuality will routinely be. The 'getting of sex' may be a more general problem, but for the diversities it is initially a seemingly insurmountable one. How can a woman find another woman? How can you find someone to beat? How can you find a well-worn black stiletto heel shoe to fondle? How can an elderly man find a young girl as an emotional and sexual companion? How can you find the surgical tools to turn yourself from a man into a woman? In all cases, the struggle is on to make available what culture has rendered unavailable. Many will not believe the effort is worth the making and indeed may take their worry quietly to their grave. Others may briefly experiment, find the price too high and give up. Still others may find ways of flirting with the experience throughout their lives – never quite making it central, and never quite giving it up. Still others will pursue the problem until their need is regularly and routinely available to them.

A fourth, and final, problem centres upon identity. In our culture (and many would argue in all), distinctions based on gender go to the very heart of our identity, and gender is presumed to be closely correlated with sexual experience. The idea that what one experiences sexually may be disentangled from one's biological sex and social definitions of gender is not usually part of conventional wisdoms. A 'principle of consistency' seems to be at work (Ponse 1978; Barrett 1980; Plummer 1981a). Hence, once any anomaly in gender or sexual experience is sensed, questions will be posed about identity. The struggle is on to find out who one really is. Given the centrality of these experiences in building identities, it is very easy for them to be transformed into a being; for potential to become personhood, for doing to become an essence, for an encounter to become an orientation. Whatever one's diversity – to worship feet, to adore encasement – it starts to be connected to one's identity and thereby is given a centrality and importance. What could just be a 'hobby' may ultimately come to be the core of one's being.

Personal reactions to stigma

It is these four problems – all fundamentally social in origin – that serve as the materials out of which modern 'perverts' are made. How a person copes with these problems helps to form the character of the sexual variations: at the very least they are likely to generate substantial worry for the person pondering them. Thus a self-amplifying process is set in motion by which guilt may generate more guilt, secrecy leads to greater isolation and more secrecy, and lack of access leads to a greater sense of frustration. Worrying about worrying can turn minor problems into much bigger ones; and sometimes the sexually diverse may spend their entire adult lives in a state of anxiety generated by their inability to solve these problems.

How may the problems be resolved? Four great strategies seem available (undoubtedly there are others); denial, treatment, neutralization and 'coming to terms'. Only in the latter is there a clear and positive acceptance of the diversity.

For some, and until recently this has been the most likely response, the answer is simply to leave well alone: denial. An attempt is made to block this 'secret' from one's life. From time to time little 'moral holidays' may occur – some may occasionally wear female undergarments or purchase pornographic magazines harbouring their secret fantasies; but this reawakens all the old guilt and panic, and very quickly the undergarments or magazines are burnt or destroyed; and the cycle can start again. Paradoxically, brute denial may serve to strengthen the problems and lead to the diversity remaining a powerful experience.

Others may take their problems into the public domain and seek 'help'. Their central coping strategy is to turn to 'experts' and professionals who claim to be able to help them with their problem. Since until recently such 'experts' were the only way a person could easily move from their private secret to another who knew about their problems, a considerable industry of 'cure' and therapy developed around these variations in the middle period of this century. Whether such treatments actually cured many people is a matter of great dispute: but they certainly performed the function of giving the 'patient' an opportunity to have their thoughts on diversity reorganized (often made even more negative!). Most recently this strategy has become less common with the perversities, but it has grown with the sexual dysfunctions. A multi-million-dollar industry has developed to restructure people's private worries about dysfunctioning. These in general claim very high success rates (unlike the diversities); but they may also be seen as moments when sexualities are brought into a wider communication process and hence restructured.

A third strategy entails the neutralization of the experience. Here, the behaviour occurs whilst the meaning is denied. Paedophiles may have relationships with children but blame it on drink (McCaghy 1968), exhibitionists may say they were caught out and had to urinate (McDonald 1973), transvestites may restrict dress-wearing to acceptable occasions like parties and men may rape whilst denying the woman as a victim (cf. Weis and Borges 1975; Jackson 1978). Crucial here is the existence of an 'account' which can permit the behaviour but give it a meaning that is not threatening.

It is only with the fourth coping strategy that a reorganized identity occurs. This strategy can, quite literally, be called 'coming to terms'. What is important to grasp here is that an experience is not necessarily an identity. Thus sexual experiences and fantasies do not automatically announce themselves as well-coded and well-understood categories. Many experiences remain ambiguously uncrystallized until circumstances permit or demand their codification: a person may very dimly sense that sex is better when a certain piece of dress is near at hand but in no way comprehend (or even know) the term fetishism; a person may be dimly aware of the fondness experienced in the company of certain children, but in no way see this (or know the term) paedophilia; a person may dimly know that their favourite sexual experiences are enhanced if they bring to it their own 'peculiar' little fantasy, but in no way is this little quirk to be read as a sign of perversion (however odd it may sound if it was actually revealed). It is very important to grasp that there is a great deal of sexual diversity which never gets coded into our existing categories. Many people are not even aware of their own secrets, let alone capable of working to hide them from anyone.

Nevertheless, for many people, the solution to their problems is to find a suitable category in which to place themselves. For finding a name – even if it does not capture one's experiences correctly – can be very useful. It allows one to think what until then was probably unthinkable; it puts one in a class, a group, and potentially bridges isolation; it is the first hint of a public world beyond one's private secret; it may give an order to a hitherto chaotic world. No matter that later this very label may bring its own problems: for the time being it is a most potent unifying force.

There are many routes available for this process of coming to terms – through friends or counsellors, magazines and books, films and meetings – and such voyages of discovery are now well documented.[11] An interesting example – interesting because it comes from a woman discovering her masochism – is Maria Marcus's feminist study *A Taste for Pain* (1981). Books and literature of all sorts, from the earliest childhood stories like *Uncle Tom's Cabin* through to the most intense readings of Freud, Kinsey and the like, played a particularly prominent role in the building of her identity – she shows quite vividly how each 'reading' gave her new senses, new ideas, new images to play with and build upon. From Fabricus Mollar's book she gets the term 'masochism' ('so there was a name for it. . . . I think I was pleased to have a name as if I were no longer floating about in the air' – p. 21) but also a sense of the furtive little bands of perverts she belonged to ('there I was together with a whole series of other abnormal phenomena' – p. 20):

> But the most important thing I have gained was the simple matter of having acquired a name. So I was something definite. I was included in a definite category. I had my own place. The drawer I belonged in didn't smell quite so nice as the others but it was a regular drawer with a label on it. In some way or other, this seemed conforting, a kind of acknowledgement. . . . Being given a name seemed to be the first act of consciousness raising, as if a whole disorganised mess of granules had gathered themselves into a solid picture, not only something definite, but also something special – something not really as it should be. Not quite like a crime, but something close to it. . . . I consulted many more books wanting to know much more. . . . (Marcus 1981, pp. 25–6)

Marcus takes her readers step by step through the literature that she, like so many of the sexually different, explored. Finding those authors who saw it as normal; looking out for the figures on how many there were; scanning pictures to find herself; looking at the way which 'childhood experiences bound up with humiliating sadistic forms of punishment have been the cause' (p. 51); and finding new terms for herself ('algolagnia – for a moment I felt homeless, but then I saw I was surrounded by all my usual friends' – p. 53). It is through this long cultural search that she slowly comes to assemble her masochism.

Collective reactions to stigma

There is a strong tendency in modern thought to see sexual diversity as a feature of individuals. As I have suggested earlier, the nineteenth century transformed sexuality into a gallery of individual types – with their own aetiologies, their own particular traits and their own potential cures. Largely through the work of medical science and psychiatry, the possibility of seeing the social nature of sexual diversity was increasingly lost. Diversity became perversion; perversion was symptomatic of individual malfunctioning; it hence became individualized, pathologized and controlled (cf. Foucault 1979; Szasz 1981).

This is, however, only one way of approaching the problem. For since human sexuality usually involves the seeking of partners and always involves the use of social symbols, sexuality can just as plausibly be viewed in social terms: it is not much fun being a pervert on your own. Although, then, at certain historical moments the whole issue can be thoroughly individualized, there remains a constant possibility for the sexually diverse to come together in groups and this can be a major way of coping with diversity. There is much evidence, for instance, that people seeking same-sex experiences created some kind of 'gay subculture' in ancient Rome and in Europe during the middle ages (cf. Boswell 1980) as well as in Renaissance England (Bray 1982); and that from the eighteenth century onwards many cities came to possess their own gay taverns and bars (cf. Bullough 1976, p. 607; Adam 1979, p. 286). These subcultures did not have the same meaning as those of today, but they nevertheless indicate the existence of collective forms of coping with diversity.

Variant subcultures do not exist in all societies – there seems little evidence for their existence in contemporary China or USSR. And indeed it is likely that it is only under capitalism that such subcultures have really proliferated. Altman, talking about the modern gay culture in America, for instance, could remark that 'this development was only possible under consumer capitalism, which for all its injustices has created the conditions for greater freedom and diversity than are present in any other society yet known' (Altman 1982, p. 104). Indeed, since the 1960s, American social scientists have documented most of the nooks and crannies of different sexual subcultures from bars to baths to bordellos (cf. Achilles 1967; Read 1980; Delph 1978; Humphreys 1975; Weinberg and Williams 1975; Styles 1979; Stein 1974; Stewart 1972). They have described the culture, roles, argot and codes of conduct experienced in nudist camps (Weinberg 1965) and on nudist beaches (Douglas and Rasmussen 1977); at swingers' parties (Bartell 1971) and in student bathrooms; in pornographic bookstores (Karp 1973; Perkins and Skipper 1981) and in massage parlours (Rasmussen and Kuhn 1976); at transvestite meetings (Feinblom 1976) and at drag shows (Newton 1973); in sadomasochistic gatherings (Weinberg and Falk 1980) and paedophiliac groups (Rossman 1979; Plummer 1981d). Very little, it seems, has been left unexplored.

The clearest example of sexual diversity becoming subculturalized is that of male homosexuality in the western world during the 1970s and 1980s. In most large cities, gays have created their own communities comparabie to those of immigrant groups who create their own ghettos (cf. Lee 1979; Levine 1979; White 1980; Altman 1982). Gay communities appear to be the most developed and advanced form of subculturalization amongst erotic minorities, and insofar as they may provide a blueprint for others to follow, their growth can be seen as passing through three waves (cf. Weeks 1977).

In the first wave, covert meeting places and networks were established. As early as the eighteenth century, taverns existed where homosexual men – often effeminate men – gathered. They had a slow growth, and often were akin to brothels or, at the other extreme, gentlemen's clubs. Whilst some homosex-uals could therefore meet, they were strictly taboo and their hallmarks were probably secrecy and silence. By the middle of the nineteenth century, a few groups in Europe and American attempted to organize themselves more politically (cf. Lauritsen and Thorstad 1974): in France, André Gide's 1911 defence of homosexual love, *Corydon*, and the subsequent *Arcadie* group; in England, Edward Carpenter's 1894 pamphlet *Homogenic Love*; in America, more ambivalently, the work of Walt Whitman – especially his 1860 *Leaves of Grass* and the much later Chicago Society for Human Rights (Katz 1976, pp. 385f.); in Germany, the creation by Magnus Hirshfield of the 'Scientific Humanitarian Committee' in 1897 and later the first Institute of Sexual Science (to be destroyed when Hitler came to power). Bullough comments of the latter: 'In a sense, the committee, the group behind the clinic, journal and research centre, came close to being an association of homosexuals, and it has sometimes been regarded as the first effective organization of homosexuals' (cf. Bullough 1976, p. 645).

Throughout Europe and America, then, the first few decades of the twentieth century began to see the emergence of something more than just covert meeting places: the beginnings of the translation of homosexuality from medical to political terms was under way. Self-declared homosexuals were of course few, organizations subject to constant harassment and closure, reputations severely at risk: but the elements were there.

The second wave began in the decade immediately following the second world war: Europe and America witnessed a slow and cautious proliferation of homosexual movements and law-reform lobbies (the latter often arising outside overt homosexual groups). In America, a social club – the Veteran's Benevolent Association – was established in 1945 and lasted until 1954, by which time many organizations had been founded: SIR (Society for Individual Rights), Mattachine and the Daughters of Bilitis being the longest lasting and each producing their own fairly continuous (but much harassed) magazines. In England, the Homosexual Law Reform Association was set up in the wake of the Wolfenden Report (HMSO 1957) and worked assiduously so that a decade later the Sexual Offences Act was finally passed decriminalizing homosexual acts by men over 21 in many circumstances. The final symbolism of nearly thirty years of organization came in the Stonewall Riots, 28 June 1969. This marked a distinctive change from the days of the early homophile movement – gays showing active resistance to police harassing a local Greenwich village bar, with a two-day street battle following. From this moment on the approach to homosexuality shifted. Whereas before it had largely been apologetic, it was now 'glad to be gay'; whereas before it had been secretive, now it was 'coming out'. Homosexuality drastically increased in visibility and the language surrounding it began to shift from one of disease to one of politics and 'rights'. A year later a small group of students met in a room at the London School of Economics and the English Gay Liberation Front was born. By that time, it had indeed become an international political movement, and it has remained so ever since.

The central issue of this third wave was 'coming out' and a politicization of sexual diversity, and it has led to an ever increasing poliferation of gay institutions. Whereas once the secret bar and the clandestine 'cottage' were all that existed for homosexuals, the 1970s witnessed the growth of gay publishing, gay industries, gay bath-houses, gay counselling services, gay switchboards, gay churches, gay trade unions, gay political parties, gay fashion, gay discos, gay ramblers – gay everything. Sexual diversity had become the explicit, overt organizing point of hundreds of thousands of lives (Lee 1978; White 1980; Altman 1982). Whole communities in America and Canada became colonized into 'gay ghettos'. Whatever evidence there was for 'gay subcultures' in the middle ages or for institutionalised homosexuality amongst certain tribes, it seems likely that world history has never seen the organization of stigmatized sexual diversity on such a massive scale before. And arguably it has set a model for other sexually diverse experiences to follow. The model suggests that in a first phase there must be minimal conditions for some like-minded people to come together – usually in secrecy and shame. From this, a gradual case can be made for changes in attitudes or law: this will be a low-key debate, virtually silenced in the public sphere. By now, though, two crucial conditions will have been established: that people experiencing diversity can meet and that arguments can be made in their defence. It becomes therefore increasingly plausible to accept and extend the diversity until a third phase is (unexpectedly) reached: the take-off into coming out and mass political protest. Once sexuality enters this sphere, the conditions are ripe for the proliferation of many institutions for the sexually different – and coping with such diversity ostensibly becomes much easier.

Few other patterns of sexuality have been either so visible or so successful in their organizing and campaigning as the gay movement, but most have made some attempts. In general they remain lodged at the first two stages of development – providing services and supports for a small group of interested members and creating the beginnings of a legitimation. Transvestism, transexualities, paedophilia, sadomasochism, prostitution, fetishism, group sex, and nudism have all created such mini-worlds.[12]

This collective way of coping with sexual diversity seems a distinctively modern development, a feature indeed of advanced capitalist societies. Small coteries may have existed in the past, and in some cases extensive subcultures; but never before in history has there been such an extensive proliferation for such diverse groupings. That paedophiles should now have become organized (admittedly in a small way) in most western countries, and that prostitutes should have set up their own union would have been unthinkable a century ago.

There is nothing particularly surprising about the evolution of so many collective forms of sexual diversity. It is completely congruent with the proliferation of subcultures more generally that seems to have accompanied industrialization (cf. Yinger 1960; Irwin 1977): it is part of the wider process of social differentiation that has been a key concern of sociologists since the work of the founding fathers. It could be seen, following Weber, as evidence of the increasing rationalization of our sexual lives – taking it out of the domain of the unpredictable and even the unavailable into the domain of the orderly, the rational and the available (and the potentially disenchanted). It could be seen, following Marx, as evidence of the ever increasing commoditization of sex; removing sexuality from the realm of spontaneous experience into the realms of marketing, packaging, selling. Certainly, many of the subcultural forms develop their own mini-economies. It could be seen, following Durkheim, as evidence of the increasing growth of small associations and communities which lessen the anomic experience of an increasingly differentiated society – the mini-worlds of erotic sexuality providing comfort, community and support. It could be seen, following Simmel, as evidence of the city fostering segregation and diversity side by side with indifference and tolerance – nobody is concerned about the other person's sexual quirks providing they are left to their own. And even some of the more recent cultural theorists, Lasch, Sennett, Foucault, could all explain this trend: as signs of increasing self-absorption, as the retreat from public life, as the proliferation of new discourses. One day a hefty study could be made of such developments: for the time being it will suffice merely to comment that there is nothing surprising about the growth of such erotic subcultures of diversity. The sexual life flows and meshes with the very texture of changes in the wider society.

Political reactions to stigma

From the foregoing, it will be clear that the collective response to diversity has been accompanied by an increasing politicization. In one sense, this is nothing new. Throughout history there have been sexual heretics – from Socrates to de Sade – who have challenged the orthodoxy and brought about change. The political edge of sexual conduct has long been recognized – and not least by those who seek to contain it. But this century has slowly witnessed the transformation of a political edge for the few into a front-line battle-field for the many. Two major forces seem to be at work. One, the gay movement, has provided a blueprint for many other sexual minorities to follow – and there have been organized attempts to legitimate most patterns of sexual and gender diversity – from paedophilia and sadomasochism to transvestism and transexuality. The other, the second wave of feminism, has become much more acutely concerned with 'examining the role of sexuality in the construction of male domination and female subordination' while creating a 'space in which women can refuse sexual exploitation' and 'reflect on our (their) own desires' (*Feminist Review* 1982). Often with widely divergent – even contradictory – arguments, these two movements have created a major alternative response to the problem of sexual diversity. At base, however, they all refuse to countenance the stigma that has been their historical birthright; they gain strength from the solidarity of working together for a common goal; and – to greater or lesser degrees – they have shifted the public rhetoric of sexuality from the individual and medical sphere to the public and political one.

Disregarding the positions of the conservative and the liberal lobbies,[13] the main debate is currently set up between the politics of desire (the sexual liberationists) and the politics of sexism (the gender liberationists). Both attack the traditional views of sexuality, and the assumed connections between heterosexuality, procreation, marriage and the normal, and seek alternative constructions of sexuality. But the former seek a proliferation of new forms of sexualities, while the latter seek a reduction of gender inequalities. The former centres around debates to 'liberate' paedophilia, sadomasochism and the fetishisms and to make pornography more freely available: it wants to extend the claimed successes of the gay movement (and indeed the so called 'permissive era') to other areas of sexuality. Desire can come in many wondrous forms and should be experienced as such: it is only because we are still suffering from our historically repressive view of sexuality that we fail to see how much joyful sexuality could be constructed.[14] In contrast, the politics of sexism centres around the same debates but draws different conclusions. Paedophilia and boy-love is 'a euphemism for rape' (Morgan, in Califia 1981, p. 137); sadomasochism is the perpetuation of male power games and displays the delusion that life and its meaning can be contained in an orgasm' (*Woman's Touch*, cited by Valverde 1980); pornography is 'propaganda for and a tool of sexual suppression of women that is unbelievably powerful in its effects' (Dworkin 1982, p. 26). More than this, even male homosexuality becomes deeply suspect – as a celebration of male desire and an ignoring of women (cf. Stanley 1982).[15]

Both these positions claim to be 'progressive' and provide political responses to the issue of sexual diversities. But they are diametrically opposed – since the former seeks to liberate a male model of desire while the latter sees this as the very source of oppression. A deep antagonism appears, and all the earlier medical perversions become a battle-ground for redefinition: as positive sexuality or oppressive to women. A complex debate is likely to emerge on this in the next few decades; but at least one writer has suggested the need for a reconciliation. Thus Gayle Rubin comments: 'Both the mobilization of the sexual fringe, and the increasing politicization of sexuality, challenge feminism to develop a political union which can be pro-sex while remaining anti-sexist' (Rubin 1981, p. 115).

In conclusion, I hope the preceding discussion demonstrates the extent to which human sexual diversity is not a timeless given: it twists, grows and refashions itself as the culture of which it is a part constantly changes. The early days of medical writing on sexuality can now only be viewed with amusement or alarm: who can say how our current constructions of sexual diversity will appear in a hundred years from now?

NOTES

1   The debate about values and ideology in social science generally has a long and complex history. I have found the discussions by Mills (1943), Gouldner (1971) and Douglas (1970) especially influential. More particularly, for different positions on the study of sexuality see Sagarin (1968), Trilling (1954), Masters et al. (1977) and Morin (1977). Whatever else they achieve, they certainly indicate the multifarious values – usually hidden – within 'sexology'.

2   Earlier studies like those of Allen (1969), Rosen (1964) or Storr (1964) exemplify this point. One problem here is that each generation of researchers seek what they

believe to be objective and neutral terms – only to find the next generation has rendered them pejoratives.

3   In some earlier writings I have spoken as if biology was insignificant – I now think it is very important: but *not* as important for human life as the symbolic. The thesis that man is twin born – that we are 'little Gods who shit' – has been most stimulatingly put for me in the work of Ernest Becker (e.g. Becker 1973, 1975).

4   The most prominent recent tradition in approaching human sexuality through society and symbolism is that of symbolic interactionism. I have outlined this orientation in Plummer (1982), but the key text is that of Gagnon and Simon (1973). In psychology, the nearest parallel is that of cognitive theory, e.g. Rook and Hammen (1977).

5   This problem of interpretation is, of course, a central one in all social science and there is not space in a short chapter such as this to deal with the deeper issues. Two issues would be crucial, however, for a full analysis. Firstly, the problem of human nature – whilst there may be a unity of humankind, is there in fact a sexual 'essence' that transcends time and place? Secondly, the problem of epistemology and relativism – whilst there may be limited truths from particular perspectives, is there any way in which a whole truth maybe grasped – one which is non-relative and independent of all positions? These are age-old questions which still generate heated debate. See, for example, Glassner (1980); and for its applicability to homosexuality see especially Boswell (1982), which advocates a middle position.

6   Annabel Faraday (1981) has recently analysed the literature on female same-sex relationships in the social science literature and shown how they have been informed by male bias. Most notably, such experiences are discussed within the framework of *male* homosexuality, instead of within the framework of female sexuality. It is a point hinted at, but not adequately developed, in the paper by Gagnon and Simon (1967). A much more personal and polemical view of this problem of separating out male and female homosexuality is to be found in Stanley (1982).

7   Some have argued that there is a pornography for women in romance magazines – but since pornography is defined through male drives it is not recognized as such. See Faust (1982).

8   It is only very recently that 'female deviance' has become a significant area of enquiry. See, in particular, Smart (1976), Hutter and Williams (1981).

9   It is beyond my scope to deal with the full range of such experience – with the victims of diversity (e.g. Burgess and Holmstrom (1974); Burgess et al. (1978); Finkelhor (1979); Rush (1980); Scacco (1982)), and the friends and families of those close to the sexually diverse (e.g. Warren (1976); Maddox (1982)). Rather I will deal only with a specific cluster of experiences – I will call them the socially stigmatized diversities – where a broadly comparable set of problems and solutions have been detected. The model for this mode of thinking has been developed most fully in studies of male homosexuality during the 1960s and 1970s, but in fact it is substantially applicable to other experiences – transvestism, sadomasochism, paedophilia, prostitution, lesbianism and fetishisms. In the broadest terms, it attempts to understand the diversities on a social level (rather than on a clinical one) and suggests that many of the distinguishing features of sexual diversity arise not

from the experience itself but from the stigma and procreative assumptions in which it is enmeshed. For these generate problems, which if not resolved will transform the experience into something much more significant and damaging than it would otherwise be. I have dealt with some of these matters in detail elsewhere (Plummer 1975, 1981a), so here my aim is to provide a broad overview.

10 For a general discussion of such legitimation processes, see G. Marshall (1981). For specific application to the sexually different, see, for example, Feinblom (1976) and Plummer (1975).

11 I have discussed this in detail elsewhere as a series of career stages. See, in particular, Plummer (1975, pp. 135–52); Plummer (1981c).

12 For specific discussions of such movements, see Sagarin (1969); Greene (1974); Feinblom (1976); Gosselin and Wilson (1980); Plummer (1981d); and McLeod (1982).

13 For example, see the polarization of positions over pornography set out by Ellis (1980). There is a vast 'conservative' and 'liberal' literature on sexuality which is relatively commonplace: I have elected to describe the more radical fringe here because it is less well known.

14 For a sample of these debates see O'Carroll (1980), Tsang (1982); Lee (1978); Altman (1982) and Samois (1982).

15 There are some very powerful statements of this view but see in particular Dworkin (1981); Raymond (1980); Stanley (1982); Linden et al. (1983); Lederer (1980) and the earlier classic statement by Brownmiller (1975).

REFERENCES

Achilles, N. (1967). The development of the homosexual bar as an institution. In J. H. Gagnon and W. Simon (eds), *Sexual Deviance* New York: Harper & Row.

Acton, W. (1857). *The Functions and Disorders of the Reproductive Organs*, London: Churchill.

Adam, B. (1979). A social history of gay politics. In M. P. Levine (ed.), *Gay Men: The Sociology of Male Homosexuality*, London: Harper & Row.

Allen, C. (1969). *A Textbook of Psychosexual Disorders* (2nd edn), Oxford: Oxford University Press.

Altman, D. (1982). *The Homosexualisation of America and the Americanisation of the Homosexual*, New York: St Martin's Press.

Banks, O. (1981). *Faces of Feminism*, Oxford: Martin Robertson.

Barrett, M. (1980). *Women's Oppression Today: Problems in Marxist Feminist Analysis*, London: Verso.

Bartell, J. D. (1971). *Group Sex*, New York: Wyden.

Bayer, R. (1981). *Homosexuality and American Psychiatry: The Politics of Diagnosis*, New York: Basic Books.

Beach, F. A. (1974). Human sexuality and evolution. In W. Montagna (ed.), *Reproductive Behaviour*, New York: Plenum Press.

Becker, E. (1973). *The Denial of Death*, New York: Free Press.

Becker, E. (1975). *Escape from Evil*, London: Collier Macmillan.

248   Ken Plummer

Berger, P. S. (1977). Sociology and freedom. In P. S. Berger, *Facing up to Modernity*, New York: Basic Books.

Bloch, I. (1965). *Sexual Life in England*, London: Corgi.

Boswell, J. (1980). *Christianity, Social Tolerance and Homosexuality: Gay People in Western Europe from the Beginning of the Christian Era to the Fourteenth Century*, Chicago: University of Chicago Press.

Boswell, J. (1982). Revolutions, universals, categories. *Salmagundi*, No. 58–9, 79–113.

Brake, M. (ed.) (1982). *Human Social Relations: A Reader*, Harmondsworth, Penguin.

Bray, A. (1983). *Homosexuality in Renaissance England*, London: Gay Men's Press.

Brown, J. (1952). A comparative study of deviations from sexual mores. *American Sociological Review*, 17, 135–46.

Brownmiller, S. (1975). *Against Our Will: Men, Women and Rape*, New York: Simon & Schuster.

Bullough, V. (1976). *Sexual Variance in Society and History*, Chicago: University of Chicago Press.

Bullough, V. (1979). *Homosexuality: A History*, New York: New American Library.

Burgess, A. W., Groth, A. N., Holmstrom, L. L. and Sgroi, S. M. (1978). *Sexual Assault of Children and Adolescents*, Lexington, Mass.: Lexington Books.

Burgess, A., and Holmstrom, L. L. (1974). *Rape: Victims of Crisis*, Maryland: Brudy.

Burke, K. (1966). *Language as Symbolic Action*, Berkeley: University of California Press.

Califia, P. (1981). Man/Boy love and the Lesbian/Gay movement. In D. Tsang (ed.), *The Age Taboo: Gay Male Sexuality, Power and Consent*, London: Gay Men's Press.

Christensen, H. T. (1966). Scandinavian and American sex norms: some comparisons with sociological implication. *Journal of Social Issues*, 22, 60–75.

Comfort, A. (1968). *the Anxiety Makers*, London: Panther.

Coward, R. (1983). *Patriarchal Precedents: Sexuality and Social Relations*, London: Routledge & Kegan Paul.

Davies, C. (1982). Sexual taboos and social boundaries. *American Journal of Sociology*, 87, 1032–63.

Delph, E. W. (1978). *The Silent Community: Public Homosexual Encoutners*, London: Sage.

Diethelm, O. (1750). *Medical Dissertations of Psychiatric Interest Printed Before 1750*, Basel: Karger (1971).

Douglas, J. (ed.) (1970). *The Relevance of Sociology*, New York: Appleton Century-Crofts.

Douglas, J. D., and Rasmussen, P. K. (1977). *The Nude Beach*, London: Sage.

Douglas, M. (1970). *Purity and Danger: An Analysis of Concepts of Pollution and Taboo*, Harmondsworth: Penguin.

Durkheim, E. (1964). *The Rules of Sociological Method*, New York: Free Press of Glencoe.

Dworkin, A. (1981). *Pornography: Men Possessing Women*, London: The Women's Press.

Dworkin, A. (1982). Interview by Elizabeth Wilson. *Feminist Review*, 11.

Edwards, S. (1981). *Female Sexuality and the Law*, Oxford: Martin Robertson.

Ehrenreich, B., and English, D. (1979). *For Her Own Good: 150 Years of the Experts' Advice to Women*, London: Pluto Press.

Ellis, J. (1980). On pornography. *Screen*, 21, 81–93.

Erikson, K. T. (1966). *Wayward Puritans*, London: Wiley.

Etture, B. (1980). *Lesbians, Women and Society*, London: Routledge & Kegan Paul.

Faderman, L. (1981). *Surpassing the Love of Men: Romantic Friendship and Love Between Women from the Renaissance to the Present*, London: Junction Books.

Faraday, A. (1981). Liberating Lesbian research. in Plummer 1981a.

Faust, B. (1982). *Women, Sex and Pornography*, Harmondsworth: Penguin.

Feinblom, D. H. (1976). *Transvestites and Transsexuals*, New York: Delta.

Feminist Review (1982) *Sexuality*, No. 11.

Finkelhor, D. (1979). *Sexually Victimised Children*, London: Collier Macmillan.

Ford, C. S., and Beach, F. A. (1952). *Patterns of Sexual Behaviour*, London: Methuen.

Foucault, M. (1979). *The History of Sexuality*, 1: *An Introduction*, London: Allen & Lane.

Freud, S. (1975). *Civilisation and its Discontents*, London: Hogarth Press.

Gagnon, J. H. (1977). *Human Sexualities*, Illinois: Scott, Foreman.

Gagnon, J. H., and Simon, W. (eds), (1967) *Sexual Deviance*, New York: Harper & Row.

Gagnon, J. H., and Simon, W. (1973). *Sexual Conduct: The Social Sources of Human Sexuality*, Chicago: Aldine.

Gide, A. (1911). *Corydon*, Paris: Gallimard

Glassner, B. (1980). *Essential Interactionism*, London: Routledge & Kegan Paul.

Gosselin, C., and Wilson, G. (1980). *Sexual Variations: Fetishism, Transvestism and Sado-masochism*, London: Faber & Faber.

Gouldner, A. W. (1971). *The Coming Crisis of Western Sociology*, London: Heinemann.

Greene, G., and C. (1974). *S–M: The last Taboo*, New York: Grove Press.

Hare, E. M. (1962). Masturbatory insanity: The history of an idea. *Journal of Mental Science*, 108, 452.

Henriques, F. (1960). *Love in Action: The Sociology of Sex*, London: MacGibbon & Kee.

Herdt, G. H. (1981). *Guardians of the Flute: Idioms of Masculinity*, London: McGraw-Hill.

HMSO (1957). *The Report of the Committee on Homosexual Offences and Prostitutes*, Command Paper 247.

Humphreys, L. (1975). *Tearoom Trade* (2nd edn), Chicago: Aldine.

Hutter, B., and Williams, G. (1981). *Controlling Women: The Normal and the Deviant*, London: Croom Helm.

Irwin, J. (1977). *Scenes*, Beverley Hills: Sage.

Jackson, S. (1978). The social context of rape: sexual scripts and motivation. *Women's Studies International Quarterly*, 1, 27–38.

Karp, D. (1973). Hiding in pornographic bookstores. *Urban Life*, 1, 427–35.

Katz, J. (1976). *Gay American History: Lesbians and Gay Men in the U.S.A.*, New York: Thomas and Cromwell.

Kessler, S. J., and McKenna, W. (1978). *Gender: An Ethnomethodological Approach*, Chichester: Wiley.

Kinsey, A., Pomeroy, W., and Martin, C. (1948). *Sexual Behavior in the Human Male*, Philadelphia: Saunders.

Kinsey, A., Pomeroy, W., Martin, C., and Gebhard, P. (1953). *Sexual Behavior in the Human Female*, Philadelphia: Saunders.

Krafft-Ebing (1886). *Psychopathia Sexualis*, London: Mayflower-Dell (1965).

Lauritsen, J., and Thorstad, D. (1974). *The Early Homosexual Rights Movement, 1864–1935*, New York: Times Change Press.

Leach, E. (1982). *Social Anthropology*, London: Fontana.

Lederer, L. (1980). *Take Back the Night: Women on Pornography*, New York: William Morrow.

Lee, J. A. (1978). *Getting Sex: A New Approach – More Fun, Less Guilt*, Ontario: Musson Books.

Lee, J. A. (1979). The gay connection. *Urban Life*, 8, 175–98.

Levine, M. P. (ed.) (1979). *Gay Men: The Sociology of Male Homosexuality*, London: Harper & Row.

Linden, R. R., Pagarno, P. R., Russell, D. F. M., and Starr, S. L. (1983). *Against Sadomasochism: A Radical Feminist Analysis*, New York: Frog in the Wall Press.

Lyman, S. M. (1979). *The Seven Deadly Sins: Society and Evil*, New York: St Martin's Press.

McCaghy, C. M. (1968). Drinking and deviance disavowal: the case of child molesters. *Social Problems*, 16, 43–9.

McDonald, J. M. (1973). *Indecent Exposure*, Illinois: Thomas.

MacDonald, R. H. (1967). The frightful consequences of onanism: notes on the history of a delusion. *Journal of the History of Ideas*, 28, 423–31.

McIntosh, M. C. (1968). The homosexual role. *Social Problems*, 16, 182–92.

McLeod, E. (1982). *Women Working: Prostitution Now*, London: Croom Helm.

Macnamara, D. E. J., and Sagarin, E. (1977). *Sex, Crime and the Law*, London: Free Press, Collier Macmillan.

Maddox, B. (1982). *The Marrying Kind*, St. Albans: Granada.

Mannheim, H. (1966). *Comparative Criminology Vols. 1 and 2.*, London: Routledge & Kegan Paul.

Marcus, J., and Francis, J. (eds) (1975). *Masturbation: From Infancy to Senescence*, New York: International University Press.

Marcus, M. (1981). *A Taste for Pain: On Masochism and Female Sexuality*, London: Souvenir Press.

Marcus, S. (1966). *The Other Victorians*, London: Weidenfeld & Nicolson.

Marshall, G. (1981). Accounting for deviance. *International Journal of Sociology and Social Policy*, 1, 17–45.

Marshall, J. (1981). *Pansies, Perverts and Macho Men*. In K. Plummer (ed). *The Making of the Modern Homosexual*, London: Hutchinson.

Marshall, D. S., and Suggs, R. C. (eds) (1971). *Human Sexual Behaviour: The Range and Diversity of Human Sexual Experience Throughout the World*, New York: Basic Books.

Masters, W. H., Johnson, V. E., and Kolodny, R. C. (1977). *Ethical Issues in Sex Therapy and Research*, Boston: Little, Brown.

Matza, D. (1964). *Delinquency and Drift*, Chichester: Wiley.

Midgley, M. (1979). *Beast and Man: The Roots of Human Nature*, London: Methuen.

Mills, C. W. (1943). The professional ideology of social pathologists. *American Journal of Sociology*, 49, 165–80.

Morin, S. F. (1977). Heterosexual bias in psychological research on lesbianism and male homosexuality. *American Psychologist*, 32, 629–37.

Newton, E. (1973). *Mother Camp: Female Impersonators in America*, Englewood Cliffs: Prentice-Hall.

O'Carroll, T. (1980). *Paedophilia: The Radical Case*, London: Peter Owen.

Ortner, S. B., and Whitehead, H. (1981). *Sexual Meanings: The Cultural Construction of Gender and Sexuality*, London: Cambridge University Press.

Padgug, R. A. (1979). Sexual matters: on conceptualisations and sexuality in history. *Radical History Review*, 20, 3–23.

Pearsall, R. (1969). *The Worm in the Bud*, London: Weidenfeld & Nicolson.

Perkins, K. B., and Skipper, J. K. (1981). Gay pornographic and sex paraphernalia shops: an ethnography of expressive settings. *Deviant Behaviour*, 2, 187–99.

Plummer, K. (1975). *Sexual Stigma: An Interactionist Account*, London: Routledge & Kegan Paul.

Plummer, K. (ed.) (1981a). *The Making of the Modern Homosexual*, London: Hutchinson.

Plummer, K. (1981b). Paedophilia: constructing a sociological baseline. In M. Cook and K. Howells (eds), *Adult Sexual Interest in Children*, London: Academic Press.

Plummer, K. (1981c). Going gay: identities, lifecycles and life styles in the male gay world. In J. Hart and D. Richardson (eds), *The Theory and Practice of Homosexuality*, London: Routledge & Kegan Paul.

Plummer, K. (1981d). The paedophile's progress: a view from belcur. In D. Taylor (ed.), *Perspectives on Paedophilia*, London: Batsford.

Plummer, K. (1982). Symbolic interactionism and sexual conduct. In M. Brake (ed.), *Human Social Relations: A Reader*, Harmondsworth, Penguin.

Ponse, B. (1978). *Identities in the Lesbian World*, New York: Greenwood Press.

Rasmussen, P., and Kuhn, L. L. (1976). The new masseuse: play for pay. *Urban Life*, 5, 3 (reprinted in C. Warren (ed.) *Sexuality: Encounters, Identities and Relationships*, London: Sage).

Raymond, J. (1980). *The Transsexual Empire*, London: The Women's Press.

Read, K. (1980). *Other Voices: The Style of a Male Homosexual Tavern*, California: Chandler & Sharp.

Rich, A. (1981). *Compulsory Heterosexuality and Lesbian Existence*, London: Only Women Press.

Robinson, P. (1969). *The Sexual Radicals*, London: Temple Smith.

Robinson, P. (1976). *The Modernisation of Sex*, London: Elek.

Rook, K., and Hammen, C. L. (1977). A cognitive perspective on the experience of sexual arousal. *Journal of Social Issues*, 33, 7–29.

Rosen, I. (1964). *The Pathology and Treatment of Sexual Deviation*, Oxford: Oxford University Press.

Rossman, P. (1979). *Sexual Experience Between Men and Boys*, London: Temple Smith.

Roth, J. (1963). *Timetables*, Indianapolis: Bobbs-Merrill.

Rowse, A. L. (1977). *Homosexuals in History: A Study of Ambivalence in Society, Literature and the Arts*, London: Weidenfeld & Nicholson.

Rubin, G. (1981). Sexual politics, the new right and the sexual fringe, in D. Tsang (ed.), *The Age Taboo*, London: Gay Men's Press.

Rush, B. (1892). *Medical Inquiries and Observation upon Diseases of the Mind*, New York: Hafner Publishing.

Rush, F. (1980). *The Best Kept Secret*, Englewood Cliffs: Prentice-Hall.

Sagarin, E. (1968). Ideology as a factor in the consideration of deviance. *Journal of Sexual Research*, 4, 84–94.

Sagarin, E. (1969). *Odd Man In: Societies of Deviants in America*, Chicago: Quadrangle.

Samois (1982). *Coming to Power*, Boston: Alyson.

Sarnoff, S. and I. (1979). *Sexual Excitement: Sexual Peace: The Place of Masturbation in Adult Relationships*, New York: Evans.

Sayers, J. (1982). *Biological Politics: Feminist and Anti-Feminist Perspectives*, London: Tavistock.

Scacco, A. M. (1982). *Male Rape: A Casebook of Sexual Aggressions*, New York: AMS Press.

Scott, R. A. (1972). A proposed framework for analysing deviance as a property of social order, In R. Scott and J. Douglas, *Theoretical Perspectives on Deviance*, London: Basic Books.

Sherfey, M. J. (1972). *The Nature and Evaluation of Female Sexuality*, New York: Random House.

Shorter, E. (1977). *The Making of the Modern Family*, London: Fontana.

Singer, I. (1973). *The Goals of Human Sexuality*, London: Wildwood House.

Smart, C. (1976). *Women, Crime and Criminology*, London: Routledge & Kegan Paul.

Spector, I., and Kitsuse, J. (1977). Legitimating homosexuality. *Society*, July/August, 52–6.

Stanley, L. (1982). Male needs: the problems of working with gay men. In L. Friedman and E. Sarah (eds), *On the Problems of Men*, London: The Women's Press.

Stein, N. L. (1974). *Lovers, Friends, Slaves . . . The Nine Male Sexual Types*, New York: Putnam.

Stewart, G. L. (1972). On first being a John. *Urban Life and Culture*, 1, 255–74.

Stoller, R. J. (1979). *Sexual Excitement: Dynamics of Erotic Life*, New York: Pantheon.

Stone, L. (1977). *The Family, Sex and Marriage in England, 1500–1800*, London: Weidenfeld & Nicolson.

Storr, A. (1964). *Sexual Deviation*, Harmondsworth: Penguin.

Styles, J. (1979). Outsider/insider: researching gay baths. *Urban Life*, 8, 135–52.

Symons, D. (1979). *The Evolution of Human Sexuality*, Oxford: Oxford University Press.

Szasz, T. (1981). *Sex: Fact, Frauds and Follies*, Oxford: Basil Blackwell.

Thompson, E. P. (1979). Happy families. *Radical History Review*, 20, 42–50.

Trilling, L. (1954). The Kinsey Report. In *The Liberal Imagination*, New York: Viking Press (reprinted in D. P. Geddes (ed.) (1954) *An Analysis of the Kinsey Report*, New York: Mentor Books).

Trudgill, E. (1976). *Madonnas and Magdalens: The Origins and Development of Victorian Sexual Attitudes*, London: Heinemann.

Tsang, D. (ed.) (1981). *The Age Taboo: Gay Male Sexuality, Power and Consent*, London: Gay Men's Press.

Valverde, M. (1980). Feminism meets fist-fucking: getting lost in lesbian S–M, *Body Politic*, February.

Warren, C. (1976). Women among men: females in the male homosexual community. *Archives of Sexual Behavior*, 5, 157–69.

Warren, C. (1977). *Sexuality: Encounters, Identities and Relationships*, London: Sage.

Weeks, J. (1977). *Coming Out: Homosexual Politics in Britain from the 19th Century to the Present*, London: Quartet Books.

Weeks, J. (1981). *Sex, Politics and Society: The Regulation of Sexuality Since 1800*, London: Longman.

Weeks, J. (1982). The development of sexual theory and sexual politics, In M. Brake (ed.), *Human Social Relations: A Reader*, Harmondsworth: Penguin.

Weinberg, M. S. (1965). Sexual modesty and the nudist camp. *Social Problems*, 12, 311–18.

Weinberg, M. S., and Williams, C. J. (1975). Gay baths and the social organisation of impersonal sex. *Social Problems*, 23, 124–36.

Weinberg, T. S., and Falk, G. (1980). The social organisation of sadism and masochism. *Deviant Behaviour*, 1, 379–93.

Weis, K., and Borges, S. (1975). Victimology and rape: the case of the legitimate victim. In L. S. Schultz (ed.), *Rape Victimology*, Springfield, Illinois: Thomas.

White, E. (1980). *States of Desire: Travels in Gay America*, London: Deutsch.

Wolf, D. G. (1979). *The Lesbian Community*, Berkeley: University of California Press.

Yinger, J. M. (1960). Contraculture and subculture. *American Sociological Review*, 25, 625–35.

Notes on Contributors

Dr Harry Brierley has worked as a clinical psychologist in prisons and in the British National Health Service. Formerly he was Area Psychologist with the Newcastle Health Authority and Associate Teacher at the University of Newcastle. Currently he is in private practice as a psychotherapist. He has had extensive experience over 20 years in counselling transsexuals and in social skills training of sex reassignment cases. He is the author of *Transvestism: A Handbook for Counsellors* (1979).

Dr Philip Feldman is currently Visiting Professor of Psychology at the Hebrew University of Jerusalem. Prior to this he was Reader in Clinical Psychology and Head of Training in Clinical Psychology at the University of Birmingham (England). His many publications include *Homosexual Behaviour: Therapy and Assessment* (1970) and (with M. J. MacCulloch) *Human Sexual Behaviour* (1980).

Dr Chris Gosselin is now a freelance research psychologist and writer. He worked previously at the Institute of Psychiatry in London and has studied patterns of sexual behaviour throughout his academic life. He is co-author, with Dr Glenn Wilson, of *Sexual Variations* (1980).

Dr Kevin Howells is a Lecturer in Psychology at the University of Leicester and a practising clinical psychologist. He worked previously in the United States and in one of the English Special Hospitals, specializing in the assessment and treatment of aggressive (including sexually aggressive) offenders and patients. His current research interests include the management of anger in everyday life and the psychological sequelae of sexual victimization. He is the author (with Mark Cook) of *Adult Sexual Interest in Children* (1981) and of a number of articles and chapters on the clinical aspects of social deviance.

Dr Derek Jehu is a Professor in the Psychological Service Centre, University of Manitoba, where his responsibilities include the Directorship of the Sexual Dysfunction Clinic. Before emigrating to Canada in 1976, he lectured at the University of Liverpool and held a chair at the University of Leicester. He is a practising clinical psychologist and has published a number of books, including *Sexual Dysfunction: A Behavioural Approach to Causation, Assessment and Treatment* (1979).

Dr D. R. Laws currently directs the Sexual Behavior Laboratory at Atascadero State Hospital in California and is a member of a private practice organization providing outpatient services to sex offenders. Dr Laws has been actively involved in the assessment and treatment of people with sexual problems for over 13 years, and has frequently contributed to the literature on sexual variation.

Dr Ken Plummer is a Lecturer in Sociology at the University of Essex. He has researched into various aspects of sexual conduct and is interested in the development of symbolic interactionism. The author of *Sexual Stigma* (1975), *The Making of the Modern Homosexual* (1981), *Documents of Life* (1983), and many articles, he is currently researching into the social aspects of sexually transmitted diseases.

Dr Patrick Tyler has been a researcher and teacher in universities in both North America and Britain. He is currently a Lecturer in Psychology at the University of Birmingham, England. His main publications are in the genetics of learning and motivation in animals. His research interests lie in the study of genetic differences in social behaviour and in the experimental testing of sociobiological models.

Dr Glenn D. Wilson was born in New Zealand and is now Senior Lecturer in Psychology at the Institute of Psychiatry in London. He has researched extensively in the area of personality and social psychology. In recent years his prime interest has been the study of sexual attraction, love and marriage, and sexual deviation. He has written a large number of articles and books, many of them in the field of human sexual behaviour, including *The Psychology of Sex* (1979), *Love and Instinct* (1981) and (with D. Cox) *The Child Lovers: A Study of Paedophiles in Society* (1982).

Author Index

Subject Index